Three's a Crowd

Three's a Crowd

Pentecostalism, Hermeneutics, and the Old Testament

JACQUELINE GREY

PICKWICK *Publications* · Eugene, Oregon

Pickwick Publications
An Imprint of Wipf and Stock Publishers
199 W. 8th Ave., Suite 3
Eugene, OR 97401

www.wipfandstock.com

ISBN 13: 978-60899-805-0

Cataloging-in-Publication data:

Grey, Jacqueline.

Three's a crowd : Pentecostalism, hermeneutics, and the Old Testament / Jacqueline Grey.

viii + 212 p. ; 23 cm. Includes bibliographical references.

ISBN 13: 978-60899-805-0

1. Pentecostalism. 2. Hermeneutics—Religious aspects—Pentecostalism. 3. Bible. O.T. Isaiah—Criticism, interpretation, etc. 4. Bible—Hermeneutics. I. Title.

BR1644 G65 2011

Manufactured in the U.S.A.

Contents

Diagrams and Tables

Acknowledgments

THE MOTIVATION FOR THIS exploration in Pentecostal hermeneutics came from my own initial uncertainty as a new teacher. I was tasked with lecturing Old Testament studies to Pentecostal and charismatic students at Alphacrucis College (Sydney, Australia). As I began to look for resources and models for reading the Old Testament, I found that there was no unique model for teaching and reading the Old Testament within my faith community. Rather than lament the lack, I embraced the situation as an opportunity to explore the issues raised by this educational task for myself. Throughout this process I have been encouraged by my colleagues and friends: Dr. Shane Clifton, Dr. Mark Hutchinson, Dr. David Parker, Pastor Stephen Fogarty, Dr. Chris Simon, and other staff of Alphacrucis College. Many of these friends and scholars have been involved in the editing of this thesis. In particular, Mark Hutchinson, David Parker, and Linda Percival have been invaluable in this process. It was also through the practical generosity of Alphacrucis College in providing sabbatical leave that I was able to research and prepare this work. I also extend my thanks to the numerous faculty, staff and students of Charles Sturt University, who have assisted and encouraged me in this endeavor.

Part of the vision of this study was to *describe* the actual reading practices of the Pentecostal-charismatic community, and from this platform *prescribe* a model for reading. This description was based on the collection of data from numerous sources, including actual discussion groups. My thanks to those who assisted in the process of acquiring this data: Linda Percival, Kristy Rigg, Brooke Pipes, Aaron Stevens, Larissa Nay-Brock, Tina Brown, Gibson Sebastian, and Mark Hutchinson.

Portions of chapter 5 have been published in *Australasian Pentecostal Studies Journal*, and in Jione Havea and Clive Pearson, eds., *Out of Place: Doing Theology on the Crosscultural Brink* (Equinox, 2011), though it appears here in a substantially revised form. Material from chapter 7 has been utilized for the publishing of a populist study in Pentecostal Hermeneutics entitled *Them, Us & Me: How the Old Testament Speaks to People Today* (published through both Australasian Pentecostal Studies and Wipf & Stock). My thanks to all of the copyright holders for permission to adapt this material. And also to Planetshakers for permission to include the lyrics of two of their songs.

Finally, I would like to acknowledge and thank my close friends, housemates, and family for their grace and patience to me throughout this process. Their continual encouragement and inspiration has been a beacon of hope. In particular, I'd like to thank my parents, John and Nancye Grey and my sister, Brooke Pipes (and her husband Allen). This thesis is for "me," "them," and "us."

Jacqueline Grey
Alphacrucis College, Sydney

1

Beginning the Conversation

BEGINNING A CONVERSATION WITH a stranger requires boldness and skill. To transform that first awkward introduction into a new friendship can require skills rivaling the artistic brilliance of Renoir or Manet. A skill so desirable, that there are countless books, courses, and websites with creative conversation-starting hints. While the first line may be rehearsed, the dialogue that follows cannot be predicted. It is a journey to a brave new world where hobbies and mutual interests are discovered with an eager intensity. Will there be an instant, easy connection with this new acquaintance, or will the ongoing relationship require effort? Is this person mutually interested in future friendship, or does the conversation end here? A scenario perhaps even more challenging is when three friends—who all know each other separately—meet together for the first time. The introduction of a three-way dialogue changes the dynamic of how the individual friendships have previously functioned. The former camaraderie and individual style of relating within the earlier partnerships must change for the three friends to each be included in a mutually stimulating dialogue.

I experienced this personally when I recently moved into a rental house with two friends I knew from different spheres of my life. While three separate friendships were maintained between us three housemates, we had to also form a single, unified fellowship. While respecting the individuals and their friendships, we chose to prioritize the unity of the household as a fellowship of three. This required deliberate effort and accommodation to the strengths and weaknesses of each friend. From this experience, I learnt that it is a challenge to the maturity of individual friendships to include the contribution of a new party. Will one party be excluded or will all three voices be heard? Do two people make company, but "three's a crowd"?

PURPOSE OF THE CONVERSATION

The purpose of this book is to introduce three friends, and so potentially produce a three-fold fellowship of Pentecostalism, hermeneutics, and the Old Testament. Each of these "friends" are well-known areas of theological research and critical enquiry (at various levels of sophistication). Yet while each of these areas of research has engaged in partner discussions, they have rarely met together as a threesome. Despite their common interests and potential for engaging dialogue, there has been little development in acquainting all three areas of research in an interconnected discussion. The youngest member of the fellowship is Pentecostalism. Having recently joined the academic dialogue, Pentecostals have found a ready connection with hermeneutics. However the burgeoning field of Pentecostal hermeneutics has been focused primarily on the New Testament to the exclusion of adequately addressing issues unique to the Old Testament. As a result, Old Testament studies have remained outside the discourse of Pentecostal hermeneutics. In contrast, while there is a long-standing friendship between hermeneutics and Old Testament studies, Pentecostalism has remained disconnected from their discussion. Separate to both these conversations is the untempered admiration of the Old Testament by the Pentecostal community, without the critical consideration offered by hermeneutics. It is the integration of these three areas of research that prompts this study. Rather than maintain three separate conversations, the aim of this book is to engage these three voices in a mutually informing dialogue; not excluding one in favor of the other but creating a conversation for three.

Of course, the concept of a triune fellowship is not new to biblical studies or to the theological enterprise. The resurgence of interest in trinitarian theology in recent decades is reflective of the interest in symbols of community and inclusion. In particular, this interest is marked by the concern and a future hope for the retrieval of relationality. The doctrine of the Trinity has metamorphosed from a symbol of hierarchical power to a proponent of egalitarianism. Historical descriptions of the Trinity, particularly the Cappadocian use of *perichoresis*, have been adopted to define the Triune God by social rather than political terminology. Therefore the inter-relatedness of the Trinitarian community is emphasized over their actions or function.[1] This model emphasizes the importance of triune fellowship, not only within the Godhead, but also in the Christian communities that reflect this mystery. The endeavor of Christian communities to demonstrate this concurrent unity and diversity is not an easy task, particularly when the partners do not come to the triune conversation without history or agenda.

To expect that the three partners—hermeneutics, the Old Testament, and Pentecostalism—can engage in a conversation without recognition of their prior histories

---

1. The economic Trinity is understood in the history of salvation revealed to humankind. The immanent Trinity attempts to define the relationship of God to God's self outside of temporality. Likewise, it is the name ascribed to the Triune God "as he is in himself" according to Moltmann (*Trinity and the Kingdom*, 151). Although they are inextricably linked, since the God who is love cannot be indifferent to the world (ibid., 152), God is not limited to his salvific revelation, as LaCugna concludes (LaCugna, *God for Us*, 25). So these two descriptions of God must be distinguished. However, the mystery of the triune God is fixed in the revelation and reality of salvation history. However, Anthony Thiselton questions the theological insistence in this resurgence of the social trinity. He writes: "If our theological understanding of Trinity calls into question our social assumptions, this is as it should be. If, however, we are tempted to opt for a "social" Trinity in order to legitimate an egalitarian view of society, this becomes manipulation in the service of power-interests and ceases to be a quest for theological truth" (Thiselton, *Interpreting God and the Postmodern Self*, 156–57).

together is to be remiss. How do Pentecostal readers interpret the Old Testament? According to a lay member of an Assemblies of God[2] church in Sydney, Pentecostals "just read it and believe it." This response reflects the belief among the Pentecostal community that their reading processes are "simple" and faithful to the Scriptures. Yet further examination reveals that if their reading processes are simple, they are not simplistic. The Pentecostal community does not read the biblical text with unqualified belief, but approaches the text through a sophisticated symbolic interaction of literalism and the dynamic of Spirit-experience. The Pentecostal reader anticipates an encounter with God in their reading of Scripture that leads to a transformation within their own life. It is this process of reading the Old Testament by Pentecostals that will be examined in this book. However it is not the aim of this study to close the conversation unresolved. Once the differing factors and concerns that contribute to the voice of the "Pentecostal reader" are determined, a responsible reading approach to the Old Testament can be developed. This proposed model must reflect the values and strengths of the community while addressing the weaknesses inherent in their practice. A corollary of the dialogue between Pentecostals, hermeneutics, and the Old Testament is the broadening of Pentecostal scholarship to the wider academic community. This triune conversation will assist those outside the movement to understand the community and its "voice" in the broader Christian dialogue.[3]

While charismatic experience is generally recognized by scholars as a core value of a Pentecostal hermeneutic, there is no consensus as to how this element interacts with other pieces of the hermeneutical puzzle in the reading process. As the development of both the Pentecostal and Charismatic movements is only a relatively new phenomenon, the evolution of a reflective scholarship is even more recent. The emerging Pentecostal scholarship is attempting to integrate and locate itself in this additional context of the academic community. With particular reference to hermeneutics, the last two decades have witnessed an explosion of discussion among Pentecostal scholars attempting to find a "voice" within the categories of wider academic scholarship. This surge of interest represents an understanding by Pentecostal scholars of their responsibility to be active in the academic community. As representatives of a global movement[4] they are required

2. The Assemblies of God is one of many Pentecostal denominations within the Pentecostal movement in Australia. It is the largest of the Pentecostal denominations in Australia.

3. The location of the Pentecostal-Charismatic community within the wider ecumenical community is important. While the Pentecostal-Charismatic community emphasizes the importance of the baptism of the Holy Spirit, it is not considered essential for salvation but an empowering to be witnesses to the gospel of Jesus Christ. As Land writes in *Pentecostal Spirituality: A Passion for the Kingdom* of the earlier North American Pentecostal community, "There was a constant mention among early Pentecostals of the importance of walking in all the light you had. Other believers (non-Pentecostals) would not be condemned, because they were walking in all the light they had. They would, of course, miss the full blessings of Pentecost; but they were, nevertheless, Christians" (Land, *Pentecostal Spirituality*, 77).

4. While the origins of the Pentecostal movement are identified in Azusa Street, Los Angeles, the movement has spread globally as represented by the recent work by Dempster, et al., *Globalization of Pentecostalism*. As the editors write in their introduction, the Pentecostal community has evolved from a small band of Christian believers to a world-wide movement of an estimated 450 million adherents in 1999. Current scholarship suggests that Azusa Street is more symbolic than genetic in its relationship to a multicentric, almost instantly global movement.

to be a voice both within their own community and within the dialogue of Christian ecumenism.[5] However, to engage with and contribute to the broader dialogue of biblical studies (and eventually scholarship in general, including philosophy), Pentecostals must seek first to understand their own tradition and current values in biblical readings and, secondly, locate their own reading within existing methodological frameworks.

In contemplating this circular debate, it seems that Pentecostal academics have "taken the mountain to Muhammad and not Muhammad to the mountain." Most scholarship on Pentecostal hermeneutics (both within and outside the movement) tends to begin with an ideal or "most appropriate" hermeneutical category, as defined by the academic community, and then proceeds to mould a description of Pentecostal readings into this image. This means their analysis tends to be prescriptive rather than descriptive; such scholars do not attempt to describe the hermeneutical processes utilized by the Pentecostal community, but rather suggest (or prescribe) reading methods based on a different set of interpretations about the value of experience. This is a "Word Plus" solution, which ignores the integration intrinsic to the Pentecostal worldview. However, this does raise questions concerning the consequences of this location: does the translation of Pentecostal readings and experience into general methodological and philosophical frameworks skew the explication of the experience so that its particularity is compromised?[6] In this sense, the uniqueness and complexity of Pentecostal readings have been distorted to fit whatever category of the wider academy each scholar considers most appropriate, whether that be postmodern, evangelical or otherwise. This approach tends to distance Pentecostal scholarship from its community: it sabotages their intention of describing an actual Pentecostal hermeneutic, and so diminishes their unique contribution to a "triune fellowship." This is not to censure the attempts of Pentecostal scholars to "speak" to the academic community, but recognizes the costs of their approach. This book will be an attempt to begin with "the mountain"; to study the reading approaches of Pentecostal groups, including pastors[7] and lay readers, and so determine the principles or values which are actually inherent in their hermeneutic. This will provide a vehicle for the "voice" of the Pentecostal *community* (as distinct from the aspirations of its academics) to emerge within the three-way dialogue, in the prescription of an effective reading model of the Old Testament.

An application of this approach is the attempt to make a practical contribution to Pentecostal-Charismatic practice itself, by helping the members of the Pentecostal community understand themselves and their reading practices more critically through the formulations of guidelines to improve their reading practice while maintaining their distinct values.[8] Although these emerging voices of the Pentecostal community will still need to be categorized according to the context of the academic community, the priority is to reflect the voice of the Pentecostal community. While it is recognized that the indi-

5. Yong, *Discerning the Spirit(s)*.

6. Ibid., 184.

7. The term "pastor" is the title given to the office of minister or professional clergy in Pentecostal movements.

8. Parker, *Led by the Spirit*, 17.

vidual context of readers influences the reading process, the generalization of these influences among the Pentecostal community is inevitable. Therefore the aim of this book is not just to adopt blindly the values of the Pentecostal community; to do so is to read from uncritical impulses, such as social conformity or intellectual intimidation[9] and so ignore the voice of hermeneutical enquiry in the three-fold fellowship. Instead, the aim of this study is to develop a reading model of the Old Testament that is reflective of the "voice" and values of the Pentecostal reading community through critical reflection on their actual practices. As Stroup notes, it is the role of the scholar to bring critical analysis to the reading process of the community in order that they might better understand their own practices, correct their mistakes, and live more faithfully to the gospel they profess.[10] This is not an attempt to change who they are, but rather a process of assisting them to realize "who they are" in a more fulsome manner.

The metaphor of "voice" has been used by scholars—particularly feminist and liberationist scholars—to symbolize the emancipation of a previously suppressed minority. Just as feminist scholars, including Loades[11] and Exum,[12] attempt to dislodge the androcentricism which defines males and their experience as a standard against which females and their experience is considered a deviation,[13] so also a Pentecostal-Charismatic interpretation attempts to highlight the experience of the charismatic not simply as a nice deviation or a matter of "personal experience" but as a necessary voice in the conversation of biblical hermeneutics. While Feminist, Womanist, and other criticisms (such as post-colonial approaches) have mainly been concerned to challenge the church and academy over culturally "legitimate" and "authorized" interpretations that exclude groups outside the boundaries of legitimacy,[14] they have paved the way for a similar challenge by Pentecostal scholarship to the boundaries of legitimacy that exclude charismatic experience. This questions the presupposition of a foundational "sameness" (irrespective of social and historical location) with which communities of faith approach reading biblical texts. This challenge to reflect the culture of a particular community is also demonstrated in Geertz's development of the theory of "thick description."[15] Within this theory, voiced from the discipline of anthropology, the ethnographer attempts to reflect the social customs and values of the "people." Through interviews and observation, the ethnographer attempts to understand and describe a people's culture, however incoherent it may be. Therefore this book attempts to include not just the semi-abstracted experience of Pentecostal scholars, but also the "voice" of Pentecostal communities (the "people"), with all their inconsistencies.[16]

9. Moore, "Deuteronomy and the Fire of God." 16.

10. Stroup, *Promise of Narrative Theology*, 87.

11. Loades, "Feminist Hermeneutics," 81–94.

12. Exum, "Feminist Criticism, 65–90.

13. Loades, "Feminist Hermeneutics," 82.

14. Exum, "Feminist Criticism," 67.

15. Geertz, *Interpretation of Cultures*.

16. This concern for understanding the experience of the readers and their community is reflected in many reader-response criticisms. In particular see McKnight, "Reader-Response Criticism."

WHY I WANT TO SEE THIS TRIUNE FELLOWSHIP DEVELOP

Speaking "for" the community requires an understanding of the values, symbols and be-havior of the community.[17] This recognition of the context of biblical studies, however, also emphasizes the subjective relationship between the examiners and examined. The Pentecostal community and their reading practices of the Old Testament are not "voiced" objectively, but are influenced by the context of the hearer. So, as McKinley writes, "I need to ask: who am I, where am I situated, and what are the communities that have formed and continue to form who I am, because all of these factors will dictate the interests that I carry with me into my reading, and influence my interpretation."[18]

Situation and community count. I am a young Australian woman teaching Old Testament studies in a Pentecostal theological college (Alphacrucis College) in the western suburbs of Sydney, Australia. Having been raised in a Charismatic Uniting (Methodist) church, I transferred to the Assemblies of God while studying Linguistics and Australian literature at Sydney University in the early 1990s. Therefore, I identify with and am a member of the Pentecostal community. However, I also identify with, and am a member of, the academic community.

It is the integration of these two communities that prompts this study. Rather than separate conversations of Pentecostal practices from academic reflection, my desire as a Pentecostal scholar is to engage these elements to form a mutually-informing voice. This concern was intensified when I was presented with the task of teaching Old Testament texts to Pentecostal students in preparation for entering pastoral ministry. Recognizing the alien nature of many of the "scholarly" methods (such as historical-critical ap-proaches) to Pentecostal readers, I wanted to be able to teach my students skills in critical thought without extinguishing the values and enthusiasm distinctive of the Pentecostal community. Like many post-modern and contextual approaches, this process began to expose the limits of many "academic" readings, such as the historical-critical approach. Yet, the employment of critical reflection also began to expose to the students the limita-tions of their own undefined, but instinctive, Pentecostal reading practice. What could I offer? Moving from questions of "why" to "how," a reading model was needed that, while critical of both, embraced both the voice of the Pentecostal community and the voice of the academic community in reading Old Testament texts.

DEVELOPING THE FRIENDSHIP

As already noted, by beginning with a study of Pentecostal reading processes, it is the in-tention of this book to voice the hermeneutical methods of the Pentecostal community, particularly with regard to the Old Testament. In the current surge of debate regarding Pentecostal hermeneutics, most of the current discussion focuses solely on the interpre-tation of the New Testament without reference to the Old Testament/Hebrew Bible.[19] In

---

17. Geertz, *Interpretation of Cultures* .95.

18. McKinlay, "What Do I do with Contexts?" 159–71.

19. This is exemplified in the recent doctoral dissertations and publications of both Mathew Clark and Kenneth Archer respectively. See Clark, "An Investigation into the Nature of a Viable Pentecostal Hermeneutic"; and Archer, *Pentecostal Hermeneutic for the Twenty-First Century*.

a tradition for which Scripture is constitutive, it is crucial that the "voice" of the community also reflects the reading processes of the Old Testament rather than solely the New Testament. This book aims to explore the relationship between the text and experience in Pentecostal readings by using *Isaiah* as a paradigmatic model. Although *Isaiah* is not representative of all texts or trends, it is a starting point in the discussion of the reading processes of the Pentecostal community in approaching the Old Testament.

Yet, why *Isaiah* and not another Old Testament text? The decision to adopt *Isaiah* as the paradigmatic text in which to view Pentecostal hermeneutics of the Old Testament began as an arbitrary choice. It was primarily dictated by the relatively limited publishing activity of the Pentecostal community. As there is minimal published material, this text bulks the larger as one of the most discussed texts in the few Pentecostal publications (however limited that output may be in comparison to other traditions). This indicates that, for Pentecostals, the prophetic and messianic elements of the book may have given it a greater centrality than other elements of the Old Testament. It is a particularly useful text for providing appropriate metaphors. The prophet Isaiah (although one with access to the royal court) shares much with Pentecostal readers in being an "outsider" who represents the interests of the community to the elite. This book is also an attempt to represent the interests of the community rather than just its scholarship. Just as Isaiah's lips are described as "unclean," so too the "uncritical" voice of the Pentecostal community is considered "unclean" by the academic community. However—and perhaps most importantly—it is a text that is close to the values and heart of the Pentecostal community. The "call narrative" of Isaiah (Isa 6) encapsulates the elements of divine transcendence, supernatural calling, charismatic gifting, and a disenfranchised prophet. The history and self-identity of Pentecostal communities reflect these key elements perceived in the text.

However, there are also limitations to this approach; "*Isaiah*" is not the "Old Testament" but one section of this corpus. Yet, the principles observed in the reading practices of the Pentecostal community rather than the "meanings" can help isolate the values of their readings and guide the development of a reading model that is both reflective and critical. It is a critical study of the hermeneutic employed by a particular community of a particular text (in this case, *Isaiah*), but is not intended to be a critical study of the text itself. Neither is this a history of exegesis, such as Evans'[20] history of the exegesis of Isaiah 6:9–10. Rather it is a study of current approaches in the context of charismatic Christianity either unexamined by critical scholarship or whose contribution has yet to be incorporated into critical scholarship.

The employment of *Isaiah* as a case study to construct a reading model for the entire Old Testament also raises questions concerning the limits of the study. What is the "Old Testament" that the reading model describes—or more pertinently—*whose* "Old Testament"? While the title "Old Testament" has been utilized by Christians from the very early centuries, its usage has been brought into question in recent years. In the past, this term has implied the judgment that the older testament is an antiquated writing,

---

20. Evans, *To See and Not Perceive.*

superseded by the "New" Testament.[21] Instead, many biblical scholars prefer to use the designation of "Hebrew Bible" to reflect the roots of the text in Judaism. However, as Holmgren notes, "We find then that the traditional designations of "Old Testament" and "New Testament" are titles that preserve the important dual witness of the Christian movement; that is, (1) a newness inherent in the new covenant brought about by Jesus and (2) a newness shaped by the traditions of the old or older covenant."[22] This affirmation does not blind Holmgren to the vulnerabilities of the use of the two titles, but suggests that the misunderstanding inherent in the designations require correction, rather than mere replacement with other expressions which contain their own misunderstandings. Just as the unique "voice" of the older covenant should not be denied, so also the impact of the Christian faith on the approach of the Pentecostal community to the older covenant text should not be denied. In the transparent experiential approach of Pentecostal readers, the "Bible" is an object which has two major divisions, both of which are objective constituents of the material whole.[23] While the term "Hebrew Bible" may help readers recognize the origins of the text in the faith of Judaism, the canon of the Hebrew Bible is quite different to the corpus adopted by the Protestant community, including the Pentecostal community. Therefore, the term "Old Testament" has been adopted rather than "Hebrew Bible," in order to reflect the canonical form of the corpus used by the Pentecostal community.

To describe and analyze the reading approaches to *Isaiah* of the Pentecostal community I will adopt two concurrent methods. The first is a meta-critical[24] study of the hermeneutical approaches observed in the history of Pentecostal publications.[25] These publications will be classified as either populist publications of journals and books, or academic publications of journals or books. While this task may seem enthusiastic (a distinctively Pentecostal attribute), the material is not as copious as it may seem due to the lack of published material in Pentecostal communities. The minimal publishing activity of the Pentecostal community is not symptomatic of a disinterest in biblical texts, but rather a reflection of its predominantly oral culture. While their publishing activity may be limited to a few journals and books, Pentecostals have primarily shared their interpretation of biblical texts through their liturgy. The worship service is the central event of the Pentecostal community. Like the reading process, the community expects to encounter God through the ritual of singing, prayer and the preaching of the word. The

21. Holmgren, *Old Testament and the Significance of Jesus*, 119. Holmgren also reflects on the ambiguities of this designation. He notes, "Christians believe that they have experienced something new in Jesus Christ and that this newness is reflected in the New Testament. How may one speak of this newness without undervaluing it or being guilty of overreaching?" (ibid., 127).

22. Ibid., 136.

23. Generally, the revisionist argument does not tend to occur to the average Pentecostal or Charismatic reader.

24. While the use of such language as "meta-critical" may be offensive from a post-modern perspective, it is deliberately used to represent the location of the Pentecostal community self-identified as "paramodern." This is a concept that will be discussed in chapter 2.

25. The meta-critical approach is also adopted by Davies in *In Search of "Ancient Israel"*; and in Fishbane, *Garments of the Torah*.

sermon teaches "biblical truth" as it speaks to the contemporary needs of the Pentecostal community.[26] Massey describes the role of the sermon in the liturgy of the Pentecostal community, "sermons are still a major part of the public services on Sundays and often at mid-week Bible studies. Pentecostal preaching tends to be enthusiastic and challenging, frequently occupying some thirty minutes of the service time. Above all, it is usually biblically centered with a traditional text or short passage as its base."[27]

For this reason it would be remiss in a study like this to neglect the role of sermons in informing the reading process of its members. In an oral culture, the sermon is a form of Pentecostal "literature." This method also recognizes that hermeneutics is not just a written phenomenon, but is also spoken. By combining the reading approaches in the limited published with this much larger oral material on *Isaiah,* we will be able to describe the Pentecostal hermeneutical process.[28] Yet while observations from the product (sermons, songs, publications)[29] of the clergy and leadership of the community is helpful in appreciating the public guidance given to reading biblical texts, it still only represents a *sample* of the membership. The "voice" of the silent majority of lay readers still must be considered.[30]

The approach to describing the actual reading processes of the Pentecostal community is the adoption of an "ethno-methodological" approach.[31] This method seeks to highlight the attitudes of sample groups as representative of the community. Priority is given to the actions or practices of the faith community as the beginning point for critical reflection and construction. As Parker[32] suggests, in the development and construction of a practical method it is crucial to represent the Pentecostal community that the actual community's voice be heard, by drawing normatively on Pentecostal experience. It is imperative to *critically reflect* upon the practices of a community of faith if a method is to truly represent and inform that community. Through the use of guided group discussion[33] from statistically "normal" populations (see Appendix A) I will compare their reading

26. Albrecht, *Rites in the Spirit*, 229.

27. Massey, "The Word of God."

28. This is also an appropriate reminder of the nature of biblical texts that began their "life" in oral circles.

29. Bird, *Bible as the Church's Book*, notes the use of scripture in worship and song in contemporary churches. She writes, "Scripture is heard in our worship in yet more ways, as a word sung as well as spoken . . . The hymns remind us too that the Scriptures played this role not simply, or even primarily, as a document from the past, but as a living word, evoking new responses and new interpretations from each generation" (ibid., 17–19).

30. Land in particular notes the important contribution and active participation of lay members of the Pentecostal community. Although he describes their involvement in the earlier Pentecostal movement, this value of lay involvement is still fundamental to the contemporary Pentecostal community. Land writes, "The whole congregation was involved in the process of formation. The singing, preaching, witnessing, testifying, ordinances (baptism, Lord's Supper, foot washing), altar calls, prayer meetings, gifts of the Spirit, all the elements of corporate worship prepared people for and called them to new birth, sanctification, Spirit baptism and life of missionary witness" (Land, *Pentecostal Spirituality*, 75).

31. Mackay, *Reinventing Australia*.

32. Parker, "Studies in Pentecostal Bible Reading," 10.

33. Mackay, *Reinventing Australia*, 312.

and reasoning processes in interpreting the text of *Isaiah*. This qualitative method is preferred over quantitative questionnaires that rationalize the measurement of attitudes and values of sample groups, as in fact there may not *be* a known "reason" for the processes that groups adopt. Qualitative research investigates the underlying attitudes of people in the attempt to explain their behavior or processes.[34] Through guided discussion, the reading processes exhibited by the representative sample of existing and divergent[35] social groups will be described, compared and contrasted. By interviews and observations, hermeneutics becomes a "process" rather than just an event. For Pentecostals it is not the event or formulations of *the* reading that counts, but the experiencing of God and of revelation that unfolds in the reading process. This could metaphorically be described in Keswick language, an antecedent of Pentecostalism, as "bringing into light."

Hugh Mackay highlights three features of a group discussion technique necessary to the success of this method. First, it must be a group of existing social networks and regular interaction.[36] In other words, it must be a real group, such as a bible study or cell group. The discussion must, secondly, be located on the "home ground of the group."[37] It must be located in a place that inspires familiarity and trust. Thirdly, the discussion must proceed uninhibited and spontaneously, as Mackay writes, "without any inference or any structure being imposed upon it by the researcher."[38] In this way, the attitudes and reading processes of the community can be "voiced." Once again, although there is the potential for numerous readings to emerge from the divergent groups, it is necessary to make general observations from these approaches and publications to conceptualize the hermeneutical processes of the community in a unified "voice." Although this description does not pretend to be the "real" voice of Pentecostals but a scholarly artifice, it is an attempt to bring academic analysis of Pentecostal hermeneutics in touch with the lives and practices of its community.

Since a community shares principles of interpretation which reflect its values, viewing Pentecostal interpretations (traditional and present) through the prism of *Isaiah* will highlight the values consistent within the development of the movement, and so throw light on this development for future analysis. This self-analysis will assist the Pentecostal community to understand their own methods of reading biblical texts, helping them to be accountable for their own method and the boundaries of their charismatic readings. For the wider academic community, this process of describing and evaluating Pentecostal hermeneutics assists those outside the movement to understand the community. In describing the "voice" of the community through readings of *Isaiah*, its speech can be

---

34. Ibid.

35. Due to the narrow sample of the qualitative method Mackay affirms that the representative groups should be diverse. He writes, "The fundamental rule is that each group and individual interviewee should be as different as possible from every other group and interviewee in the study in terms of characteristics such as age, socio-economic status, position in the life-cycle, geographical locations, etc. In data analysis, one of the primary aims is then to discern the *range* of attitudes emerging from that highly diverse sample" (ibid., 314).

36. Ibid., 312.

37. Ibid.

38. Ibid.

translated for the wider academic world. This allows Pentecostal hermeneutics to have a "voice" in the wider Christian community. The translation process, however, inevitably demands that the indigenous speech of the Pentecostal community be interpreted into the paradigm of hermeneutical methods already recognized within the academic community. The purpose of the translation proposed in this study, by contrast, is to locate Pentecostal readings in the matrix of contemporary methods and reading approaches, and to highlight the unique features that a Pentecostal reading of the Old Testament can bring to the dialogue of the ecumenical community.

PREPARING TO TALK

From the study of the real practices of the Pentecostal community in the readings of *Isaiah,* the "voice" of the community can be heard. Yet this does not mean that their interpretations are consistent with the biblical text or even productive of responsible interpretations. The voice of the community in reading Old Testament texts must engage in serious dialogue with the voice of hermeneutics. Pentecostal scholar, Gordon Fee notes, "as readers we are already interpreters of Scripture, whether we realize it or not. The real question is whether we do it *well*."[39] The readings of the Pentecostal community must be critiqued and evaluated to determine the strengths and weaknesses of their approach. From this foundation, a reading model for the Old Testament can be developed and proposed for the employment of the Pentecostal community. To achieve this, consistent with the pragmatism of the Pentecostal community, a structure for this dialogue must be followed.

Chapter 2 is an introduction to Pentecostalism—both as ideology and movement—as a dialogue partner. While Pentecostalism may be known to the other dialogue partners through reputation (or dis-reputation!) it is a burgeoning global movement that highlights the theological distinctive of "baptism in the Holy Spirit" to empower believers for witness. This presupposition of pneumatic experience or encounter with God in all areas of life, including the reading of biblical texts, is a defining feature of Pentecostal and charismatic communities. This results in a tendency toward counter-intellectualism, so that Pentecostal and charismatic communities have previously lacked the self-reflection required for academic dialogue. This is not to say that there has been no "intellecting," but rather that the community developed its identity in part by rejecting the institutions and processes which, in the 1910s and 1920s, were the normal modes of intellectual-*ism.* Yet, according to Pentecostal missiologist Allan Anderson, Pentecostalism is "fast becoming the dominant expression of Christianity and one of the most extraordinary religious phenomena in the world of any time."[40] So with this massive global growth of the community comes the responsibility of Pentecostalism to engage in both serious reflection and meet new "friends" in the fellowship of academic dialogue.

---

39. Fee, "History as Context for Interpretation."

40. Anderson cites Barrett to note that in 1997 Pentecostals-Charismatics made up approximately 27 percent of the world's Christian population and projects this will rise to approximately 44 percent by 2025 (Anderson, "Introduction: World Pentecostalism at a Crossroads," 19).

Having introduced Pentecostalism, the next chapter engages with the current conversation between Pentecostals and hermeneutics within the academy. As noted previously, while there has been an emerging interest in the development of a unique Pentecostal hermeneutic among Pentecostal scholars, there has been little reflection on the Old Testament or the actual reading practices of the community. For this reason chapter 3 also introduces the role of Scripture, particularly the Old Testament texts, to the recent conversations of Pentecostal hermeneutics in order to expand the discussion to a three-fold "fellowship."

The three-way dialogue begins in earnest in chapter 4 as the Old Testament speaks up. The critical analysis of Pentecostal readings of *Isaiah* highlights the value of New Testament faith as the readers view the Old Testament christologically. The Old Testament is viewed through the interpretative lens of the New Testament (or the Jesus story), including the baptism of the Holy Spirit narrated in its pages. However, this creates potential conflicts of interest in its questioning of the relationship between the testaments. In particular, it asks how a christological lens may hamper the discernment of the original historical witness.

In chapter 5, the Pentecostal readings of the Old Testament find a common interest with hermeneutics, particularly Semiotics. The analysis of the actual readings of *Isaiah* by the Pentecostal community highlights their practice of permitting multiple meanings from identical texts. These readings are identified as "dynamic" as the same text is used to delineate a variety of meanings and applications. The dynamic quality of the readings understands the text as a symbol or pointer to the reality of God's interaction with, and laws governing, the world. Pentecostal readers project themselves and their experience onto the text in order to discover themselves (and their experience) within its story. The purpose of their reading is not for theologizing or for historical insight, but for living the Christian faith.

However, this reading practice of the Pentecostal community also demonstrates a literalist tendency that appropriates the imagery of the biblical text without recognition of the differences in cultural location between the reader and text. This is where the conversation shifts between hermeneutics and Pentecostalism in chapter 6. As with any growing friendship, differences of opinion and perspectives must be shared in an open discussion to benefit and strengthen each member of the fellowship. In contrast to the practice of Pentecostalism, hermeneutics generally recognizes that the cultural location and world-view(s) of the biblical writers are fundamentally different from the worldview of the Pentecostal community. The recognition of the cultural and historical context of the text is thus crucial if one is to avoid irresponsible readings. The significance of the text to the original community helps provide boundaries of reasonable interpretation.

A resolution to the questions raised by the dialogue partners is explored in chapter 7. From this critical reflection on the goals of a Pentecostal hermeneutic of the Old Testament, a model for reading is proposed. This shifts the focus from the "why" of hermeneutics to the "how" of method. The method incorporates the values of the Pentecostal community previously identified. The proposal acknowledges the self-identification of the Pentecostal community as part of the continuity of God's people, from creation to the present, by proposing a model of reading the Old Testament text from the perspectives of *me, them,* and *us.* The dynamic quality of Pentecostal readings (from chapter 5) is recognized by the concern to apply the biblical text to the context of the reader—what it means to *me.* However, the inherent literalism (of chapter 6) of Pentecostal readings can be addressed in the identification of the significance of the text for *them,* the community of the people of God represented in the text. The continuation of this community in the New Testament must not quench the unique voice of the Old Testament text, but its voice must also be sought for in the significance of the text for *us*—New Testament believers who have experienced something new in Jesus Christ[41] (chapter 4) and the new covenant which he has inaugurated. The proposed model invites the participation of these three voices (me, them and us) in a mutually informing dialogue.

Chapter 8, as a conclusion, reflects on the implications of this study for both the Pentecostal community and the wider, ecumenical Christian church. The hope for an ongoing triune fellowship requires from each dialogue partner deliberate effort and potential adjustment. This includes a continued commitment from the Pentecostal community to reflection and responsible reading practices, and a real openness from the academic community. Yet as each friend contributes to the ongoing discussion and addresses prevalent issues in the relationship, it establishes a foundation beyond the mere identification of common interests, perhaps to become friends for life.

41. Holmgren, *Old Testament and the Significance of Jesus,* 127.

2

Introducing Pentecostalism

As the youngest member of the budding conversation, Pentecostalism has only recently learnt the scholarly vocabulary and theologizing tone that unlocks the ivory gate to the academic conversation. Yet, while it has attempted initial connection with new friends within academic circles, introducing and defining this "voice" of Pentecostalism is fraught with difficulties. One main obstacle is the elusive description of "Pentecostalism," since the term refers interchangeably to a spirituality, a diffuse social movement, a theological projection of the action of God, and a set of scholarly presuppositions about new religious movements. Yet this lack of clear classification for the purposes of academic discussion has not stopped the growth of Pentecostalism nor been of concern to its grassroots adherents. From its inception in the early twentieth century, the leaders of the Pentecostal movement have traditionally been uneducated and uninterested in "theologizing." Connection with academia was deemed of little importance and a distraction from their focus on missional activity. Leadership credentials instead were (and continue to be) based on a sense of "calling" and impetus through personal experience of the Holy Spirit. Because of this experiential orientation and restorationist location and intention, Pentecostals have historically reckoned it more important to pray than to study or organize. This, along with the diversity of Pentecostal movements that have permeated every area of the globe, has meant that Pentecostalism has eluded definition. As Anderson notes, "It is not always easy to define what is meant by 'pentecostal,' as the term refers to a wide variety of movements scattered throughout the world, ranging from the fundamentalist and white middle class 'mega-churches' to indigenous movements in the Third World that have adapted to their cultural and religious contexts to such an extent that many western pentecostals would probably doubt their qualifications as 'Christian' movements."[1]

---

1. Anderson, "Introduction: World Pentecostalism at a Crossroads," 19.

While the emergence of the charismatic renewal (from the late 1950s) has given the experience of Spirit baptism a new respectability in Western societies, its most significant growth continues to be in the Third World. As a consequence, this diverse "voice" of Pentecostalism is currently represented to the academic community by the newly emerging scholarship. While this, mostly Western, Pentecostal scholarship is more inclined to "theologize, study, and organize" than their predecessors, they do not always have much influence as voices to their movement. Therefore it is imperative that Pentecostal scholars attempt to describe, rather than just prescribe, the nature of Pentecostalism as both a spirituality and a movement, if only so that others may ultimately more accurately prescribe the academic categories which will be used about the movement in the future.

PENTECOSTAL SPIRITUALITY

The Pentecostal worldview has been described by sociologist Margaret Poloma as an anomaly; maintaining a tension between the "rational cognitive and the affective experiential."[2] It developed within the zone of engagement between the premillennial, healing and Holiness movements of the nineteenth century and theological modernism, emerging from sectarian isolation to eventually become a worldwide fellowship of multiple variations and with various degrees of organization.[3] There are two distinct features of Pentecostal spirituality, namely, the experiential orientation of their epistemology and the doctrinal appropriation of this in the "Baptism in the Holy Spirit." The orientation toward and through experience can be described as an epistemology in which religious truths are not objects of abstract belief (i.e., belief as cognition), but are living facts experimentally known as personal, first-hand knowledge (i.e., belief as comprehension).[4] Ellington writes, "Doctrines may be challenged and even overturned without striking at the very heart of Pentecostal faith because the central emphasis of Pentecostalism is not a teaching which must be believed or a proof which can be deduced and defended against all challenges, but a God who must be reckoned with in direct encounter."[5]

Pentecostalism does not dismiss doctrine, but emphasizes its praxis rather than its creedal representation. While Pentecostals do not claim to be the only group who experience God, their experience is different in its orientation to other traditions within the wider ecumenical dialogue. This is due to their emphasis upon direct intuition and experience of God, as interpreted through historical restorationism. According to Albrecht, this situates Pentecostal spirituality within the Christian mystical tradition, though Pentecostals would not, as a whole, accept the subjectivism which such identification entails.[6] The experiential knowledge of Pentecostalism argues for a truth outside the realm of scientific rationalism, however much it interacts with that realm through "evidences"

---

2. Poloma, *Assemblies of God at the Crossroads*, 8.

3. These include classical and charismatic; Catholic and Protestant; Third World, North American, Hispanic, Asian; Trinitarian and Oneness.

4. Albrecht, *Rites in the Spirit*, 14–15.

5. Ellington, "Pentecostalism and the Authority of Scripture," 17.

6. Albrecht, *Rites in the Spirit*, 238.

(tongues, prophecy, healings, etc.). It does not negate reason, nor deify sensory experience, but recognizes them as sources of knowledge and the means of being embraced in God's greater movement. Bridges-Johns and Johns describe Pentecostal epistemology by the Hebrew term *yāda* "to know," which is generally "treated as knowledge which comes through experience."[7] Therefore, Pentecostalism will emphasize a relational knowledge of God, impelled by the fellowship with the Holy Spirit who is known through direct and supernatural encounter.

While the "mystical" references within Pentecostal epistemology emphasize its individual nature, the importance of anti-subjective reflexive "evidence" results in ritual which roots Pentecostal experience within the community.[8] The high participation level of adherents recorded by Poloma in her study of the North American AG[9] reflects the importance of ritual participation within Pentecostalism. The worship service has traditionally played a central role as the outlet for community participation. It is in this corporate event—which in part provides legitimate space for bodily realization of the invisible through spiritual "performance"—that individuals seek for a divine encounter, and the group seeks divine legitimization of its normativity. The liturgy of the service, according to Albrecht, deliberately aims to create pathways into the direct and intimate presence of God as each worshipper is facilitated and impacted by fellow worshippers.[10] Albrecht identifies three media functions that transmit the communal experience within the worship service: biblical, oral and kinesthetic/musical.[11] The use of biblical images and symbols to describe the Pentecostal experience is fundamental to its liturgy. Albrecht asserts, "The biblical symbols provide the primary medium through which the community understands itself and communicates that understanding; biblical images contain and carry the Pentecostal spirituality."[12]

As Pentecostalism is orientated to the affections, biblical images such as "fire," "power," and "wind" are often used to articulate the experience. These elemental images are used to describe the individual experience to the community, usually through the medium of oral testimony or preaching. According to Albrecht, the oral emphasis in Pentecostalism not only describes its spirituality but also prescribes it. It creates expectation within the community that their own experience—understood through these elemental biblical images—will in turn provide future testimony in the ongoing oral transmission of liturgies and moral codes within the community.[13] The third medium is the dual dimension of kinesthetic/musical. Music and movement are an important reflection of the communal experience of God, from lifting hands to dancing. Often the musical lyrics and dance express and represent these elemental biblical images experienced by the community. Movement and worship are also a means of response to

7. Bridges-Johns and Johns, "Yielding to the Spirit," 112.

8. Albrecht, *Rites in the Spirit,* 245.

9. Poloma, *Assemblies of God at the Crossroads,* 13.

10. Albrecht, *Rites in the Spirit,* 149.

11. Ibid., 246.

12. Ibid.

13. Ibid.

God by the community in its ritual participation. Physical stances and representations of surrender to the divine are encouraged. Physical acknowledgment of a transcendent encounter with God is encouraged by responses such as altar calls or kneeling.[14] Therefore knowledge of God in Pentecostalism, both individually and communally, is a transcendent experience, usually requiring a physical response and described through the media of biblical imagery.

This presupposition of pneumatic experience or encounter with God through the liturgy and worship of the community includes the reading of biblical texts.[15] As Pentecostal readers bring this presupposition of charismatic experience to their reading of biblical texts, there is also an expectation that the Spirit will be encountered in the reading process. They anticipate being challenged by the text for personal transformation and change, as well as to experience God. The Spirit speaks through the text beyond the original meaning or original context of the biblical passage to the contemporary situation of the Pentecostal reader. The experience of the Spirit provides meaning, not just application; and since the experience of the Spirit differs according to the community and the individual members of the community, so also the meaning of the text differs according to the individual context in which it is read. This provides multiple interpretations according to the individual's experience and potentially results in multiple meanings.[16] These meanings are the result of the interpretive methods employed by the Pentecostal community, however intuitively or subconsciously they are adopted. Biblical scholar, Conrad, writes, "Meaning arises when readers bring to the text interpretive strategies, which themselves are conventions employed by the community of interpretation to which the reader belongs."[17]

This interaction of Spirit and text to produce meaning in the Pentecostal reading community can be exemplified by reference to Pentecostal literature and liturgical testimony. This process was instanced in a recent prophecy given by Norm Armstrong, leading Pentecostal evangelist and church planter, based on the words of Deuteronomy 1:6–8. The passage begins, "The LORD our God spoke to us at Horeb, saying, '*You have stayed long enough at this mountain.* Resume your journey, and *go into the hill country* of the Amorites as well as into the neighboring regions'" (emphasis added).[18] Understood as a prophetic message, this text was interpreted as an instruction from God for the national Assemblies of God Bible College in Australia (Alphacrucis College, then known as Southern Cross College)[19] to relocate from the peripheral Blue Mountains (Katoomba)

14. Ibid., 247.

15. In this sense, this paper shares the concern of Melugin in "use theory"—concern for what the text is used to *do* (Melugin, "Introduction" to *New Visions of Isaiah*, 27. This is also consistent with some of the interest of speech-act theory and performative linguistics—see Austin, *How to do things with Words* and Searle, *Speech-Acts*.

16. It will be discussed in subsequent chapters whether these multiple meanings produce conflicting interpretations.

17. Conrad, *Reading Isaiah.* 325.

18. Emphasis from Fogarty, "Toward a Pentecostal Hermeneutic," 7.

19. Alphacrucis College is the national training college for the Assemblies of God in Australia.

to suburban Chester Hill.[20] The commands of the text were read through contemporary experience, as inspired by the Spirit, rather than within its original context or possible authorial intention. This suggests that the dynamic experience of the Spirit, central to the identity of the Pentecostal community, contributes to the interpretive process (a concept to be tested in this study). While it is not the intent of this book to describe the theology[21] or epistemology of charismatic experience, a central interest is in how the experience influences the reading of biblical texts. As "experience" is a core element in various reading approaches in general scholarship (such as feminist and reader-response theories)[22] it is also the experience of and values which flow from the "charismatic encounter" that distinguish the Pentecostal community.

In the attempt to describe the contribution of a dynamic experience of the Spirit to the Pentecostal worldview, some scholars, such as Macchia,[23] have adopted the symbol of "tongues."[24] The symbol of "tongues" is utilized to represent a charismatic experience crucial to the identity of the community. It symbolizes the empowerment of the Spirit as witnessed by the Christian community in Acts 2 to perform the task of building the kingdom of God. The spirit empowers the Pentecostal community to be witnesses of the gospel of Jesus Christ in and through the outpouring of *charismata*. These gifts of grace, according to 1 Corinthians 12, include tongues, prophecy, and healing. The Pentecostal community identifies itself as being in continuity with the early church in the outpouring of these gifts of grace and the ongoing expansion of God's kingdom.[25] For this community, the testimony of Spirit empowerment in Acts is normative; the text is understood as a literal description of the ministry of the early church that should be

20. Fogarty, "Toward a Pentecostal Hermeneutic," 7.

21. The development of a unique Pentecostal theology is discussed by Russell Spittler who writes, "Interest in developing a distinct theology proper: So far as any published 'systematic theology' is concerned, a self-conscious effort to frame religious truth for the Pentecostal tradition within its own time and space—something even remotely comparable to Donald Gelpi's work for Roman Catholic charismatics, not to mention Karl Barth's magisterial *Church Dogmatics* [emic] for the Reformed tradition—there simply is no such Pentecostal theology. Even the interest to produce such a work has barely surfaced" (Spittler, "Scripture and the Theological Enterprise"). However, other Pentecostal scholars such as McKay are defensive of this critique of the movement for its supposed lack of theological reflection. McKay asserts, "It is often said that charismatics are strong on praise, but weak on theology. I would rather say that they are strong on praise and strong on their own brand of theology, but unhappy about the sort of dispassionate, uncommitted theology one frequently encounters in an academic setting" (McKay, "When the Veil is Taken Away," 19).

22. For example, see A. Loades and C. Exum.

23. Macchia, "Groans Too Deep for Words," 153.

24. For further examination on the use of "tongues" as a symbol, see Amos Yong and Frank Macchia. However, as Clifton notes, this is not all that the Pentecostal community has to offer academic scholarship. He writes, "While the Pentecostal church has been shaped by the emphasis on *glossolalia* and subsequence, we have perhaps reached the point where we ought to be able to recognise the irony of the 1999 publication of the *Asian Journal of Pentecostal Studies*, the theme of which was 'Initial Evidence, Again.' It is also apparent that non-Pentecostal theologians seem to believe that Pentecostals have little else to contribute" (Clifton, "Pentecostal Theological Method: A Colourful and Creative Approach," 9.

25. According to Land, the responsibility felt by the Pentecostal community for evangelism and mission extends from their Wesleyan/Armenian theological roots which emphasized the personal agency and responsibility of the believer (Land, *Pentecostal Spirituality*, 76).

likewise adopted by contemporary believers. Perhaps the most controversial application of the gifts of the Spirit as described in Acts and Corinthians has been the "restoration" of the gift of "tongues," which has become a symbol of this normative experience of Spirit empowerment.

While there has been little critical reflection on the experience-orientation of Pentecostal spirituality, the second distinctive feature of Pentecostalism has been thoroughly theorized within the tradition. Although there are as many definitions of Spirit Baptism as there are Pentecostal groups (in which a general discussion may not be representative of all views of Pentecostalism), their syntax would usually include "baptism," "empowering," "power" or "infilling" to describe this phenomenon. Within the Australian AG, "Baptism in the Holy Spirit" can be defined as an experience subsequent to salvation. Their statement of belief affirms that the baptism of the Holy Spirit according to Acts 2:4 is given to believers who ask (Luke 11:13). The doctrine of Spirit Baptism is based almost exclusively on a reading of Luke-Acts, which is generally considered by Pentecostals to be a normative record of the early church. It is the fulfillment of the prayer of the Son for the Holy Spirit to be sent (Matt 3:11; Mark 1:8; Luke 3:16; Acts 1:5) to empower them to witness. Like salvation, it is not dependant on the merit of the recipient, neither is it an automatic endowment: the believer must ask and receive (Acts 19:2). Spirit Baptism is also separate to the work of the Holy Spirit in sanctification. Its purpose is the glorification of Jesus Christ and the edification of the body of Christ. Just as the Holy Spirit's empowering was the connection between the kerygma of Christ and the early church, a correlation to be reciprocated by the contemporary church.

The empowering of the believer by Spirit Baptism is witnessed by the physical bestowal and experience of the *charismata*, understood by Pentecostals to be identical to the "spiritual gifts" of 1 Corinthians 12. These gifts (such as the demonstrative gifts of healings and miracles) can act as signs to the unbeliever of the power of God, while other gifts (such as prophecy) are for the edification of the body of Christ. According to the Australian AG, Spirit baptism is evidenced primarily by the initial gift of tongues (*glossolalia*). A definition for this gift is presented by Frank Macchia: "Glossolalia is an unclassifiable, free speech in response to an unclassifiable, free God."[26] Apart from the syntax used to describe Spirit baptism, the main distinction between Pentecostal and "charismatic" doctrine is the formers' insistence of *glossolalia* as the *initial* evidence of Spirit baptism. However, the impact of the charismatic renewal upon classical Pentecostal groups such as the Australian AG and the institutionalization process continues to threaten the doctrinal "sacred cow" of *glossolalia*. A recent survey of Australian AG women pastors indicates only fifty percent "strongly agreed" that tongues were the initial evidence of Spirit baptism.[27] This suggests to some that the distinctive features of Pentecostalism are threatened, but on the other hand (a more likely scenario) it may simply reflect the shift of experiential focus to other areas, particularly the encounter of euphoric worship in the Pentecostal service, in ways not verbalized in our current theology. As global

26. Macchia, "Groans Too Deep for Words," 61.

27. Grey, "Torn Stockings and Enculturation," 12.

Pentecostalism reflects upon these distinct features of its spirituality, and the impact of this experience-orientation upon its developing theologies, they can begin to join the fellowship of ecumenical dialogue.

A corollary of the spirit experience central to the Pentecostal community is the rejection of intellectual*ism* and doctrinar*ism*. This tendency toward non-intellectualism in favor of embracing the spiritual dynamic highlights the Pentecostal community as existing outside the dominant modernist culture of Western society.[28] Experiencing God is considered the priority, rather than dealing with God intellectually.[29] The pneumatic experience of Pentecostal spirituality has previously not been seen as compatible with a rigid doctrinal system that prescribes liturgy in words and deeds.[30] Instead, a bittersweet value of the Pentecostal community is a pragmatism that makes the movement more action-orientated than reflective. According to Macchia, this lack of critical scholarship in Pentecostalism is reflective of its eschatological expectation of the soon-coming Christ and evangelistic fervor.[31] As Johnston notes, this was typified in the statement of Michael Harper—made when he was editor of the British charismatic magazine *Renewal*—who wrote, "The world awaits a fresh manifestation of Christ within His Body, the Church. It is tired of . . . airy-fairy doctrines of theologians. 'Show us,' the world yells at the Church. 'Let us see you do it. Then we'll listen to your words.'"[32] The anti-intellectualism of Pentecostalism is reinforced by the fact that until recently there were no educational requirements attached to holding ministerial credentials in many of the formal organizations, including the Australian AG. Spirit-gifting is perceived to be the main factor in ministry rather than the educational qualifications of the pastor, because "spirit gifting" is functional—it makes ministry and churches work.

This pragmatic value also extends to the reading of biblical texts that reject the intellectual pursuit of a scientific hermeneutic in favor of a pragmatic approach: obey what should be taken literally and allegorize the rest.[33] Again, Pentecostal scholars such as Land recognize the centrality of the sign of "tongues" as a symbol of this anti-intellectualism. Land writes, "Outsiders focused quickly on tongues as indicative of a whole movement of irrational, revivalistic, hysterical protest by the disinherited and illiterate."[34] That said, it is important to note that the anti-intellectualism of early Pentecostals was not intrinsic to their theology, but rather driven by their ecclesiological isolation. Born in the fight of mainline denominations over theological modernism and fundamentalism, Pentecostals incorporated "theological modernism" as an element of "the world" which their spiritual dualism rejected. The activity of the mind—seen in a brilliant pulpit performer (e.g., F. B. Van Eyk), a respected journal editor (E. N. Bell) or prophetic teacher (Donald Gee)—was seen as the concomitant of ministry. What they rejected were intel-

28. Poloma, *Assemblies of God at the Crossroads*, 5.

29. Roelofs, "Charismatic Christian Thought," 227.

30. Ibid., 227.

31. Macchia, "The Struggle for Global Witness," 8.

32. Johnston, "Pentecostalism and Theological Hermeneutics," 53.

33. Cargal, "Beyond the Fundamentalist-Modernist Controversy," 165.

34. Land, *Pentecostal Spirituality*, 61.

lectuals as a class claiming the right to judge the church, and intellectualism as a process which undermined certainty.

For the Pentecostal community, their pneumatic experience provides a testimony and focus for daily life. As Parker notes, "Pentecostals give exuberant testimonies to their experience, citing them as evidence of the presence of the Holy Spirit."[35] The biblical text was not only to be read but lived, spoken, prophesied, sung, and preached as an active force. As noted above, the prolific use of testimonies, preaching and narratives in the Pentecostal community (in particular, the worship service) highlights its nature as an oral culture. Albrecht highlights the importance of the oral nature of the Pentecostal community in the expression of the biblical text. He writes, "Pentecostals recognize the voice of God, the word, in biblical messages (e.g., sermons, teachings, exhortations), testimonial narratives and charismatic words."[36] This means that the theology of the Pentecostal community is transferred primarily through oral rather than written communication. Pentecostal spirituality is "caught" rather than "taught." As Smit writes, "In a particular social location we read with particular interpretive interests and according to particular methods, because we have seen other people in that location, in that community and in that tradition, do it in that way."[37]

Yet, most Pentecostal readers are unaware of the values or reading practices of their own community; they think it is the obvious and natural way to read.[38] This is an important consideration for the expression of the actual practices of the Pentecostal reading community and highlights the need for the "voice" of the Pentecostal community to be heard and understood.

While strict adherence to the literal meaning or "face value" of the biblical text is theoretically maintained by Pentecostal readers, it is not the original context or scientific factors that interest them. This is particularly highlighted by the theological distinctive of the movement, baptism in the Holy Spirit, which empowers believers for witness. Just as the bible describes the experience of receiving the Holy Spirit in Acts 2 as a divine gift to the New Testament community, so the Pentecostal community expects to receive the gift in their contemporary context. The Pentecostal community appropriates pneumatic experiences, such as the charismatic gifts (especially the gift of tongues) as part of their present-day Christianity.[39] Theories of authorial intention or original context are subordinate to their expectation of charismatic encounter through the text.[40] Pentecostal

35. Parker, *Led by the Spirit*, 21.

36. Albrecht, *Rites in the Spirit,* 229.

37. Smit, "Biblical Hermeneutics," 303.

38. Ibid.

39. Like Land (*Pentecostal Spirituality*, 78) the word "experience" will be used with varying degrees of care, varying from transient feelings to the most common usage of a pneumatic encounter in which the presence of God is realized or felt in the believer's life. However, whatever degree of emotion or Spirit-impact, the term "experience" represents a crisis or encounter.

40. This expectation of "charismatic encounter" relates both to the spiritual gifts (as identified in 1 Cor 13) and a spiritual or ontic encounter. The use of "encounter" and "experience" in this sense will be used interchangeably through this book.

readers expect to encounter the living God in their approach to the biblical text.[41] The rejection of theorizing and critical reflection by the early Pentecostals certainly resulted in anti-intellectualism at the movement's popular level, though less so at the level of its intellectual leadership, a group which has expanded with the growth of specifically Pentecostal institutions.

The anti-intellectualism and social marginalization of the Pentecostal movement is particularly noted by M. Poloma in her sociological study of the Assemblies of God, USA. As noted above, Poloma describes the Pentecostal worldview as a protest against Modernity, in that its definitions of reality are outside the interpretations of the dominant secular and modern views,[42] including the normative experience of the paranormal.[43] Poloma isolates four key characteristic traits of the Pentecostal-Charismatic movement: "the norm of experiencing the sacred in the midst of a profane world; the norm of expecting divine guidance for both personal and institutional concerns, standing in contrast to rational and bureaucratic methods; a reticulate organization that refuses to immortalize tradition and the past; and personal participation of the vast majority of adherents in the charismata movement."[44]

Throughout her study, Poloma draws upon the observations of Weber, who identifies the first stage of formation of a religious community (the "prophetic stage") as generally receptive of the charismata and alternative ministry, including that of women—an emphasis which rarely goes beyond that initial phase.[45] According to Weber's thesis, when this routinization sets in, pneumatic manifestations come to be regarded as disreputable. As Poloma's study suggests, this "routinization of charisma" and process of institutionalization is a potential threat to the dynamic values of pneumatic experience that have marked the Pentecostal movement. David Martin points out that the Pentecostal response to liberalization and bureaucratization is downward mobilization—to find a constituency that is prepared to accept pneumatic phenomena as empowerment as opposed to de-statusization.[46] This can be constructed as anti-intellectualism—though the flipside to this construction is the intellectual politics of exclusion. However, there is hope among Pentecostal scholars that this anti-intellectualism inherent in the origins of the community is shifting, and a deliberate attempt to manage the shift so that it does not result in the de-naturing of Pentecostalism. The values of critical reflection and Spirit-experience are no longer mutually exclusive to the community. Ironically, this is perhaps due to the institutionalization and shifting social location of Pentecostalism in many Western nations, away from the margins into the respectable middle class. While the process of institutionalization has come with certain costs (particularly for women ministers outside the margins of respectable

41. Ellington, "Pentecostalism and the Authority of Scripture," 17.

42. Poloma, *Assemblies of God at the Crossroads*, 5.

43. Ibid., 6.

44. Ibid.

45. Ibid., 102.

46. Martin, *Pentecostalism*.

middle class society),[47] it has produced a positive shift towards the acceptance of critical reflection. As one of the earliest students of Pentecostalism, Walter Hollenweger notes "it is now possible to speak in tongues and to be a critical thinker at a university at the same time—this was not possible in the past."[48]

PENTECOSTALISM AS A GLOBAL MOVEMENT

While the spirituality of Pentecostalism emphasizes the experiential nature of the movement, this is similarly reflected in its growth and organization. Initially, Pentecostalism grew from the testimony and sharing of experience that was later organized into what is described as a dynamic "movement" (rather than denomination). The consequence or overflow of the Pentecostal experience was the missionary and evangelistic drive that has led to its phenomenal growth worldwide. It is what Hollenweger describes as an "oral missionary movement."[49] Therefore it is the purpose of this section to understand the features of the origins and growth of Pentecostalism as a global movement,[50] to help locate it in the triune dialogue with hermeneutics and the Old Testament. While the history of Pentecostalism and its predecessor, the Wesleyan-Holiness movement, are well-documented by the scholarship (particularly in the Western context), it is not the purpose of this section to duplicate their historical research. The aim of this section—along with the previous description of its core ethos and spirituality—is to create a sense of the general history and variations of Pentecostalism globally that contribute to its "voice." Although there are significant parallels between the development of global Pentecostalism and its American counterpart (including the routinization of charisma and emerging professional male clergy), it is also important to realize that there are significant differences. It is therefore crucial to understand the beginnings of Pentecostalism in the twentieth century, its development, and diversity as a global movement.

What has been particularly interesting within the intra-dialogue of Pentecostalism as a global movement is the drive toward exclusivity of definition by some North American scholars. While many of the indigenous movements in various global contexts have adapted Pentecostal teaching and spirituality to their cultures to such a degree that some Western scholars question their "Christian-ness," it is the common adoption of the "spirituality" of Spirit experience that includes these groups within the broad definition of "Pentecostalism." While the classical Pentecostal movements in North America tend to define themselves doctrinally (particularly in relation to the doctrine of "initial evidence"), the Pentecostal movement globally primarily defines themselves in relation to the experience of the working of the Holy Spirit and practice of charismata.[51] For this

---

47. For a description of this cost of institutionalisation in the Australian context, see Grey, "Torn Stockings"

48. Hollenweger, "The Black Roots of Pentecostalism," 33.

49. Ibid., 42.

50. While the exact size of the movement is unknown, it was estimated in 1997 that the Pentecostals/charismatic movement worldwide exceeded 497 million people (Anderson, "Introduction: World Pentecostalism at a Crossroads," 19).

51. Ibid., 20.

reason, scholars such as Hollenweger and Anderson argue for the inclusion of groups that *practice* the spirituality as genuinely Pentecostal movements.[52] Freston notes that there is a politics of comparison among Pentecostals, with first world countries including as "Pentecostal" those abroad who are unlike themselves because Pentecostal churches grow more quickly outside the first world, while two-thirds world churches include the bureaucratized first world church because of its influence and financial resources.

The characterization of Pentecostalism as a global movement is due to its common "spirituality" of spirit experience.[53] Pentecostalism has grown at various rates in all areas of the world, irrespective of nation-state boundaries. As a religious movement, Pentecostalism is defined not only by its origin, but also by its regionalized development and identity. While the subsequent chapters of this book focus on the Australian expression and context of Pentecostalism, the attempt to define the "voice" of Pentecostalism must take into account this global presence. To do so, the identity of Pentecostalism within six regions of the world will be examined in a general overview. While this is not intended to be a comprehensive account of the history and growth of the global movement, this generalized study does highlight the shared and diverse features of the movement that each contribute to the nuanced voice of Pentecostalism.

North America

While it is assumed by most North American Pentecostal scholars that contemporary global Pentecostal groups find their origin in the 1906 Azusa Street revival in Los Angeles, this supposition is not necessarily supported by international research, particularly within the Australian context.[54] Moreover, it is not the case for Pentecostal Holiness denominations, such as the Church of God (Cleveland), which traces its origins back to the Cherokee County revival of 1896.[55] Nonetheless, the importance of this event as a *symbol* or organizing principal for global Pentecostals cannot be denied.[56] The beginnings of Pentecostalism in North America are thus generally traced to two significant events.[57] The first event was in Topeka, Kansas, when Agnes Ozman, on 1 January, 1901, received prayer at a small Bible training institute founded by Charles Fox Parham—a prayer which resulted in Ozman speaking in tongues (*glossolalia*). This "outpouring" continued among the other students in the following days. The second event occurred five years later in a Bonnie Brae Street prayer meeting, and then relocated to a disused African-American

52. Ibid., 20.

53. Klaus, "Pentecostalism as a Global Culture," 127.

54. For example, Barry Chant suggests that, in the Australian context, "there is little evidence that Pentecostalism was imported" but was an indigenous movement with interaction with similar international groups.

55. Viz. Hunter, "Spirit-baptism and the 1896 Revival in Cherokee County, North Carolina." For a formal response to the Azusa Street claim, see Creech, "Visions of Glory," 405–24.

56. Clifton (an Australian theologian) suggests that the Azusa Street revival functions globally as a symbol of the Pentecostal identity and theology in Clifton, "Pentecostal Theological Method."

57. While scholars continue to debate for a single "birthplace" of Pentecostalism, it is the suggestion of this book that such distinction is unnecessary when understood as a diverse and complex movement. For an overview of this debate see Hollenweger, "The Black Roots of Pentecostalism," 33–44.

Methodist Episcopal church on Azusa Street, Los Angeles. The catalyst was the preaching of William Seymour;[58] a student of Parham's who was proclaiming this message of Spirit baptism. When Seymour and seven other seekers received this Spirit baptism, the legend of the Azusa Street revival was born.[59] The revival at the Azusa Street Apostolic Faith Mission became a centre for early Pentecostalism as it combined the white American holiness traditions with the expressive worship of the African-American community.[60] It was here that Pentecostalism is credited with the beginning of its enormous impact—not only throughout the United States, but also around the world, sponsoring missions to Canada, Europe, Africa, Asia, and South America.[61] The features of Spirit experience that marked this birth of the Pentecostal movement in North America continued to distinguish the movement for the rest of the century.[62]

According to Synan, the revival swept many holiness denominations into the new movement, including the Church of God in Christ.[63] However the revival began to splinter into separate groups reflecting the various social contexts of its disciples. The formation of the Assemblies of God in 1914, for instance, was seen partly as a racial separation when ministers who had previously been licensed by the largely black COGIC separated to form a distinct organization.[64] The church groups that formed early in the revival, including those as late as the "International Church of the Foursquare Gospel" founded by Canadian preacher Aimee Semple McPherson in 1923, came to be known as "Classical Pentecostalism." However after World War II, Pentecostalism in Northern America began to merge with dominant Evangelicalism for the verbalization of their doctrinal position. While the Pentecostal movement dwelt among the fringes of Evangelicalism, it was not until the Charismatic renewal beginning in the 1950s that the wind of Spirit-experience was carried into mainline denominations, with both Roman Catholic and Protestant expressions emerging in this trans-denominational renewal.[65] This blending of Spirit experience with the culture and theological values of some mainline denominations also led to the development of independent or "third wave" charismatic groups, exemplified by the "Association of Vineyard Churches" founded by healing evangelist John Wimber. The various cultural and theological differences between Pentecostal and Charismatic groups will be discussed below. Like the global impact of the Azusa Street revival, this second

58. William Seymour is described by Owens as "Born in Louisiana, the son of former slaves, Seymour was a short, stocky African-American man who was blind in one eye and graced by a meek and humble spirit." In Owens, "The Azusa Street Revival," 46.

59. Albrecht, *Rites in the Spirit*, 30–33.

60. Synan, "The Pentecostal Century," 4.

61. Ibid., 7–8.

62. Albrecht, *Rites in the Spirit,* 35.

63. Synan also notes that the Church of God continues to be the largest Pentecostal denomination in the US with a membership in 2001 of almost six million (Synan, "The Pentecostal Century," 6).

64. This was intensified by the 1916 controversy of "Oneness" or Jesus-only theology that led to a further split within the movement.

65. Albrecht, *Rites in the Spirit,* 37. According to Albrecht, this second stage of the Pentecostal movement is variously defined as "Neo-Pentecostalism," the "Charismatic Movement" or the "Charismatic Renewal."

phase of the Pentecostal movement in the North American context has had enormous impact on the shape of Christianity globally.

South America

The introduction of the Pentecostal movement to South America was not a mere import from Azusa Street but, as Sepúlveda suggests regarding the Chilean experience, a merging of independent yet contemporary revivals with that described in Northern America.[66] The same indigenous Pentecostal experiences seen at Azusa Street are reported to have occurred in Brazil and Argentina in 1910 and other Latin American nations shortly thereafter.[67] The Chilean experience had direct links to Mukti, in India, while Argentinean and Brazilian movements were connected to both indigenous and diasporic links to global movements, including indirect connections to Azusa Street. What the South American experience does have in common with Azusa Street is that Pentecostalism was (and continues to be) associated disproportionately with the poor and less educated.[68] However as the movement has grown, there is currently a shift away from the earlier anti-intellectualism among some sectors of Pentecostalism in South America as some from prominent church groups in Chile and Argentina engage in academic discussion and scholarship.[69] This embracing of education in major centers of South American Pentecostalism is also reflective of the shift in class values and recruitment from middle-class Catholics and Protestants.[70]

The current growth rate of Pentecostalism in South America during the last two to three decades is described by Cleary as "explosive," particularly at the grassroots level.[71] He estimated in 1999 that the general Protestant population in Latin America and the Caribbean was 40 million (in a population of about 400 million). Pentecostals comprise 75–90 percent of the Protestant figure, a percentage which is growing. However, while this gives a general overview, the distribution of Pentecostals is localized and not even across the continent. For example, Protestants in Puerto Rico and Guatemala (most of them Pentecostals) comprise approximately 40 percent of the population, whereas Pentecostalism is not prominent in other nations such as Costa Rica, where they make up less than 10 percent of the general population.[72]

Central to this growth is the Spirit experience in both individual piety and communal worship where the *charismata* are present and expected. Because of this experiential nature and spirituality of Pentecostalism, it has spread throughout South America as primarily an indigenous movement[73] with little cultural adjustment. The growth has been so

66. Sepúlveda, "Indigenous Pentecostalism and the Chilean Experience," 113.

67. Cleary, "Latin American Pentecostalism," 134.

68. Freston, *Evangelicals and Politics in Asia, Africa and Latin America*, 194.

69. Cleary, "Latin American Pentecostalism," 135.

70. For example, Cleary notes that approximately 40 percent of Pentecostals in Chile belong to the middle classes (ibid., 136).

71. Ibid., 134.

72. Ibid.

73. As Martin notes, this does not ignore the massive investment of both funds and personnel (mis-

phenomenal that South American Pentecostalism is now being exported to other groups around the world, particularly through movements such as the revivalism of Juan Carlos Ortiz and Carlos Annacondia, and through the G12 cell church structure founded in Bogotá, Colombia. However this massive growth of Pentecostalism in recent decades cannot be mentioned without recognition of the resurgence of Catholic Christianity. Considering some of the commonalities of their spirituality, this perhaps suggests a wider religious awakening of which Pentecostalism is a part.[74]

Africa

Unlike the South American experience, Pentecostalism was birthed and developed in Africa as a post-Azusa Street missionary emphasis from North America.[75] Azusa Street was itself in part an extension of developments in African-American spirituality, and re-flex missions from this directed at the post-Civil War restoration of slaves to Africa. For example, Seymour, it will be remembered, was initially called to Los Angeles to replace Julia Hutchins, who was intending to leave on mission to Sierra Leone. After arrival, the movement rapidly indigenized. The growth in sub-Sahara Africa in recent decades within the region is likened to the explosive expansion in South America. According to Hollenweger, this growth has occurred not because of the doctrinal particularities but because of its roots in the spirituality of the nineteenth century African American slave religion.[76] These roots emphasize the experience of Pentecostalism and practice of the *charismata*, particularly divine healing, exorcism, and glossolalia. Pentecostalism has adapted and emerged in the African context as an authentic expression of indigenous African Christianity.

Again the majority growth of Pentecostal groups in sub-Sahara Africa has oc-curred in the last two to three decades; a decade later than the explosive growth in Latin America.[77] The groups that have emerged in this time tend to combine elements of Christian tradition with indigenous African culture. With emphasis on the interac-tion between the supernatural and material worlds that the Pentecostal "spirituality" and practice of Spirit baptism permit, it is has been developed as an ideal candidate for a "Christian" expression within Africa. In this sense, it is also a very pragmatic gospel as it seeks to address practical needs such as sickness, poverty, unemployment, and oppres-sion from evil spirits.[78] For example, in South Africa, 38 percent of all Christians can be found in the proto-Pentecostal African Independent Churches. In a nation where (in

---

sionaries) by Pentecostal churches in the U.S., but that the main thrust is local. (Martin, "Evangelical and Charismatic Christianity in Latin America," 77.)

74. Ibid., 135.

75. While Cox recognizes the existence of African Independent churches prior to the Azusa Street re-vival, he suggests that it was not until post-Azusa Street revival preachers (such as John G. Lake in 1907) arrived in Africa that these churches became influenced by Pentecostal worship style and spirituality. Cox, H. *Fire from Heaven*, 249.

76. Hollenweger, "The Black Roots of Pentecostalism," 36.

77. Martin, *Pentecostalism: The World Their Parish*, 133.

78. Anderson, "Global Pentecostalism in the New Millennium," 127.

1991) 75 percent of the population are Christians, this indicates that Pentecostalism is fast becoming the new "mainline."[79]

The influence of South Africa on the development of Pentecostalism in Africa cannot be underestimated. Most of the early missionaries to Central and Eastern Africa post-Azusa travelled through South Africa where there were important links established by parallel Pentecostal church groups. Like Azusa Street, the Pentecostal movement began in South Africa in a black township within Johannesburg.[80] While it began as a non-racial movement, it did not take long for it to splinter into groups based on ethnic boundaries leading to struggles for unity.[81] The majority growth of Pentecostalism in contemporary South Africa continues amongst the black population found in what Anderson describes as "African initiated churches" rather than the classical Pentecostal denominations such as the "Apostolic Faith Mission."[82]

In comparison, the region known as North Africa and the Middle East has been in general hostile to contemporary Pentecostalism and Christianity in general. Although the birthing ground for three major world religions (Judaism, Christianity and Islam) and an area of growth and importance in Early Christianity, this region has come to generally be dominated by the presence of Islam. While there is a relatively small expression of Pentecostalism in this is North Africa and Middle East area, it has become a focus in recent years of heightened missionary endeavor.

Europe

This explosive growth in South America and Africa is described by Jean-Daniel Plüss as a challenge to Pentecostalism in Europe[83] which in most areas has experienced marginal growth. While European Pentecostals adhere to the doctrinal emphasis of Spirit-experience, it seems the practice of this spirituality has been scrutinized by leaders concerned that it is an obeisance to consumerism. In commenting on recent a survey of European Pentecostal leaders, Plüss notes: "While there is a basic openness toward experiences of the Spirit, even among the more critical respondents, there was also a cautiousness in placing an ideological significance on these experiences as well as understanding their cross-cultural impact."[84] The indigenization of Pentecostalism in the context of secular Europe has resulted in a focus of individualization, which includes the experience of the Spirit as both an individual and individually interpreted.[85]

Yet, while many Pentecostal groups in Europe may have lost momentum in the last two to three decades, there have been pockets of growth. For example, while from 1985 to 1990 there was a decline in mainline churches in the UK, there was a 30 percent growth

79. Freston, *Evangelicals and Politics in Asia, Africa and Latin America*, 166.

80. LaPoorta, "Unity or Division," 162.

81. Ibid, 162–63.

82. Anderson, "Dangerous Memories for South African Pentecostals," 89.

83. Plüss, "Globalization of Pentecostalism or Globalization of Individualism? A European Perspective." 170.

84. Ibid, 177.

85. Ibid, 178.

among "independent Christian churches," which Cox notes includes mainly Pentecostal and Charismatic groups.[86] This growth is particularly evident among migrant African and Caribbean groups. The theme of the prominence of Pentecostalism among the poorer classes, migrants and women continues in the study of Europe. Pentecostalism came to Italy in 1908 when a migrant worker returned from the U.S. to share this new faith. By 1929 there were 149 Pentecostal congregations, and by 2001 over 300,000 members.[87] While it continues to be the largest non-Catholic religious group, its adherents continue to be drawn primarily from the middle to lower classes.[88] Among these groups, Pentecostalism tends to reflect the innate catholic spirituality and folk religion of the people that has allowed the growth of sect-like groups such as Pentecostalism and even cult groups such as the Jehovah's Witnesses. This leads Cox to suggest that where Pentecostalism has not by-passed regions of Europe it has been indigenized and infused with what he described as a "primal spirituality."[89]

Asia

Like each of the regions already discussed, Asia is an area of social and cultural diversity. Common also to the previous regions is the growing recognition among scholars identifying Pentecostalism not as an import but an indigenous awakening independent to yet contemporary with the revival in Northern America. This is particularly emphasized by recent studies in manifestations of Pentecostal spirituality in India, Sumatra, Myanmar, and China prior to Azusa Street.[90] This is exemplified by the description of the revival at Mukti Mission in Maharashtra as the birthplace of Pentecostalism in India in 1905.[91] At the same time, the influence of Azusa Street revival for Pentecostal activity in Asia, such as providing missionary and evangelistic endeavors, cannot be de-valued. Yet despite almost a century of Pentecostal Asian presence, the introduction of Pentecostalism to the various sections of Asia has had varying impact. While the impact has been significant in Korea, Malaysia, Philippines, and Singapore, not every nation has been receptive to Pentecostalism.[92] While there are approximately 135 million Pentecostal and Charismatics in Asia, the majority of these are Han Chinese and Indians within indigenous independent groups rather than traditional Pentecostal assemblies, such as the Assemblies of God.[93]

The most prominent example of the success of Pentecostalism in Asia is the remarkable growth of the movement in Korea. Pentecostal groups in Korea have experienced massive growth and social influence in the last three to four decades. The most promi-

---

86. Cox, *Fire from Heaven*, 187.

87. Burgess and van der Maas, *New International Dictionary of Pentecostal and Charismatic Movements*, 132.

88. Cox, *Fire from Heaven*, 197.

89. Ibid., 204.

90. Hwa, "Pentecostalism and the Asian Church," 43.

91. Bergunder, "Constructing Indian Pentecostalism," 186.

92. Julie Ma, "Pentecostal Challenges in East and South-East Asia."

93. Hwa, "Pentecostalism and the Asian Church," 38.

nent example is the expansion of Yoido Full Gospel Church led by Rev. Cho Yong-Gi. Tapping into Korean communalism and shamanistic substratum, Cho preaches towards peoples' felt needs, as Lee notes, "they need health, wealth, fertility, and success in their life ventures. Cho Yong-Gi's preaching meets those needs exactly: 'Anything is possible if you have faith.'"[94] Again, Pentecostalism has adapted to the cultural context as it presents a very pragmatic gospel addressing practical needs. The release of the ministry for women has also played a crucial factor in the growth of Cho's church. However Lee notes that the majority of quantitative growth among Korean churches such as Cho's occurred in the post-Korean war period of the 1970s and 1980s when there was also massive national economic expansion. The rate of growth has declined since.[95] It also highlights the challenge in defining Pentecostalism as "adaptive." Is adaption for transformation within a culture or a capitulation to existing interests within cultures being reformed by other forces? This same concern, particularly as relates to the challenge of syncretism, exists among some Pentecostal groups within Central and Southeast Asia. In her review of the appropriation of Pentecostalism among the Kankana-ey tribe in the northern Philippines, Julie Ma notes that they "seem to bring in some of the old religious orientations and enhance them in the new religious setting."[96] For example, their practice of *charismata* and Spirit experience particularly focuses on prayer for healing. She notes that while a power encounter may open the heart, an allegiance encounter is needed to abandon their former loyalties of ancestral worship and embrace allegiance to their new-found Savior.[97] However this process of indigenization continues to be a controversial issue in the intra-Pentecostal dialogue. As Wonsuk Ma notes, the role and influence of shamanism upon Asian Pentecostalism is still heavily debated.[98]

Australia & Pacific

The current impetus among Pentecostal studies to identify the indigenous features of the origins of the movement is also reflected in the work of Australian historians. Unlike many other regions, this sense of distinctness is supported by the fact that Pentecostalism in Australia originated among middle-class and rural groups. According to Barry Chant, "in Australia, its origins were among people of relatively comfortable socio-economic status."[99] During the earliest stages of the development of Australian Pentecostalism in the early 1900s, the movement was marked by the prominent involvement of women. By 1930, twenty of the thirty-seven Pentecostal churches were initiated by women.[100]

94. Lee, "*Minjung* and Pentecostal Movements in Korea," 146–47.

95. "Pentecostal Challenges in East and South-East Asia," 147–48.

96. Julie Ma, "Comparison of Two Worldviews," 288.

97. Ibid., 290.

98. Wonsuk Ma, "Asian (classical) Pentecostal Theology in Context," 69.

99. Chant also demonstrates the middle-class beginnings of Pentecostalism by a comparative study of occupations, which "shows that the percentage of Pentecostals involved in professional occupations in the 1930s was roughly double that of the community while the percentage of labourers was approximately half" (Chant "The Spirit of Pentecost," 38).

100. Ibid., 428.

Currently in Australia there are seven main Pentecostal denominational fellowships[101] and numerous smaller groups, the largest being the Assemblies of God (AG) which was officially formed as a fellowship of autonomous congregations in 1937. A certain emphasis placed on church growth and "success" (usually defined by church growth rather than church health) has resulted in competitive and uncooperative elements within Pentecostal transdenominational dialogues, as has the slow recognition by the unusually strong mainline denominations that there was another player on the block.

Having grown from a cult-like status to one of the most frequented denominations by weekly attendance, the Australian AG has emerged from adolescence to face a new battle: institutionalization. As Australian Pentecostalism has grown, so has the need for an institutional framework to ensure its continued growth. The establishment of the Australian Assemblies of God (AG) itself is an example of this cultural process. While women were constitutionally able to continue in leadership, a cultural pattern of "men only" leadership emerged in the following years that have continued to dominate the fellowship.[102] In contrast to the early stages, women currently comprise 16.8 percent nationally of credentialed AG ministers, with only 3.7 percent of women in the leadership position of senior pastor. While ordination is not the only avenue for ministry within Pentecostalism, it represents the recognition by the Pentecostal community of both the minister and the ministry. Yet the prominence of women as worship leaders and songwriters in the rise of international music ministries (such as the Hillsong label), suggest alternative avenues for women to express their leadership gifting.

By comparison, the place of Pentecostalism in many of the islands of the Pacific can be likened to that of Latin America (without the "explosive growth"). The social mobility offered by Pentecostalism is attractive to many of the younger generation, along with its experiential spirituality. As Martin notes, "What the Pentecostal churches offer to uprooted young people is warmth and personal experience, authoritative guidance, participation, lively music, spiritual power, and (perhaps) prospects of prosperity."[103]

Central to Pentecostalism in Australia, New Zealand, and the Pacific is the experience of the Spirit—both in individual piety and communal worship—where the *charismata* is present and expected.

Global Commonalities and Challenges

While this brief overview highlights the diversity of global Pentecostalism, there are also core commonalities evident. Common to global Pentecostalism is an emerging scholarship that is reflective of the upward social and economic mobility of its adherents. While Pentecostalism began in most regions among the lower, poorer classes, this social location has begun to shift. In some areas, such as Korea, it appears that Pentecostalism has grown in tandem with economic development. This shift in social mobility is especially reflect-

---

101. These include Assemblies of God, Apostolic, Christian City Church, Foursquare, Christian Revival Crusade, Christian Outreach Centre, and Betheseda. The AG and Apostolic formed a network in 1999 called Australian Christian Churches.

102. Grey, "Torn Stockings and Enculturation," 1.

103. Martin, *Pentecostalism*, 165.

ed in the common interest in academic research on both the present and past natures of contextualized Pentecostalism. While most scholars acknowledge the importance of North America as a key symbol and mediating point for much of the global movement, its dynamic growth particularly in the Two-Thirds World means that the movement has primarily situated outside the West. As the movement has globalised, it has taken on local forms that have become interested in defining their particular identities. They have done so through contextualized histories and theologies increasingly in dialogue with theologians and scholars of other traditions. Yet a corollary of this drive towards academic dialogue and increased social presence is reflected in widespread interest in political and governmental influence. While early Pentecostalism tended to lack political involvement or was pacifist, the winds have shifted toward a sense of socio-political responsibility. However, typical of the fissiparous and glocalizing nature of Pentecostalism, while there is a common global interest, there is no uniform nature and expression of socio-political perspectives. There is thus no single Pentecostal political group or perspective. As Martin writes, "Pentecostalism is very specifically a cultural revolution, and one undertaken from below, with no political theory to guide it and no political ideology to promote. What motivates the rival religious entrepreneurs who guide the revolution is pursuit of a particular kind of personal transformation."[104]

Instead, the expression of Pentecostal spirituality in global politics is ambiguous at best, and tends to vary according to the context.[105] In Western societies, the drive toward political power tends to uphold conservative middle-class values. In comparison, the expressions of socio-political interest within some Latin American areas have included the promotion of both left and right wing ideologies.[106] Similarly, some Pentecostals in South Africa promoted apartheid whilst others sympathized with the liberation movements. As Anderson notes, these political differences tended to be drawn on racial lines, indicating that most political interest usually contains an element of self-interest.[107]

Despite the rise of an academic reflection that reverses much of the earlier anti-intellectualism of Pentecostalism, it is clear that the academic voice does not necessarily represent the global voice of the Pentecostal movement in all its diversity. With such varying expressions, it is not only difficult to define "Pentecostalism" but also to represent the "voice" of this movement. One of the challenges this raises is not only "who" speaks for this diversity of Pentecostalism but who decides what is a Pentecostal voice? While Pentecostalism remains a global phenomenon representing a massive grassroots movement, an academic elite is perhaps not the appropriate vehicle for its voice. It is a movement driven by experience rather than an articulated theology, by a spiritual rather than an intellectual meritocracy. It is crucial therefore that the vehicle for this "voice" of Pentecostalism engages its grassroots constituency that it may be reflective of the community for which it claims to speak.

104. Martin, *Pentecostalism*, 167.

105. Anderson, "Global Pentecostalism in the New Millennium," 210.

106. Ibid.

107. Ibid.

Throughout this overview of the global phenomenon, it is clear that the definition and boundaries of "Pentecostalism" are still hotly debated. As the Spirit experience is indigenized, the expression of Pentecostalism varies greatly between the global communities. In almost of all of these regions, there is recognition of the value and importance of the indigenization of Spirit experience. While this experience looks different in each context and is not uniform in its expression, it highlights the adaptability of Pentecostalism. As Anderson writes, "In varying degrees, Pentecostals in their many and varied forms, and precisely because of their inherent flexibility, attain an authentically indigenous character which enables them to offer answers to some of the fundamental questions asked by indigenous peoples."[108]

While some scholars seem to reject this indigenization as syncretistic, scholars such as Hollenweger suggest a distinction is necessary between theologically responsible and theologically irresponsible syncretisms.[109] While the charge of syncretistic irresponsibility is generally directed towards Third World Pentecostals, these latter can rightly object to the competitive and market-driven elements of their Western counterparts as equally irresponsible. After all, do they not syncretize their spirituality with the "success" ethic of capitalism? As Harvey Cox suggests, perhaps Pentecostals need more sermons on Acts 5 (the ethic of communal sharing) than on Acts 2.[110] Yet this highlights that, in whatever context, experience of the Holy Spirit, encountering God and practice of charismata are generally far more important to Pentecostalism globally than a fully articulated doctrine. However, if much of the indigenization of Pentecostalism is a rejection of traditional western models and groups in favor of more local expressions impacted by the charismatic renewal, should these groups be defined as "charismatic" rather than "Pentecostal"? Is there a difference?

THE EMERGING CHARISMATIC MOVEMENT

Mark Cartledge describes the Charismatic movement as a continuation of the Pentecostal spiritual tradition outside of organized Pentecostal denominations.[111] While the new millennium has found Pentecostals concluding their first century, Charismatics are concluding their first generation.[112] If the beginnings of the Pentecostal movement, in all its diversity, can be symbolized by the Azusa Street Revival, then the charismatic movement can be symbolized by the healing crusades of North American John Wimber (as part of the later "third wave" movement).[113] As the founder of the Vineyard movement, Wimber emerged in the 1970s with an emphasis on a Spirit-experience not linked to *glossolalia*, but the demonstration of signs and wonders. The Charismatic, or neo-Pentecostal move-

---

108. Ibid., 217.

109. Hollenweger, "The Pentecostal Elites and the Pentecostal Poor," 212.

110. Cox, "Pentecostalism and Global Market Culture," 395.

111. Cartledge, "Charismatic Prophecy," 79.

112. Spittler, "Are Pentecostals and Charismatics Fundamentalists?" 105.

113. I think JohnWimber verbalized the charismatic values and theology which had previously been intuitively felt by the community but not expressed as explicitly as they later were by Wimber.

ment, is identified as the "breaking out" of Spirit-experience from classical Pentecostalism into the mainline Christian denominations, both Protestant and Catholic. Cerillo has identified this "wave" as beginning the mid-1950s to 1990s,[114] but most prominent in the 1960s and 1970s. Yet while Pentecostalism historically was associated with sect-like groups among the lower classes with little theological reflection, the charismatic movement could be portrayed as more theologically moderate and non-sectarian as it attempted to bring renewal into the mainline middle-class churches.[115] Because of their social location, the identification of Pentecostal groups with charismatics has lent the former a certain respectability not previously achieved.

It is this common emphasis on the centrality of spirit-experience and charismatic gifting that unites the Pentecostal with the Charismatic community despite the diversity in expression, theological understanding, and historical development that they represent.[116] For example, the Charismatic movement in Australia is predominantly located within established denominations, such as Anglicanism and Catholicism. While these groups demonstrate charismatic spirituality, they tend to still express this emphasis through the cultural traditions of their denomination. However the shared Spirit-experience of Pentecostals and Charismatics also distinguishes the latter from their original denomination, leading occasionally to rifts and separations.[117] It represents the boundaries of the community: a "Charismatic Anglican" is identified because their experience of the charismatic distinguishes them from a generic "Anglican," particularly in locations, such as Sydney, where there are distinct congregations of charismatic and non-charismatic within the Anglican community.[118] As Spittler notes, the word "Charismatic" usually functions as an adjective describing mainline believers, hence one might claim to be a "Charismatic Catholic," a "Charismatic Uniting," or a "Charismatic Anglican."[119] With

---

114. Cerillo, "The Beginnings of American Pentecostalism: A Historiographical Overview," 249.

115. Ibid., 250–51. That this was a matter of socially-constructed perceptions can be seen in Tom Smail, Andrew Walker, and Nigel Wright, *Charismatic Renewal*, where Smail bewails the excesses of the Charismatic movement, and idealises the wisdom of the older Pentecostal denominations, particularly the British Elim and AG movements.

116. The Holiness-Wesleyan origins of the Pentecostal movement is noted by several scholars, particularly Land, *Pentecostal Spirituality*, 47–53 and Dayton, *Theological Roots of Pentecostalism*, 35–62. This has produced a culture within Pentecostalism that is concerned with external and internal purity and forms of purity such as abstinence from alcohol and gambling; attitudes and mores reflective of the Holiness movement. Land writes of the practices of the Holiness movement that have been adopted by North American Pentecostalism: "The holiness practices and restrictions from the nineteenth century were retained by most North American Pentecostals for almost half a century. Even today they remain conservative on most issues, though of course now that certain luxuries are more affordable they are not seen as quite the compromise with the world that they once were" (Land, *Pentecostal Spirituality*, 66). Similarly, a study by Grey on women ministers in the Australian AG discovered that "there is also a significant shift from the Pentecostal tradition of holiness and segregation from expressions of worldliness, including social dancing, movies, drinking (alcoholic beverages) and gambling" (Grey, "*Torn Stockings and Enculturation*," 11).

117. See for instance Emilsen and O'Connor, *Exploring the History of a Uniting Church Congregation*.

118. However, I acknowledge the great variety and permutations of global Anglicanism.

119. The definition of "Pentecostal" and "charismatic" groups is similarly discussed by Del Colle, also noting the distinctive work of the Holy Spirit as the definitive feature. He writes, "By "Pentecostal" I mean that which has to do with the effusion of the Holy Spirit within and upon the believer as a constituent ele-

this in mind, the term "Charismatic" will be used to refer to Christians in mainstream denominations who have adopted certain Pentecostal beliefs and practices but have not left their own denominations as well as independent churches and new "denominational" groups (such as Vineyard) that identify with the centrality of Spirit experience and charismatic gifting.[120] The term "Pentecostal" will be used to refer to established Pentecostal groups recognized as part of the global movement, whether "classical" or "indigenized" Pentecostals groups. In comparison, since Pentecostals and Charismatics have developed a distinct spirituality based on the personal experience of the Holy Spirit; specifically Spirit baptism and its corollary of spiritual gifts (*charismata*), the term "Pentecostalism" will refer to this common and inclusive spirituality.

FINDING THE "VOICE" OF PENTECOSTALISM

Despite the elusive definition of "Pentecostalism," it is clearly identified as a dynamic and diverse movement unified by a common experience of the Spirit. Since it is a movement driven by experience rather than any particular formulated doctrine, the contribution of adherents at the grassroots level is essential in the representation of the "voice" of Pentecostalism as it engages with our dialogue partners. To adequately speak for Pentecostalism in this developing friendship with hermeneutics and the Old Testament, and to ultimately develop a reading model of the Old Testament that reflects the values and practices of the Pentecostal community, it is necessary that the voice of the community be legitimately heard. Even among the emerging scholarly discussions of a viable Pentecostal hermeneutic (explored in chapter 3), there has been little attempt—apart from academic hypothesizing upon what Pentecostal scholars *think* the community might say—to determine the practices of actual readers. The voice of the community must be considered *for* its own voice and *with* its own voice if a reading method is to genuinely reflect the values of the group. Priority must be given to the practices of the faith community as the beginning point for critical reflection and construction.[121] However, while the insights of the burgeoning Pentecostal academic community tend to be prescriptive rather than descriptive, they are essential to the developing dialogue with hermeneutics and the Old Testament as they offer critical reflection on the community at large. It is now that the conversation between the Old Testament, hermeneutics, and Pentecostalism may begin in earnest.

---

ment of Christian initiation. Commonly referred to as the Baptism of the Holy Spirit, it is that endowment with power that initiates the Christian into the powers of the new age. By "charismatic" I mean the evidence of that same power in the exercise of the charismata, or gifts of the Spirit. Also included is the heightened sense of the sanctifying work of the Spirit, whether that be understood according to Wesleyan, Reformed or Catholic models" (Del Colle, "Postmodernism and the *Pentecostal*-charismatic Experience," 99–100).

120. Spittler, "Are Pentecostals and Charismatics Fundamentalists?" 104.

121. Parker, *Led by the Spirit,* 10.

3

Pentecostalism, Hermeneutics, and the Old Testament in Dialogue

THE DEVELOPMENT OF GLOBAL Pentecostalism from the early twentieth century and the Charismatic movement from the 1960s[1] has seen their emergence as a distinct group within the broader spectrum of Christianity.[2] This distinct group has a specific emphasis on Spirit—experience that flavors all aspects of its spirituality, including Bible-reading practice. However, while this unique theology and practice has emerged, it has developed with little regard for formal theologizing[3] or academic reflection. It is only in the recent decades that Pentecostal scholarship (itself a new concept) has sought to define a distinct theology and to subsequently integrate itself in the context of the wider Christian and academic communities. The recent aim of Pentecostal scholarship has been to reflect on and contribute to the distinct features of its community to the ecumenical dialogue. The last two decades have witnessed an explosion of discussion on issues as diverse as the Pentecostal understanding of the nature of biblical texts;[4] the role of charismatic experience and spirituality in interpreting texts;[5] the development of Pentecostal hermeneutics, and Pentecostal hermeneutics in ecumenical dialogue.[6]

1. For a description of the origin, development and culture of Pentecostalism and the Pentecostal movement, see chapter 2 of this work.

2. Matthew Clark notes that while the relationship between the Pentecostal movement and other Christian denominations has not always been smooth, there is a desire on the part of Pentecostals to be a part of the Christian world and not see the working of the gifts of the Spirit as something sectarian or cultish but rather as a distinctive within general Christian theology (Clark, "An Investigation into the Nature of a Viable Pentecostal Hermeneutic," 53).

3. Johnston, "Pentecostalism and Theological Hermeneutics: Evangelical Options," 51.

4. For example, see Ellington, "Pentecostalism and the Authority of Scripture."

5. For example, see Land, *Pentecostal Spirituality*; Archer, *A Pentecostal Hermeneutic for the Twenty-First Century*; Moore, "Deuteronomy and the Fire of God"; Pinnock, "The Work of the Holy Spirit in Hermeneutic"; Spittler, "Scripture and the Theological Enterprise"; Menzies, *The Development of Early Christian Pneumatoloy with Special Reference to Luke-Acts*; Ervin, "Hermeneutics: A Pentecostal Option."

6. For example, see Karkkainen, "Pentecostal Hermeneutics in the Making"; Moltmann, "A Pentecostal

Despite the evolving discussion there has been little consensus among Pentecostal scholars on a reading approach which reflects their community's reading practices. Instead the debate continues to circle as scholars force Pentecostal reading processes into unfamiliar and perhaps incongruent categories.[7] These categories are loaded with social and political implications within the hierarchy of academic classification. To avoid the indictment of being considered "uncritical," Pentecostal scholarship has shifted toward association with the established hermeneutic practices of either Evangelical (particularly historical-critical approaches) or post-modern approaches (particularly Ricoeur's "hermeneutic of suspicion"[8]). Some Pentecostal scholars such as Davies and Moore[9] have adopted a "postmodern" or "literary" reading of Old Testament texts that skirts the issues of literalism. Others, such as Menzies and Fee,[10] prefer Evangelical categories that avoid association with the plurality of "postmodern" readings. Yet, as Cargal suggests, this limits the multiplicity of readings inherent in the charismatic experience.[11] So the debate for an appropriate description of Pentecostal hermeneutics continues as scholars attempt to integrate their Pentecostal experience into the "horizon"[12] of the text.

A SCHOLARLY DISCUSSION BETWEEN PENTECOSTALISM AND HERMENEUTICS

Of the various existing categories of academic hermeneutics that Pentecostal scholars tend to adopt, the most prominent historically and socially have been the Evangelical approaches, particularly those developed in the context of Fundamentalism. The Evangelical approach, as Clark notes, has influenced Pentecostal scholars to the greatest extent in North America where Pentecostal theology (and life) has consciously developed under the umbrella of Evangelicalism.[13] Although Clark accurately notes the lim-

---

Theology of Life"; Johns, "Pentecostalism and the Postmodern Worldview"; Menzies, "Jumping Off the Postmodern Bandwagon"; Cargal, "Beyond the Fundamentalist-Modernist Controversy"; Byrd, "Paul Ricoeur's Hermeneutical Theory"; Dempster, "Paradigm Shifts and Hermeneutics"; Sheppard, "Biblical Interpretation after Gadamer."

7. For an extended discussion on this, see Yong, *Discerning the Spirit(s)*.

8. See in particular, Ricoeur, "The Hermeneutics of Testimony."

9. Moore, "Deuteronomy and the Fire of God," 11–33; Davies, *Double Standards in Isaiah*.

10. Menzies, "Jumping Off the Postmodern Bandwagon"; Fee and Stuart, *How to Read the Bible for all its Worth*.

11. Cargal, "Beyond the Fundamentalist-Modernist Controversy."

12. Gadamer, *Truth and Method*.

13. Clark, "An Investigation into the Nature of a Viable Pentecostal Hermeneutic," 54. Evangelicalism is defined by *Larry Eskridge* as an umbrella definition that covers a diverse number of Protestant groups. However, he notes three ways that the term is used in the contemporary context. He writes, "The first is to see as 'Evangelical' all Christians who affirm a few key doctrines and practical emphases." In particular, it is the concept of "conversionism." The second sense Evangelicalism may be understood "is to look at Evangelicalism as an organic group of movements and religious tradition. Within this context "Evangelical" denotes a style as much as a set of beliefs that defines this group." This grouping includes movements as disparate Dutch Reformed Churches, Pentecostals, and Southern Baptists movements. The third sense of the term is "as the self-ascribed label for a coalition that arose during the Second World War. This group came into being as a reaction against the perceived anti-intellectual separatist, belligerent nature of the funda-

ited influence of Evangelicalism on Pentecostal communities in other continents such as South America, Africa, and Australia, the influence of North American Pentecostalism cannot be under-estimated. While the previous discussion in chapter 2 noted that not all regions of global Pentecostalism attribute their origins to the North American revival in Azusa Street, its role is still prominent as a symbol of the global movement.[14] As North American Pentecostalism is profoundly influenced by conservative Evangelicalism, its significance for Pentecostal reading approaches cannot be ignored.[15]

Since the post-Azusa Street revival meetings in the early 1900s, the Pentecostal community in North America existed on the fringes of society.[16] As demonstrated by Poloma, in order to improve their status and respectability, North American Pentecostalism tended to adopt the theology and forms of their closest cousins, Fundamentalism and Evangelicalism.[17] While Pentecostalism seemed to resonate with some of the values of these groups, such as the anti-intellectualism of Fundamentalism[18] and the "high view" of Scripture of Evangelicalism, its basis for holding these values was significantly different. The anti-intellectualism of Pentecostalism within Fundamentalism emerged as a critique of Modernism.[19] McLean suggests that this shift towards Evangelical theology and Fundamentalism was motivated by the fear of Modernist thought that denies the supernatural activity of God in a world ruled by scientific materialism.[20] Many Pentecostals emulate the literalistic readings of fundamentalists in approaching such texts as Gen 1–3. As Clark writes, "The Pentecostal movement stands in the tradition of those groups, who maintain that the record of Scripture is historically accurate, particularly in terms of the so-called supernatural stories e.g., the Noachian Flood, the ten plagues of Egypt, the crossing of the Red Sea, the virgin birth of Jesus, the resurrection, etc."[21]

This means that most Pentecostal groups adopt fundamentalist affirmations of the verbal inspiration and literal inerrancy of Scripture. As Spittler notes, while Pentecostal readers may associate with the notions of verbal inspiration and inerrancy[22] he consid-

---

mentalist movement in the 1920s and 1930s. Importantly, its core personalities (like Harold John Ockenga and Billy Graham), institutions (for instance, Moody Bible Institute and Wheaton College), and organizations (such as the National Association of Evangelicals and Youth for Christ) have played a pivotal role in giving the wider movement a sense of cohesion that extends beyond these 'card-carrying' Evangelicals" (http://www.wheaton.edu/isae/defining_Evangelicalism.html).

14. The influence of North American Pentecostalism on Australian Pentecostalism is typified by the use of Asuza Street as a theological symbol in the work of Australian Pentecostal theologian S. Clifton.

15. The big issues are not so much the origin there, but the continuing dominance of communication channels via American organizational and financial power.

16. Kärkkäinen, "Pentecostal Hermeneutics in the Making," 80.

17. The work of Chant ("The Spirit of Pentecost") on the origins of Pentecostalism in Australia notes that while it similarly developed on the fringes of Australian society, it was predominantly located in a middle-class constituency. For a detailed study on the sociological development of the North American Assemblies of God, see Poloma, *Assemblies of God at the Crossroads*.

18. Kärkkäinen, "Pentecostal Hermeneutics in the Making," 80.

19. Ibid.

20. McLean, "Toward a Pentecostal Hermeneutic," 38.

21. Clark, "An Investigation into the Nature of a Viable Pentecostal Hermeneutic," 55.

22. Ibid.

ers the formulation of a distinct Pentecostal approach to include wider concerns than simply the fundamentalist-modernist controversy.[23] The usefulness or otherwise of this adopted theology in forming Pentecostal beliefs and practice regarding Scripture will be discussed below. The anti-intellectual basis and uncritical Biblicism of Pentecostalism is not necessarily founded on a rejection of higher criticism (as per Fundamentalism), but on the democratization of the Spirit as described in Acts 2. For Pentecostal readers, the scholar-cleric does not monopolize correct interpretation as the values of their community emphasize the enabling by the Spirit for each believer to understand, interpret and minister from Scripture regardless of age, gender, race, or education. However for Pentecostal scholars such as Fee, Menzies, and Johnston,[24] the mutuality of value with which Scripture is regarded by Pentecostals and Evangelicals is enough to qualify the latter's approach as a "natural" method for Pentecostal readers to adopt (reinforcing their historical propinquity). Evangelical approaches to Bible reading tend to evidence concern for the historical meaning of the text as the primary goal of hermeneutics.[25] They attempt to isolate the probable historical context and probable intention of the author of the biblical text to determine its meaning.[26] According to Fee and Menzies, this approach is the most appropriate for Pentecostal readers to adopt.[27] It is paradoxical therefore, that in its attempt to maintain a particular faith-value (i.e., high view of Scripture), the Pentecostal community has mostly adopted the reading approach of historical criticism that resists a fundamental element of that faith-value, the continuation of the supernatural activity of God from the apostolic community to the present.

Pentecostal scholar and prolific writer, Gordon Fee particularly sees the need for Pentecostal readers to engage in responsible exegesis to avoid the excesses of some Pentecostal readings, such as the "prosperity doctrine" that is popular among segments of the Pentecostal community.[28] The model Fee provides for this responsible exegesis is the adoption of a historical-critical method to provide the "plain sense" of Scripture. According to Fee, "the antidote to bad interpretation is not *no* interpretation but *good* interpretation, based on common-sense guidelines."[29] His most well known publication (with Douglas Stuart) *How to Read the Bible for all it's Worth*,[30] advocates the Evangelical hermeneutic of authorial intention.[31] This leads the reader to bridge the "hermeneuti-

23. Spittler, "Scripture and the Theological Enterprise," 60.

24. See in particular Fee and Stuart, *How to Read the Bible for all its Worth*; Menzies, "Jumping Off the Postmodern Bandwagon"; Johnston, "Pentecostalism and Theological Hermeneutics."

25. Menzies, "Jumping Off the Postmodern Bandwagon," 116.

26. More detailed discussion on the nature of Evangelical reading methods can be found in Thistleton, *New Horizons in Hermeneutics*.

27. Interestingly, both these scholars consciously refer to themselves as "Evangelicals" as well as "Pentecostals."

28. While Fee and Stuart direct their direct at a general audience, the critique of the prosperity doctrine appears to be aimed at a Pentecostal readership.

29. Johnston, "Pentecostalism and Theological Hermeneutics," 53.

30. Fee and Stuart, *How to Read the Bible for all its Worth*.

31. The commitment to an Evangelical method is also reflected in his later works: Fee, *New Testament Exegesis* and Fee, *Gospel and Spirit*.

cal gap" between what the Scripture *meant* in its original setting and what it *means* to the contemporary reader (what Fee calls "hermeneutics").[32] To highlight the importance of responsible reading approaches, Fee cites the example of the "so-called wealth and health gospel" prominent among North American Protestants.[33] By showing that the prosperity doctrine reads Scripture out of context, Fee asserts "One may rightly question whether the plain meaning is being sought at all; perhaps the plain meaning is simply what such a writer wants the text to mean in order to support his pet ideas."[34] For Fee, the "plain meaning" of Scripture and authorial intention are synonymous. While this reading process attempts to highlight the "plain sense" of Scripture, Fee acknowledges the influential role of the pre-suppositions of the reader in determining the "plain sense" of the passage.

Another prominent Pentecostal scholar who actively seeks to locate a Pentecostal hermeneutic within the framework of Evangelicalism is Robert Menzies. The work of Menzies[35] in maintaining the importance of biblical narrative (particularly the Lukan narrative) has been extremely influential within the movement to engage Pentecostalism with Evangelical scholarship. Menzies has consistently promoted the need for Pentecostalism to re-assess its seemingly pre-critical approaches to reading by stressing the theological integrity and distinct contribution of each biblical author in the attempt to give faith to historical criticism.[36] For Menzies, the absence of a definitive Pentecostal theology negates the need for a distinct hermeneutical approach. Menzies' approach in engaging with Evangelical scholarship has been to adopt the same methods for a different subject, namely the role and character of the Holy Spirit. Menzies' interest in the work of the Holy Spirit post-Pentecost is framed by a historical-critical hermeneutic. The distinct Pentecostal experience of baptism or empowerment of the Spirit as a separate occurrence to salvation is understood in Menzies' work as being "nice" but not necessary. This results in Pentecostalism becoming the optional icing to the cake of Evangelicalism. As McLean notes, by synthesizing Pentecostal theology with Christian theology of the Evangelical persuasion, a Pentecostal approach becomes simply Evangelicalism plus the Pentecostal experience of the Holy Spirit.[37] This is hardly reflective of the reality of Pentecostal readings and values of the community that view the work of the Spirit as central to their theology and practice, not just an optional extra.[38]

The need for Pentecostal readers to base their reading practices on firm ground and avoid the pitfalls of early Pentecostal readings, including homogenous xenolalia,[39] is

32. Fee and Stuart, *How to Read the Bible for all its Worth*, 13.

33. Ibid.

34. Ibid., 18.

35. Menzies, *The Development of Early Christian Pneumatology*.

36. Menzies, "Jumping Off the Postmodern Bandwagon," 116.

37. McLean, "Toward a Pentecostal Hermeneutic," 35.

38. Perhaps this is reflective of the creeping colonization of Pentecostal thought by North American Pentecostalism with its interface with dominant Evangelicalism.

39. Xenolalia refers to the understanding within primitive Pentecostalism that the "tongues" received by the community included the ability to speak in unlearnt, foreign human languages. It was briefly considered part of the empowering for missionary service through the acquiring of unlearnt languages.

similarly presented by Johnston. He writes, "Pentecostals, suspicious of the merely formal academic enterprise, have too often accepted simple, uncritical explanations of the Bible which have proven erroneous."[40] Instead, he suggests that responsible biblical scholarship should be the guide to developing "solid biblical interpretation" which, like Fee and Menzies, he identifies with the Evangelical wing of the church.[41] Within the wider umbrella of Evangelicalism, Johnston suggests that Pentecostal hermeneutics can find a place. This approach presents both a freedom and rootedness for Pentecostal readers with its diversity.[42] While he does not present a model of reading *per se*, he does present the resonance between a developing Pentecostal theology and the value for Scripture found within Evangelical theology. Although Johnston emphasizes the diversity within Evangelical theological methodology, he also notes the commonality of approaches which a Pentecostal reading method would need to reflect. This commonality, or theological centre, is based on the magisterial role of Scripture above all tradition, reason, culture, science, or opinion.[43] However, as Johnston notes, a commitment to biblical authority is not itself a sufficient guarantee of biblical faithfulness.[44] Evangelicals have been more interested in defending Scripture than expounding it.[45] This is quite contrary to the interests of Pentecostal readers who have shown less interest in defending the theological authority of Scripture or discovering the authorial intention of a text than in affirming the active role of the Spirit in illuminating the text.

These approaches (particularly the historical-critical approach adopted by Pentecostal writers such as Fee and Menzies) have come under attack in recent years with the emergence of postmodernism as a critical movement.[46] Scholars, including some Evangelicals, now recognize the limitations of the historical-critical approach, which assumes knowledge of a past which can never be fully re-constructed and assumes the intentions of an author that can never fully be known (even if the author can be accurately identified). Since Gadamer,[47] the bubble of the Evangelical approach has begun to deflate. The confidence in the process of equating the "plain meaning" of Scripture with authorial intention has been undermined. It is now questioned: can contemporary readers really reconstruct what the author intended? For Pentecostal readers, can the text be limited to just one meaning? The multiplicity of readings inherent in the charismatic experience suggests that the limitation of the text to a singular meaning goes against the grain of Pentecostal values. Similarly, the limitation of the reader's encounter with the

40. Johnston, "Pentecostalism and Theological Hermeneutics," 52.

41. Ibid., 54.

42. Ibid., 58.

43. Ibid., 57.

44. Johnston cites the example of the Jehovah's Witnesses and the Worldwide Church of God as groups that hold to a doctrine of "inerrancy" and a strict, high view of Scripture. Yet, both these groups are widely considered by mainstream Christians to be in error (ibid., 61).

45. Johnston, "Pentecostalism and Theological Hermeneutics," 61.

46. This understanding highlights postmodernism as part of the trajectory of Modernism, from which it has emerged.

47. Gadamer, *Truth and Method.*

text to a rational, critical approach contradicts the significance of pneumatic illumination valued by the Pentecostal reader. It is these issues that inspire Pentecostal scholars, influenced by postmodern theories and approaches, to ask questions which illumine the biblical text.

In adopting an Evangelical approach to a distinct Pentecostal hermeneutic, the Pentecostal community must consider the potential theological losses along the way. The theological underpinnings of many Evangelical theories, particularly dispensationalism, are in direct conflict to the values of the Pentecostal community. The dispensationalist approach of Evangelical hermeneutics is contrary to the values and distinctives of Pentecostal theology, which affirm the ongoing validity and use of the gifts of the Spirit in the contemporary church. This creates a tension between the values of the Pentecostal community and the values inherent in its adopted theology. As McLean notes,

> On the conservative side, we have a set of exegetical and hermeneutical principles which, when rigorously followed, posit a fundamentally different mode of God's presence in and among the faithful during the formative period of the canon and today. Indeed, while some Evangelicals affirm God was an active causative agent in the biblical period, they teach that such causative activity will not again be seen until the rapture inaugurates the Great Tribulation, putting us at present in a somewhat deistic hiatus in which God's activity is for the most part limited to illuminating Scripture through the agency of the Holy Spirit and through the proclamation of the Gospel.[48]

However, despite its limitations, the Evangelical influence has not been totally negative. It has provided a connection between Pentecostals on the one hand, and charismatics from mainline Protestant denominations on the other. Evangelical language and the common experience of Spirit baptism have provided a link between the two communities.

For an emerging group of Pentecostal scholars the Evangelical quest for authorial intention limits the tradition of Pentecostal readings to an enlightenment rationalistic hermeneutic. This critique and rejection of the values of Modernism can be characterized under the banner of "postmodernity."[49] As Sheppard notes, most "postmodern" theories are built upon the radical criticisms of Modernism that arose in the social, political, and intellectual unrest of the 1960s.[50] The shift has been away from describing the role of an interpreter within the object-subject split that has characterized Modern methodological hermeneutics. In this Modern paradigm, the text is the object and interpreter the subject.[51] The aim of Modernity was to discover the objective meaning of the text by ridding it of all subjective influences and distortions by the interpreter (subject). However,

48. McLean, "Toward a Pentecostal Hermeneutic," 39.

49. Postmodernism in particular, highlights the influence of the late modern "fathers of suspicion": Freud (1886–1939), Nietzsche (1844–1900), and Marx (1818–1883). A more detailed discussion on the origins and nature of postmodernism can be found in Berger, *Facing Up to Modernity*; Docherty, *Postmodernism: A Reader*; Harvey, *The Condition of Postmodernity*; Lindbeck, "The Church's Mission to a Postmodern Culture."

50. Sheppard, "Pentecostals, Globalization, and Postmodern Hermeneutics," 290.

51. Dempster, "Paradigm Shifts and Hermeneutics," 131.

the reflexive shift within postmodernity questions the viability of this hermeneutical agenda. Instead of the text being read by a passive interpreter free from presuppositions, postmodernity recognizes the role of the reader as unstable and interested.

According to Cargal the current paradigm shift of postmodernism away from the fallacy of objectivity offers Pentecostal scholars an opportunity to explore such Pentecostal values as dynamic and multiple meanings in reading the biblical text.[52] He notes the tendency of Pentecostal reading practices to be pre-critical in nature, with what he identifies as a traditional emphasis on typological readings resulting in plural meanings and applications.[53] With this in mind, Cargal suggests that Pentecostal readings have more in common with postmodern theories than Evangelical options. Cargal charges those Pentecostal scholars (such as Fee and Menzies) who adopt the Evangelical approach as operating "within a philosophical paradigm dominated by historical concerns during a period in which Western society more generally is undergoing a 'paradigm shift' away from the historical paradigm of meaning typical of Modernism."[54] He suggests that Pentecostalism should move beyond the fundamentalist-modernist debate to engage in the contemporary context of post-Modernism and its hermeneutical theories. For Cargal, Pentecostal hermeneutics needs to be increasingly meaningful to people living in the postmodern context to avoid losing relevance in the contemporary culture.[55] This relevance includes engaging with current philosophical and hermeneutic theories.

Cargal suggests that postmodernism distinguishes itself from Modernism at the most fundamental level by its critique and rejection of the notion that "only what is historically and objectively true is meaningful."[56] Instead, he proposes that meaning is not limited by such positivistic constraints. Determining the historical origins and truth of a biblical text may actually have very little meaning for the reader. This is particularly true for Pentecostal readers, who are less interested in the historical location as they are in the "meaning" and appropriation of the text. He writes, "while critical methods can tell us some important things about the text (e.g., the history of its composition and transmission), they cannot tell us everything meaningful about a text."[57] This elevation of historical truth is further undermined by the results of higher criticism, where elements of the biblical narrative have "proven" to be unhistorical. In this case, Cargal suggests that a postmodern approach still allows Pentecostal readers to value and interpret the text regardless.[58]

Truth, according to this view, is not limited to or located exclusively in what is historically "true," but rather is located in the function of the text. This includes not only biblical narrative that may be meaningful though historically questionable, but also typological interpretations of the Old Testament found in the New. For example, Cargal

52. Cargal, "Beyond the Fundamentalist-Modernist Controversy"

53. Ibid., 165.

54. Ibid., 164.

55. Ibid., 165.

56. Ibid., 171.

57. Ibid., 177.

58. Ibid., 178.

cites the biblical presentation of Pilate washing his hands in Matt 27:24, which he suggests is important for its narratological function rather than its historicity. This action by Pilate is only recorded by Matthew; it is ignored by the other gospel writers. Cargal asserts, "The detail is meaningful because of the function it serves within Matthew's narrative which led him to include something the other evangelists overlooked because they attached no special significance to it or invent it specifically to fulfill that function. From a postmodern perspective, it is the issue of its function within the story that is more significant than its historical reliability."[59] For Cargal, this is an appropriate approach for Pentecostal readers to adopt as it reflects the current use of Pentecostal reading practices that find significance and meaning in texts outside of their historical significance or concerns for historical reliability. That God speaks through the text to the Pentecostal reader is what gives the text meaning. It allows for faith to be based not exclusively on historical viability but also in the function and meaning of the text to the Pentecostal reader.

A similar approach suggested by Ellington is one that utilizes narrative theology, treating Scripture as a story into which the reader is invited.[60] This story-world presents its own worldview that "makes claims upon the reader's perceptions of reality."[61] This approach, like the discussion of Cargal, lays aside the question of history to focus on the truth claims of the text that are visible from within the world of the story. While this appeals to the preservation of faith in the text, it forces the Pentecostal reader to adopt an ahistorical reading that denies all historical truth, including the resurrection and other events that are foundational to Pentecostal faith and identity, in the attempt to reconcile faith with some biblical record that has proven to be unhistorical. This is an area yet to be explored by Pentecostal scholars, as Ellington poignantly questions, "It is my contention that the biblical writers neither understood nor were they interested in writing history in the modern sense of that term. Neither, however, were they simply about writing creative stories without any reference to 'real events.' Where, then, is truth to be located in the biblical narrative, and how is it to be accessed and appropriated for Pentecostals?"[62] Instead he offers a model of "truth-as-testimony," along the lines originally developed by Brueggemann.[63] In this view, the truth claim of Scripture is not in its declaration (or testimony) of "historical facts" but in the testimonies themselves. Yet this does still not reconcile the validity of the historical event to the Scriptural witness.[64] It matters to the Pentecostal community whether the resurrection was a real event, or whether or not the stories of Jesus healing the sick really happened[65] in their appropriation of Scripture. This balance of "truth" and "testimony" is an important consideration for the development of

59. Ibid., 184.

60. Ellington, "History, Story, and Testimony."

61. Ibid., 253.

62. Ibid., 255.

63. Brueggemann, *Theology of the Old Testament*.

64. As my historian colleague, Mark Hutchinson, notes, these claims to lack of historicity are equally the matter of opinion as the claims to their historicity—the debate is one that theologians *using* history engage in rather than historians *per se*. This is simply because there is insufficient evidence one way or the other.

65. Ellington, "History, Story, and Testimony," 255.

a Pentecostal reading model of the Old Testament, as will be discussed further in later chapters of this book.

The relevancy of postmodern theories of interpretation of the biblical text to the Pentecostal community is similarly discussed by Israel, Albrecht and McNally.[66] Israel *et al* however do not limit the discussion of "texts" to the use of Scripture, but also describes the Pentecostal community as a Ricoeurian "text." The community as "text" is read in interaction with the biblical text rather than the community being the context of interpretation.[67] Israel *et al* write, "A Pentecostal hermeneutic, as we have argued *à la* Ricoeur and Gadamer, is the interpretive activity in which Pentecostals search for an understanding of themselves."[68] Therefore, they suggest that any development of a distinct Pentecostal hermeneutic should be considered in dialogue with the theories of postmodernism that help not only define the biblical text, but the interpreter as well. However, this approach has dilemmas for the Pentecostal reader, as observed by Harrington and Patten. They note the potential conflict for Pentecostal readers in adopting this theory of Ricoeur[69] who does not distinguish between texts that are sacred (and therefore fixed) and those that are not.[70] However, it does emphasize the role of the community in interpreting biblical texts; the Pentecostal reader is not an isolated, objective reader but part of a dynamic interpretive community.

The rising interest of Pentecostal scholars in philosophy and hermeneutic theories also reflected in the writings of Byrd.[71] Byrd looks to the preaching of the early Pentecostals at Azusa Street to emphasize their focus on the immediate meaning of the biblical text rather than on the Evangelical concern of the original cultural context of the biblical passage. Byrd suggests that Pentecostal readers require a theory and method of hermeneutics which facilitates this immediate meaning and "re-experiencing" of the biblical text.[72] He identifies the hermeneutic theory of Ricoeur as the most appropriate current option for a Pentecostal Hermeneutic. Byrd directs the Pentecostal reader through a movement of interpreting biblical narrative from Ricoeur's first naiveté of uncritical acceptance of the text through the stage of critical consciousness to the second naiveté. The process of critical reflection adopted by Byrd mirrors the Evangelical concerns for historical-critical issues. He writes, "This process of exegesis deliberately moves the interpreter from an initial understanding, through critical reflection, to culminate in presenting a text to a specific audience for the purpose of that audience 'understanding'

---

66. Israel, et al. "Pentecostals and Hermeneutics."

67. Harrington and Patten, "Pentecostal Hermeneutics and Postmodern Literary Theory."

68. Israel, "Pentecostals and Hermeneutics." 161.

69. The discussion on general hermeneutic theorists such as Gadamer, Ricoeur, and Derrida in this chapter is focused predominantly on the understanding and use of their theories by Pentecostal scholars rather than a study on their theories *per se*. The limits of this study to Pentecostal Hermeneutics does not allow for detailed discussion on general theory except where it interacts and impacts with the development of a Pentecostal reading model. For further discussion on the various general theories, see Thistleton. *New Horizons in Hermeneutics.*

70. Harrington and Patten, "Pentecostal Hermeneutics and Postmodern Literary Theory," 114.

71. Byrd, "Paul Ricoeur's Hermeneutical Theory and Pentecostal Proclamation."

72. Ibid., 205.

and appropriating the text."[73] The hermeneutic of Byrd's sermon requires the relevant imagery and symbols of the biblical text be communicated through an appropriation that allows the audience to identify existentially with the images in it and subsequently re-experience the text. While Byrd's adoption of this theory of "second naiveté" of Ricoeur may be helpful to the Pentecostal scholar traversing the rigors of critical issues, it is not reflective of the general Pentecostal reader who remains untouched by the critical reflection of the academy and who remains in the first naiveté of uncritical acceptance.

Sheppard also sees the theories of Ricoeur as a potential model for a Pentecostal reading of Scripture and "responsible theological apologetic of Pentecostal experience to the larger academic world."[74] He suggests that Ricoeur is an appropriate theorist for Pentecostal readers to adopt as he goes beyond Gadamer in the modern debate, but remains pre-deconstructionist.[75] The postmodern development of "deconstruction," particularly associated with Derrida, is the de-centering of each interpreters proposed "centre" of the text by exposing the circular logic required to overcome the semantic "gaps" characteristic of any "text."[76] In doing so, it highlights the motivations and assumptions that direct the reading of texts and the biases of each interpreter. This means there is no objective, neutral or innocent stance from which the proper interpretation of texts can be observed.[77] This hermeneutic highlights the agenda of the reader, even if that agenda is not consciously recognized by the interpreter. It proposes that the interpreter is not free from presuppositions, agendas (whether political or theological) or self-interest. The interpreter brings these elements to the reading of the text which influences the outcome of their reading. In this view, Scripture is at the service of the interpreter. As Cargal notes, "We must accept that not all the coherences of meaning the Pentecostal interpreter finds within the Bible as speaking to her or his present situation are the result of pneumatic illumination; all people are susceptible to the insidious influences of sexism, racism and classism."[78] This is an important consideration for developing a Pentecostal Hermeneutic as it recognizes the role of presuppositions of the Pentecostal reader and their community as they explore the meaning of the biblical text. However it is unsustainable in the long run because the Pentecostal community also define themselves by the God who changes not.

Harrington and Patten suggest that while the Evangelical quest for the historical reconstruction of biblical texts limits the meaning and dynamic quality of texts it does offer some important safeguards for Pentecostal scholars to consider. They write, "Indeed, limiting the meaning of the text to only what the ancient authors intended to convey to their audiences may cause the reader to miss the creative work of the Spirit in making the text relevant to life."[79] Instead Harrington and Patten suggest the importance of the frame

---

73. Ibid, 213.

74. Sheppard, "Biblical Interpretation after Gadamer."

75. Ibid., 124.

76. Sheppard, "Pentecostals, Globalization, and Postmodern Hermeneutics," 293.

77. Ibid., 294.

78. Cargal, "Beyond the Fundamentalist-Modernist Controversy," 187.

79. Harrington and Patten, "Pentecostal Hermeneutics and Postmodern Literary Theory," 109.

of reference of the reader as a crucial consideration in shaping the interpretation of the text (which is then, in turn, shaped by the text). They consider the subjectivity involved in the appropriation of the text by the reader to not only be legitimate, but inevitable.[80] This subjectivity also allows a dynamic element within the reading process. As Clark notes, "Perhaps one of the most attractive aspects of post-Modernism for the Pentecostal is that it appears to make space for an encounter with God."[81] However, both Harrington and Patten and Clark are nervous of divorcing the biblical text from its historical context because of the inherent relativization and extreme subjectivity of multiple meanings it produces. While postmodernism allows for dynamic experience and multiple meanings, it does not necessarily (according to the evaluation of Clark) call for the evaluation of these encounters. Such abandonment of criteria leaves Pentecostal readings open to the devaluing of its claims of unique and absolute truths.

The potentiality for multiple readings of the biblical text is an issue similarly explored by Pinnock.[82] According to Pinnock, the adoption of an Evangelical hermeneutic denies the illuminating work of the Spirit. Of Evangelical scholars (a camp to which he once belonged) he writes "Presumably they are telling us that, if you wish to understand the Bible, sharpen your exegetical tools and go to work."[83] He recognizes the basis of this approach to be the "strong influence of rationalism in Western culture which fosters a neglect of the Spirit"[84] and a fear of subjectivism and mysticism.[85] However, like Harrington and Patten, Pinnock is careful not to reject all the benefits of Evangelical hermeneutics in the embracing of postmodern theories. While Pinnock advocates the illumination of the Holy Spirit in reading biblical texts, the result of this inspiration is still equated with the Evangelical goal of authorial intention. The Pentecostal reader still achieves basically the same outcome as the Evangelical method of authorial intention but through the path of Spirit illumination rather than rational deduction. While it does emphasize the Pentecostal value of pneumatic experience, Pinnock's approach denies the potential for multiple readings potentially illumined by the Spirit that would be unforeseen by the human author of the text, and does not reflect the hermeneutical practices of Pentecostal readers.[86] Yet, Pinnock's work does emphasize the importance of the concept of pneumatic illumination for the Pentecostal reader. As Arrington writes, "It is God who opens eyes of faith and illuminates his Word to the human heart."[87]

---

80. Ibid.

81. Clark, "An Investigation into the Nature of a Viable Pentecostal Hermeneutic," 84.

82. Pinnock, "The Work of the Holy Spirit in Hermeneutics."

83. Ibid., 7.

84. Ibid., 8.

85. Ibid.

86. In the Pentecostal claim of pneumatic illuminations of particular meanings of a biblical text this raises several issues such as responsibility in interpretation, the feminist concern for interestedness in readings and the politics of who decides what is a legitimate reading or not. These issues will be discussed in chapter 4 of this work.

87. Arrington, "The Use of the Bible by Pentecostals," 103.

The possibilities that postmodern theories offer the dialogue of Pentecostal Hermeneutics regarding pneumatic illumination is similarly explored by Cargal. Liberated from the confines of rationalism, he writes that postmodernity "provides a philosophical space in which it is meaningful to speak of an encounter with transcendent reality, the Spirit of God. And it also permits that human 'experiences' of such 'pneumatic illumination,' as well as other human experiences and insight, can contribute to our comprehension of the meanings of the biblical text."[88] The role of experience is crucial to the reading process of the Pentecostal community. Pentecostals have recognized the role of experience in the hermeneutical circle and recognized the informative effect of Pentecostal Spirit experience on their reading. Even Fee acknowledges that "it is probably fair—and even important—to note that in general the Pentecostals' experience has preceded their hermeneutics. In a sense, the Pentecostal tends to exegete his experience."[89] This view of the role of experience, Cargal notes, is consistent with concerns raised by postmodernity.[90] It is also true to say that at the popular level, so do Evangelicals: the difference is that Evangelicals have a much more articulated formal theological establishment around which to build a "proper" approach.

Therefore, in the development of a distinct Pentecostal hermeneutic, the theories adopted and proposed by Pentecostal scholars continue to circle. While scholars such as Cargal, Sheppard and Byrd persistently oppose the imposition of Evangelical concerns onto Pentecostal readings, the Pentecostal scholars from the Evangelical school continue to defend their position from postmodern critics. As Menzies writes, "As a result of recent trends, Evangelicals are more aware of their lack of objectivity, the nature of their pre-understanding, and the need to listen to those with whom they might disagree. Yet the ahistorical stance and epistemological skepticism of postmodernism is extreme and inevitably leads to relativism . . . If we loose the meaning of the text from its historical moorings, how shall we evaluate various and even contradictory interpretations?"[91] This concern for the future development of Pentecostal hermeneutics is mirrored by McLean, "The very reasonable fear of many Pentecostal leaders and educators is that a Pentecostal hermeneutic will soon abandon or so distort the Scripture that the twentieth century Pentecostal movement will founder and cease to be Christian."[92] The dilemma yet to be addressed by Pentecostal proponents of both camps of Evangelical and postmodern theories are not only the gains of adopting alien approaches, but the threat to the distinct values and theology of Pentecostalism. For this reason, many Pentecostal scholars have looked to the development of a unique Pentecostal hermeneutic that reflects the values of the Pentecostal identity and theology rather than forcing Pentecostal reading processes into these unfamiliar and, for many Pentecostal scholars (such as Yong[93]) incongruent classifications.

88. Cargal, "Beyond the Fundamentalist-Modernist Controversy," 178.

89. Fee, "Hermeneutics and Historical Precedent," 122.

90. Cargal, "Beyond the Fundamentalist-Modernist Controversy," 179.

91. Menzies, "Jumping Off the Postmodern Bandwagon," 116–17.

92. McLean, "Toward a Pentecostal Hermeneutic," 36.

93. Yong, *Discerning the Spirit(s)*.

To do this, Johns suggests that Pentecostal scholars need to consider carefully the distinctiveness of their own worldview and its implications for the postmodern era before they buy into the paradigms and models of the emerging worldview.[94] If they do not, the resulting marriage may prove far more detrimental to the movement than the fading courtship with Evangelicalism. Pentecostal models of ministry must flow out of Pentecostal paradigms of truth, that is, a pneumatological epistemology. This includes an understanding of the distinct value of the biblical text to the Pentecostals. This questions the authentic description by Pentecostal scholars of a theology of Scripture that adequately reflects their unique theology and practice. In the absence of a developed Pentecostal theology or formulated confession, early Pentecostals tended to adopt the theologies of these established Christian groups closest to them, particularly Evangelicalism. To understand the discussion of a unique Pentecostal approach to reading the Scriptures, it is also necessary to consider the emerging discussion of a unique Pentecostal understanding of the nature of Scripture.

APPROACHES TO SCRIPTURE BY PENTECOSTAL SCHOLARS

While not discussing hermeneutics directly, Bridges-Johns and Johns[95] both address issues concerning the Pentecostal worldview paradigm which inherently concerns both hermeneutics and attitudes to Scripture. The resonance of the postmodern worldview with a developing Pentecostal worldview is acknowledged by Bridges-Johns and Johns on the basis of the acceptance by both groups of "realms of reality which exist outside objective, scientific knowledge."[96] According to Johns the Pentecostal reality is based on an "affective experience with God which generates an apocalyptic horizon. In this apocalyptic horizon the experience of God is fused to all other perceptions in the space-time continuum."[97] This is inconsistent with the worldview of Modernism that is primarily rationalistic and material in its outlook. Instead, the Pentecostal community values the supernatural element that Modernism and Evangelical models generally marginalize. Similarly, Bridges-Johns and Johns reject the association of a Pentecostal worldview with the postmodern because of what they perceive to be enormous differences. These differences include the God-centered reality of the Pentecostal worldview and the transrational nature of their reality in which "the spectrum of knowledge includes cognition, affection and behavior, each of which is fused to the other two."[98] Although this worldview is associated with "pre-critical" traditions, Johns prefer to adopt the term "para-critical" to describe the Pentecostal worldview as it has developed within and not prior to the Enlightenment vision. For this reason, many scholars such as Bridges-Johns and Sheppard consider the Pentecostal community to exist outside the socio-historical movements of Modernity and postmodernity, and they therefore prefer to refer to

---

94. Johns, "Pentecostalism and the Postmodern Worldview," 96.

95. Bridges-Johns, "A Pentecostal Perspective"; Johns, "Pentecostalism and the Postmodern Worldview."

96. Ibid., 46.

97. Johns, "Pentecostalism and the Postmodern Worldview," 87.

98. Bridges-Johns, "A Pentecostal Perspective," 47.

Pentecostals as "sub-modern"[99] or "para-modern"[100] rather than pre-modern, modern, or postmodern.

Bridges-Johns acknowledges that while Pentecostal approaches to Scripture may appear to contain a fundamentalist understanding of Scripture, there are major differences.[101] She writes, "Because there is a co-joining of God's presence with God's Word, to encounter the Scriptures is to encounter God."[102] The agent of this encounter is the Holy Spirit. The second major divergence of Pentecostal approaches to Scripture from fundamentalist understandings according to Bridges-Johns is the conceptualization of the role of Scripture. For Pentecostal readers, the Bible is a "template for reading the world."[103] Similarly, as Johns writes, "It is in the light of Scripture that the patterns of life are recognized and woven into the divine-human narrative. In this manner the Scriptures facilitate the formation of visions (pre-analytic, affective dispositions) within the believer which are perceived to conform to the character of God."[104] For this reason, scholars such as Bridges-Johns seeks to disentangle the Pentecostal understanding of the nature of Scripture from a uniquely doctrinal setting and place it in the relational context of the community of faith.[105]

This highlights the notion that, in presenting competing models of readings from Evangelicalism and postmodernism, Pentecostal scholars concentrate not on an appropriate theory, but on Pentecostal beliefs and practice regarding Scripture. Cargal, representing the postmodern camp, distances himself from the Evangelical insistence on the inerrancy of Scripture.[106] While most Pentecostal denominations affirm the inerrancy of Scripture in their doctrinal statements, this is usually an adopted fundamentalist theology of Scripture rather than a uniquely developed Pentecostal theology. The Evangelical camp provided the Pentecostal community with the vocabulary to express their high view of Scripture, but in a way not necessarily reflective of their reading practice. As Clark notes, "While Pentecostals could identify with the fundamentalist concern that the record of Scripture be taken seriously, for many it is difficult to maintain the virtual deification of the letter of Scripture itself."[107] The mechanical reception of verbal inspiration is contrary to the Pentecostal experience of the revelation of God via the charismata, making it problematic to reconcile this theology with practice. Scripture is the mirror, not the substance. Instead, Pentecostal readers tend to highlight the reliability and authority of the God to whom Scripture witnesses.[108] Pentecostal readers affirm the primacy of the Spirit who inspired, illuminates, and transforms believers through the Scriptures.

99. Sheppard, "Pentecostals, Globalization, and Postmodern Hermeneutics," 289.

100. Bridges-Johns, "A Pentecostal Perspective," 47.

101. Ibid.

102. Ibid.

103. Ibid.

104. Johns, "Pentecostalism and the Postmodern Worldview," 90.

105. Bridges-Johns, *Pentecostal Formation.*

106. Clark, "An Investigation into the Nature of a Viable Pentecostal Hermeneutic," 83.

107. Ibid., 56.

108. Ibid., 55.

These limitations of adopted Evangelical descriptions for the Pentecostal community highlight the importance of developing a unique Pentecostal theology. Of the various recent studies regarding Pentecostal understandings of Scripture, the most dynamic discussion presented in recent years is the writing of Ellington.[109] In his observations of Pentecostal students, he suggests that "Pentecostals do not found their understanding of the authority of Scripture on a bedrock of doctrine, but that, in fact, their doctrine is itself resting on something more fundamental, dynamic, and resilient; their experiences of encountering a living God, directly and personally."[110] For Pentecostal readers, the Bible is the standard by which all experience is measured and interpreted. Rather than reading *about* God, Pentecostal readers approach the Bible to meet *with* God.[111] Yet, it must also apply that the Bible is not only the measure and corrective of experience, but also the means or vehicle by which God is encountered. As Ellington notes, the Bible is considered to be authoritative for Pentecostal readers because the Holy Spirit is found to be at work experientially in and through Scripture in the lives of each member of the church community.[112] This emphasis on experience and community is resonant with the values of some postmodern theorists, such as Ricoeur, Fish, and Iser.

This understanding of Scripture presented by Ellington creates an experiential circle (or spiral). The reader encounters God in the text, and through this experience, accepts the role of Scripture to be informative and corrective in their lives.[113] The reader's experience is then evaluated in the light of the authoritative Scripture, which then creates opportunity and expectation to encounter and experience God in the text. However, this process assumes that the experience results from a reading of the biblical text, and limits the encounter of God to the reading of biblical texts. Yet, Pentecostal theology does not limit the encounter with God to reading biblical texts but allows for dynamic encounter with God through alternative vehicles such as prophetic words, prayer, and creation. If this encounter outside of reading biblical texts is still to be evaluated and corrected by Scripture, then the authority of Scripture is not realized through personal encounter but through the acceptance of the value that the community places upon the Word of God. In other words, the role of the community is much more influential in determining doctrines and values than Ellington's model anticipates. This emphasis on community in the reading process is a significant contribution to the development of a unique Pentecostal hermeneutic. However, while Ellington does affirm the role of the community of faith, he tends to emphasize the primacy of individual experience and testimony over the collective values and authority of the community in the interpretative process. The issue this concept raises concerning the potential conflict and politics between the authority of the individual reception of pneumatic illumination and the authority of the community will be discussed in chapter 4 of this work.

---

109. Ellington, "Pentecostalism and the Authority of Scripture," 6–38.

110. Ibid., 17.

111. Ibid., 26.

112. Ibid., 36.

113. Ibid., 26.

PENTECOSTAL SCHOLARSHIP OF OLD TESTAMENT TEXTS

In recent years, there has been a small but steady interest among Pentecostal scholars in the discussion of Old Testament texts. These Pentecostal scholars (including Moore, Davies, Ellington, and McQueen)[114] engaging in biblical studies of Old Testament texts generally exhibit a concern for the worldview and values of the Pentecostal community. Each adopts varying approaches to reading Old Testament texts, ranging from literary analysis and postmodern methods to historical-critical analysis; each attempting to reconcile their faith confession with biblical scholarship. This concern of the Pentecostal community with charismatic experience is particularly reflected in the reading of the Old Testament text of Deuteronomy by Moore.[115] Moore presents an approach that is self-consciously critical, yet also charismatic in his commitment to reading the text through the eyes of his Pentecostal experience, as a Pentecostal scholar.[116] Just as the book of Deuteronomy presents an act of interpretation as a voice in the wilderness, so Moore sees his work in a similar light. He writes "A self-consciously Pentecostal perspective comes to the table of modern biblical scholarship as a voice from the margin."[117] This reflects the personal journey of Moore as he recounts through testimony (a value of the Pentecostal oral tradition) his experience as a Pentecostal Bible student encountering the maze of modern biblical scholarship in a North American graduate school.

Moore poignantly describes the anxiety of many Pentecostal students who suddenly discover the bias of the academy against their previous "pre-critical" readings of biblical texts. He writes: "I knew, without it having to be explicitly stated, that to be seen as 'pre-critical' in this environment was a fate to be feared worse than death. Being relegated to the camp of the pre-critical was cursed; being admitted to the guild of the critical was blessed. I survived that time mostly by hiding in a wilderness between the curse that I feared and the blessing that I could bring myself to embrace."[118] Instead, Moore found eventual reconciliation as a Bible teacher in the adoption of literary approaches. He recalls that, "In Pentecostal scholarship this encouraged a conscious interest in the narrative orientation of Pentecostalism's own theological heritage. Story or testimony had been the prime vehicle and mode of discourse in Pentecostal faith from its beginnings, long before it had become fashionable in academic circles."[119]

For Moore this meant a conscious attempt to reconcile his faith confession with his interpretive method as he approached the text with, in the language of Ricoeur, a second naiveté. Although once a marginalized and illegitimate reading, approaching the text through "Pentecostal eyes" became legitimized through the decentralization of postmodernity. As an example of this practice, Moore adopts a literary approach for the study

---

114. Moore, "Deuteronomy and the Fire of God"; Davies, *Double Standards in Isaiah*; Ellington, "History, Story, and Testimony"; McQueen, *Joel and the Spirit*.

115. Moore, "Deuteronomy and the Fire of God."

116. Ibid., 11.

117. Ibid., 12.

118. Ibid., 13.

119. Ibid., 15.

of Deuteronomy that is organized around the theme of the "fire of God." According to Moore, the image of fire in the book represents a theophanic experience of God by the people of Israel in the context of confessional renewal.[120] The self-characterization of God in the book is as "a consuming fire" (Deut 4:24). In his literary analysis, Moore identifies chapter five as the book's defining section in which the people plead with Moses to come between them and the death they fear before the "fire of God."[121] This motif provides a literary coherence within the structure as the "fire of God" invades the community from the margins. The subsequent legal sections and conclusion of Deuteronomy, according to Moore, significantly refer to the fire motif that he identifies as significant to the book. He concludes that a Pentecostal approach to Deuteronomy is open to the experience of God speaking from the margins since it arises from personal experience of the marginalization of the Pentecostal community.[122]

Yet, it is ironic that while Moore presents a "marginalized" reading, he does not attempt to integrate other voices from his Pentecostal community. Instead his singular voice becomes the central interpretation of the biblical text while the voices of his "pre-critical" community are still left in the margins. The adoption of literary analysis and postmodern perspectives of de-marginalization similarly allows Moore to evade the issues of historical-criticism while upholding a legitimate (and politically acceptable) form of biblical scholarship. This means that pre-critical assumptions of Pentecostal readers (such as questions of authorship and dating) remain unchallenged and hidden beneath the veneer of a literary reading. While it presents an emphasis on the experience of God by the Pentecostal reader, by approaching the text through the legitimization of postmodernity Moore ignores the issues of responsibility and ethical reading standards that are inherent in a model based on charismatic experience. As Ellington notes, "postmodern hermeneutics, while offering many fresh insights into the text that are of use to Pentecostal readers, operates out of a worldview in which all truth-claims are local and relative and in which the biblical writers are viewed with a high degree of suspicion. Therefore, postmodern approaches are also limited in their applicability to the practice of hermeneutics by Pentecostals."[123]

While rejecting the *worldview* of postmodernism in his development of a Pentecostal hermeneutic, Ellington presents a Pentecostal reading of an Old Testament text (Ps 22) based on the writings of biblical scholar and postmodern critic, Brueggemann.[124] As noted above, Ellington presents a model of truth-as-testimony in which the testimony of the biblical writer is explored in relation to the experience of the contemporary reader. In this sense, the Pentecostal value of the continuing activity of God is emphasized as the fresh experiences of the Pentecostal reader (Ellington) are explored in the light of biblical experience as expressed through the testimony of the text. However, Ellington acknowledges that his model differs from current Pentecostal reading practices (as he

---

120. Ibid., 27.

121. Ibid., 28.

122. Ibid., 33.

123. Ellington, "History, Story, and Testimony," 261–62.

124. Brueggemann, *Theology of the Old Testament*.

quotes Israel) "the text points to a world, the interpreter orients himself or herself toward the claim of the text and that is where appropriation takes place."[125] Instead, Ellington suggests that Pentecostal Bible reading generally ignores serious complaint to God.[126] Therefore he attempts to correct this lack in his hermeneutic. However, the development of a hermeneutic that is helpful to the community and reflects their values and faith confession needs to be developed outside the correction of its theology.

This adoption of literary approaches to the reading of Old Testament texts is similarly reflected in the writings of Davies, who adopts postmodern methodologies, particularly deconstruction, in his presentation of divine ethics in the book(s) of *Isaiah*.[127] While his work does not address issues or an audience that is specifically Pentecostal, his publication is widely accepted by biblical scholarship and represents a new guard of Pentecostal scholars integrating with the academy. Davies' adoption of postmodern methods means that he avoids issues of historical criticism and literalism that may be misconstrued by either (or both) of the two communities of Pentecostal and academia in which he co-exists. For example, Davies considers the ethical concerns of all sixty-six chapters of Isaiah as a "redactionally—unified whole work"[128] as his study is not dependent on any particular view of the development of the book of Isaiah—an approach adopted by many Pentecostal scholars of the Old Testament. This allows Davies' study to be thematically driven, rather than loaded with the issues of source or redaction criticism.

The study of McQueen[129] presents an attempt to integrate the voice of the wider Pentecostal community into his critical scholarship. McQueen presents a threefold analysis that considers, first, the historical concerns and literary themes of the book, followed by consideration of the appropriation of those themes in the New Testament writings and in Pentecostalism. He attempts to "bring the book of Joel and its New Testament appropriation into conversation with Pentecostal tradition and scholarship."[130] McQueen highlights the role of Pentecostal experience in shaping the hermeneutical process. His concern is the dialogue between the text and the Spirit, as he writes, "To be a Pentecostal interpreter of Scripture, my confession about the text must agree with the previously evoked confession about the Spirit. It is true that the claim of the Spirit is in agreement with the claim of the text, but we come to know the claim of the text in the light of the claim of the Spirit."[131] For McQueen the claim of the Spirit must be balanced by the claim of the text. However, for Pentecostal readers, the text and the Spirit are not in dialogical opposition. According to Pentecostal understandings of Scripture, the text represents space for an encounter with God. However while it appears postmodern in its language, essentially the "claim of the text" is defined by McQueen as, essentially, the claim of historical-critical methodology.

125. Ellington, "History, Story, and Testimony," 261.

126. Ibid., 260.

127. Davies, *Double Standards in Isaiah*.

128. Ibid., 4.

129. McQueen, *Joel and the Spirit*.

130. Ibid., 107.

131. Ibid., 109.

Yet, the claim of McQueen resounds that the pneumatic illumination of the text cannot be in contradiction to the claims of the historical criticism. For McQueen, what the text meant to its original community and context cannot contradict the "claim of the Spirit." McQueen describes his journey of reading the text in which (by exploring the inherent historical concerns and literary themes) he discovered the central "claim of the text" to concern lament. He writes, "Before I began the process of research for this work, I did not 'know' the claim of the text of Joel because I had not been claimed by the Spirit the way the book of Joel presented that claim. In Joel's words, I did not know how to lament. In Pentecostal language, I did not know how to pray through. I was not made aware of this until several months into reading commentaries, monographs, and articles on the book of Joel but without a clear sense of 'knowing' the text of Joel itself."[132] While McQueen demonstrates the process of pneumatic revelation operating through the rational processes of critical analysis, this is not generally representative of the reading processes of the Pentecostal community at large. This also assumes that the connection between the "claim of the text" and the "claim of the Spirit" will be grounded on historical-critical claims. However both the New Testament appropriation of Old Testament texts (including passages from Joel such as Joel 3:1–5 applied to Acts 2), and Pentecostal readings do not always adhere to the context of the original passage as defined by historical criticism but regularly read texts with a fuller meaning (*sensus plenior*) than what was understood by the original Old Testament author.

The discussion of Old Testament texts by Pentecostal scholars highlights the need to develop a hermeneutical model that reflects the practices and values of the Pentecostal community at large. It is essential that this reading approach engage with the concerns for pneumatic illumination and charismatic experience. The Pentecostal community expects to encounter God in the text (the text representing that space for encounter), and in doing so is not bound to the historical concerns for the discovery of meaning within the text (such as the text as an artifact).[133] As Clark writes, "A Pentecostal hermeneutic is the ultimate challenge to the scholarly detachment, not because the Bible is a non-rational book demanding total intellectual surrender, but because rational and historical scrutiny of its content confronts the reader with a God who is truly there, who draws readers into his ongoing history, changing their lives, enduing them with power, and making them witnesses to the activity of God through the activity of his Spirit who testifies of the risen Lord."[134] The question, then, is how legitimate are these non-rational and pneumatically—illuminated readings and meanings discovered by the Pentecostal reader? Or more potently, *who* determines their legitimacy as a reading?

132. Ibid.

133. My thanks to Dr Jione Havea for pointing out that this parallels with Jewish tradition in that nothing exists outside the Torah. This idea is also explored by Derrida where "nothing exists outside of the text."

134. Clark, "An Investigation into the Nature of a Viable Pentecostal Hermeneutic," 299.

DEVELOPING A UNIQUE PENTECOSTAL HERMENEUTIC

The development of a distinct approach by the Pentecostal community to the nature and understanding of Scripture highlights the need for a related approach to reading methods. The confines of the adopted models (Evangelical and postmodern) make them inadequate for the full expression of the unique values and reading practices of the Pentecostal community. Instead, many Pentecostal scholars are now looking beyond the categories of Evangelical and postmodern theories to develop their distinct hermeneutic. Like Byrd, various Pentecostal scholars are now looking to their own Pentecostal heritage and theological uniqueness to develop a reading model that reflects this identity. In particular, Archer looks to reading models of classic Pentecostalism to provide a viable hermeneutic.[135] By observing past approaches he writes, "Pentecostal interpretation placed little or no significance upon the historical context of Scripture nor would it be concerned with the author's original intent (the historical-critical method). The Bible is the Word of God understood at face value."[136] This represents a shift in the discussion of Pentecostal reading models away from authorial intention to reflect the distinct understanding of Scripture within the Pentecostal community. In describing the hermeneutic of classic Pentecostals, Archer critiques the tendency of readers to associate the authority and inspiration of Scripture with infallibility. According to Archer, as the Bible is the very word of God to Pentecostals, its inspiration becomes a direct dictation to the context of the contemporary reader.[137] This results in reading approaches that accept the Bible at face value with little or no appreciation of the historical context in which it was first delivered. He notes that ironically, "this approach led to multiple dimensions of meaning" but wants to, like Fee and Menzies, avoid the affirmation of relativism.[138]

While Archer looks to the heritage of Pentecostalism, Autry considers the missing link in the Pentecostal discussion of hermeneutics to be the goal of Scripture reading and preaching.[139] Understanding the text, whether that is through methods of historical reconstruction or postmodern approaches, is not the end in itself. The goal of hermeneutics for Autry, is the "the goal identified by the canon itself: knowledge of (not simply about) God."[140] This knowledge of God is both subjective and objective as the charismatic experience of the Pentecostal reader is guided and corrected by the authoritative canon.[141] For Autry, the authoritative canon provides a map to guide the reading community into knowledge of God, and to correct their subjective experience of encounter with God. Yet as the reader brings their presuppositions and interests to their interpretation of the canon, the nature of Autry's "objective" knowledge of God must be questioned. However, while Archer and Autry highlight important *values* of the Pentecostal community, they

---

135. Archer, "Early Pentecostal Biblical Interpretation."

136. Ibid., 66.

137. Ibid., 67.

138. Ibid., 69.

139. Autry, "Dimensions of Hermeneutics in Pentecostal Focus."

140. Ibid., 42.

141. Ibid., 43.

do not provide either a specific theory or a *model* of reading for Pentecostal readers to adopt. In his later monograph,[142] Archer goes on to suggest that the most ideal avenue to pursue a unique Pentecostal hermeneutic is through the vehicle of narrative criticism.

In the attempt to reflect the oral tradition and proliferation of storytelling within Pentecostalism, Archer equates this value with the narrative method. He writes, "The Bible is not reduced to propositions but instead functions as it was intended to—as stories that grip and shape the readers while challenging them to infer from the narrative a praxis orientated theology."[143] However, Archer does not separate the value from the method. While the oral tradition of Pentecostalism and engagement with the story-world of the text (*a la* reader-response theories) is an important value to the community, narrative criticism is not a method that can be appropriately adopted to read *all* genre of texts— especially non-narratives such as poetry, law, or prophetic texts like those in *Isaiah*. Yet, it does present a model that represents the values of the Pentecostal community and can therefore potentially engage the entirety of the Pentecostal community.

The importance of the community of believers in the interpretative process is also emphasized by Thomas.[144] Adopting the Council of Jerusalem in Acts 15 as a case study, Thomas creates a hermeneutic model that integrates the experience of the community, the Holy Spirit and Scripture. The Council recognized the dynamic of each component as it heard the testimonies of the converted Gentiles, recognized the working of the Holy Spirit in this and confirmed this working of the Spirit through the Scriptures.[145] Thomas writes of the integral role of the Holy Spirit, "For not only is the final decision of the Council described as seeming good to the Holy Spirit, but the previous activity of the Spirit in the community also spoke very loudly to the group, being in part responsible for the text chosen as most appropriate for this particular context."[146] This explicit dependence on the Holy Spirit in the interpretive process clearly goes far beyond the Evangelical description of "illumination" as Thomas aptly points out.[147] Once this model based on Acts 15 is established, Thomas then applies this paradigm to the issue of women in ministry to affirm the role of women ministers in the Pentecostal community. This is vastly different from the Evangelical approaches adopted by earlier Pentecostal scholars such as Fee and Menzies as it allows a dynamic reading of Scripture separate from the authorial intention, yet still guided by the community in the Spirit.[148]

The role of the community is valued in this exercise as it allows space (like the Acts 15 model) for testimonies of the Spirit's activity that are discerned by the community in the light of Scripture. He writes, "The community can offer balance, accountability and

---

142. Archer, *A Pentecostal Hermeneutic for the Twenty-First Century*.

143. Ibid., 168.

144. Thomas, "Women, Pentecostals, and the Bible."

145. Ibid., 44–46.

146. Ibid.

147. Ibid., 49.

148. To not allow this method is to insist on the "special" (i.e., dispensationalist) nature of early revelation.

support."[149] This is perhaps (unfortunately) the ideal offered by Thomas rather than the practice of the community. The idea behind this process is to guard the interpretation of both Scripture and pneumatic experience from rampant individualism. This model allows for the study of the historical context of the passage and other important concerns highlighted by Evangelical methods, but is not limited to those concerns. However the model does tend to rely on quantitative rather than qualitative Scriptural evidence for the subject matter presented; whatever side can claim the most Bible references wins. In addition, this model suggests a prioritization of the experience of the community and the selection of texts that validate that experience.[150] In applying this model to the issue of women in ministry, Thomas concludes that "Despite the fact that a couple of silence passages do indeed exist, the powerful testimony of the Spirit coupled with numerous New Testament passages that clearly support a prominent role for women in ministry necessitate a course of action which not only makes room for women in the ministry of the church but also seeks to enlist all the talents of these largely under-utilized servants of the Lord in the most effective way possible for work in the harvest."[151]

While this model by Thomas integrates crucial values of the Pentecostal community regarding pneumatic experience, oral testimony, community interaction and significance of Scripture in a dynamic manner, it is a *pre*scription for the Pentecostal reader rather than necessarily descriptive. The rampant individualism that this model seeks to avoid in the interpretive process is an unfortunate reality of the Pentecostal community. The greatest strength of the Pentecostal community, the democratization of the Spirit, is also its greatest weakness as the individual experience of the Spirit becomes the overriding authority rather than a motive force within (as seen in the balanced approach of Thomas) the interface of the three key elements of interpretation. It is also noted that while Thomas' model underlines the importance of Scripture, his demonstration only refers to New Testament texts. Even in his discussion of the issue of women in ministry where some poignant Old Testament examples from Scripture, such as Deborah in Judg 4 and Miriam in the Exodus record, are ignored. This suggests that "Scripture" refers to primarily the New Testament writings, more specifically, the didactic texts. This lacuna clearly raises the question of the role of the Old Testament for the Pentecostal community.

One of the most recent major works on developing a distinct and viable Pentecostal hermeneutic has been presented by Clark.[152] He rejects both the Evangelical and postmodern options in his search for a viable Pentecostal hermeneutic. Like Archer, he emphasizes the importance of narrative to Pentecostal readers, not just in reading the texts, but also in the Pentecostal experience of being part of the ongoing narrative history of God.[153] He writes,

149. Ibid., 55.

150. However, what Thomas does not address the concern in the possible event of an entire community being misled and thereby not offering the balance and accountability the model requires.

151. Thomas, "Women, Pentecostals, and the Bible," 54.

152. Clark, "An Investigation into the Nature of a Viable Pentecostal Hermeneutic."

153. Ibid., 142.

> The idea that Pentecostals are involved in an *ongoing history with God*, and therefore see themselves as the people of God of the new covenant, especially as made evident in the fulfillment of the promise of the presence of the Spirit. This fulfillment is seen in the discernible presence and working of God in their midst and mission in terms of the charismata. This provides a sense of pneumatic continuity with the church community of Acts, as well as with the charismatic history of Israel.[154]

This is particularly demonstrated in the use of the New Testament narrative, particularly the book of Acts, by the Pentecostal community as a canon within the canon.[155] This is in tension with the super-canonical use of Paul by many Evangelicals. The description of the early church became the pattern or model for the early Pentecostal movement. The effort to "restore" the character and practices of the New Testament church has been highlighted by Graham as was one of the driving forces behind the early Pentecostal movement.[156] The reflection on this foundational value of Christianity, also present in the work of Clark, provides the basis for a model of reading that integrates the present Pentecostal community with the continuing activity of the Spirit and story of God's work since Pentecost. Clark then applies his approach to the text of 1 Cor 14 to demonstrate the differences between a Pentecostal and a non-Pentecostal position or approach.

By reflecting on elements of the Pentecostal experience that Clark identifies as central to developing a hermeneutic, elements such as the continuity with the apostolic church and the participation of God in that history, he highlights the continuity between the New Testament text of 1 Cor 14 and the contemporary Pentecostal community. His reading places emphasis on encouraging charismatic activity in the Pentecostal congregation so that each participant is concerned to hear God speak authentically among the whole community.[157] This assumes that charismatic activity is active in the contemporary community, a basic value of the Pentecostal community that Clark seeks to highlight in continuity with the Corinthian community. Clark similarly emphasizes the resultant promotion of evangelism and a missionary spirit among the congregation through the reading of the text from the Pentecostal position. And yet, he introduces the prescription of a safeguard for the Pentecostal reader by stressing the important role of rational methods and content in the passage. He writes, "While 1 Corinthians 14 is a charismatic chapter, from a charismatic author to a charismatic church, it does not exalt a Gnostic spirituality, nor a dualism of mind and spirit."[158] The rational argument of Paul is highlighted by Clark to prescribe to the Pentecostal reader the similar importance and application of rationality to their own situation.

What Clark presents, in essence, is a contextual hermeneutic that emphasizes the values of the Pentecostal community. He considers the meaning of the text in the context in which it was written; he then applies this meaning to the contemporary Pentecostal community in a way that is consistent with its values. This is helpful for a reading of New

154. Ibid., 295 (italics author's own).

155. Graham, "'Thus saith the Lord': Biblical Hermeneutics in the Early Pentecostal Movement," 126.

156. Ibid.

157. Clark, "An Investigation into the Nature of a Viable Pentecostal Hermeneutic," 237.

158. Ibid., 238.

Testament texts, but raises the same question as Thomas: is this approach appropriate for reading Old Testament texts? While the approach of Clark is viable for reading New Testament texts it does not engage with issues addressing the reading of Old Testament texts. While Clark acknowledges the need for a distinct approach to the Old Testament by Pentecostal readers, he does not attempt to engage this need in his discussion of the nature of a "viable Pentecostal hermeneutic." Instead, he simply highlights the discontinuity between the two testaments in his discussion of the Pentecostal experience as part of the ongoing narrative history of God. If the Pentecostal community is in continuity with the New Testament community but in relative discontinuity with the Old Testament community, this has profound implications for the adoption of Clark's model for the entire canon. He writes,

> Again the important distinctions between Old and New Testament charismatic modality cannot be ignored. On this continent [Africa] such distinction are overlooked at times in African Christianity. Set in a tribal culture, the Old Testament stories abound with isolated heroes, great leaders who stood, or fell, in a special relationship with the deity. Standing spiritually head and shoulders above the rest of the nation as they did, these men often serve as literal and simplistic role-models for contemporary African religious leaders . . . The New Testament challenges this view in many respects. It affirms the existence of a new state of affairs: there is no distinction among believers in terms of the Spirit which is at work among the people of God, although there are significant differences in ministry and calling. However, as a priesthood of believers the modern Pentecostal movement cannot encourage a too literal identification with the Old Testament pattern of exclusivity.[159]

For this reason, Clark advocates the priority of New Testament texts, particularly the stories of Jesus, in establishing models for Pentecostal experience. However, to extend the trajectory of Clark's thought, this would mean that the Old Testament texts must be read exclusively through the New Testament to establish continuity with the Pentecostal community. This model would not allow for elements of continuity between the Old Testament community and the contemporary Pentecostal community, such as the charismatic activity of the prophets, or allow for the validity of reading Old Testament texts for their unique contribution without christological lenses. This questions the use of Old Testament texts by Pentecostal scholars and the reading practices they have adopted.[160] Reading the Old Testament exclusively through the eyes of the New Testament is not only a "two-stage" reading by which the former gets absorbed into the New Testament reading,[161] but fails to recognize that connections are made from the side of the New Testament by reading *back* into the Old Testament and not the side of the Old Testament.[162]

---

159. Ibid., 155.

160. Part of the issue identified by Dr Mark Hutchinson (private conversation) is that the first generation of Pentecostal scholars tends to be driven by institutional needs to preference the New Testament over the Old Testament. In choosing this training, they therefore tend to focus and study in the New Testament and Greek, rather than in the Old Testament and Hebrew.

161. Brueggemann, *Theology of the Old Testament*, 731.

162. Ibid., 732.

It is this seeming violation of the uniqueness of the Old Testament text that will be discussed in the next chapter as the "Old Testament Speaks Up."

DEVELOPING A UNIQUE PENTECOSTAL HERMENEUTIC OF THE OLD TESTAMENT

The issue of responsibility is central to the development of a viable Pentecostal reading approach to the Old Testament. The centrality of charismatic experience and pneumatic illumination is highlighted by numerous scholars. As the model by Thomas highlights, this tends toward rampant individualism that elevates individual revelation over community evaluation. The need which is thereby highlighted is for the Pentecostal community to develop a model that embraces pneumatic illumination in a responsible form. It will be a form that allows diversity and multiplicity of readings, faith confession and expression of Pentecostal values, yet is responsible in the maintenance of this faith confession.

Common to the varied explorations of Pentecostal scholars is a cry for a model that embraces not only the interests of Pentecostal scholars but also reflects the values inherent in the practices of the Pentecostal reading community. While the concerns of the Pentecostal academic community in dialogue with hermeneutical theory are still an important consideration, theirs is not the only voice to represent the diversity of Pentecostalism in this crowded discussion. While most Pentecostal scholars present a concern to reflect the values of the Pentecostal community, there has been little attempt in their work to empirically determine how these values are reflected in practice. The voice of the community has been silenced in the determination to prescribe a Pentecostal hermeneutic by the scholars of the community. So rather than presenting a *description* of a Pentecostal reading model, most Pentecostal scholars have imposed a *prescription* that reflects their own concerns and agenda. Instead, a model is required that seriously considers the reading practices of the community, not as a tokenism, but which genuinely seeks to understand and describe their practices. From this description, a study of the key values of a Pentecostal reading of the Old Testament can be determined which lay the foundation for developing a responsible reading method. From the *description*, a *prescription* can be voiced in its logical order. One of the aims of this study—to construct a reading method of the Old Testament that reflects both the values of the community and the concerns for responsibility from academic reflection—requires the voice of the community to be heard in its own environment. This requirement is the concern of the next chapter.

4

The Old Testament Speaks Up

To allow the community to voice its reading practices, this book adopts the text of *Isaiah* as a focus for registering the "voice" of Pentecostalism as it engages the three—fold conversation with Hermeneutics and the Old Testament. While readings of this prophetic literature could conceivably provide different outcomes of meaning from readings of alternative books and genres from the Old Testament, the attempt is not to discuss the outcome of meanings or content as such, but to highlight the principles (Hermeneutics) observed in these reading practices (from Pentecostalism). Although any of the thirty-nine books from the Old Testament canon could have been selected,[1] the text of *Isaiah* was chosen for its popularity and familiarity among the Pentecostal community. This intimacy with the text means that there are multiple examples of Pentecostal readings from across a wide range of time periods, source types (sermons, magazine articles, and small group discussion) and groups within the context of Australia (professional ministers and laity).[2] Although predominantly a pragmatic choice, the various sources represent a cross-section of readers from the Pentecostal community engaging with the text of *Isaiah* (as represented in Appendix 1). This presentation is reflective of the oral culture of the Pentecostal community in which storytelling, experience, and testimony are vital elements.[3] Considering the important value of narrative to the storytelling and

---

1. It must also be acknowledged that limitations on the length of this study would not allow a comprehensive discussion of every book of the Old Testament canon; therefore one book was selected as a prototype or example for the examination of Pentecostal reading practices.

2. While a book unfamiliar to Pentecostal readers would also have produced an interesting study, and may even have highlighted further the common and dominant features of Pentecostal readings due to its unfamiliarity and non-deliberated response, the nature of an alien text also means a lack of sources and resource with which to discuss it.

3. Land, *Pentecostal Spirituality*, 73.

oral traditions of Pentecostalism, also highlighted by Archer,[4] this approach is reflective of these principles of the community.

The purpose of this description is to adequately reflect the Pentecostal community involved by engaging with grassroots readers to elucidate their practices and values in the articulation of the meaning(s) of texts, rather than imposing ideal versions and academic musing separate to the workings of the actual community. Yet the choice of *Isaiah* is significant. The text of *Isaiah*, as noted previously, can also be considered representative of the self-identification of the Pentecostal community in Australia. In Isa 6, the prophet encounters God; he is overwhelmed, his lips are burnt (the mouthpiece protecting the 'tongue'), and is transformed by the revelation of Yahweh. He then begins his missionary ministry as a rejected prophet, misunderstood. The parallel experience of history and identity of the global Pentecostal community as a marginal group in the broader context of Christianity has already been noted in chapter 2. In this sense, the experience of the prophet can act as a trope for the experience of the Pentecostal community.

While this book presents a critical analysis of the hermeneutic employed by a particular community of a particular text (in this case, *Isaiah*), it is not intended to be a critical study of the text itself. In this sense, the outcomes of the readings will not be discussed rather than the values and approach that they present. These readings of *Isaiah* are unearthed from the writings and speech of the grassroots Pentecostal community. The Pentecostal readings presented represent a mixture or nuance of "voices" from the community in Australia, including articles from populist Pentecostal publications, sermons and small group discussions as a sample of membership from professional and lay members of the faith community. The concerns, attitudes, language and even bible translations adopted reflect the concerns and choices of the community. While the reading sample is specifically from the multi-cultural community in Australia, the diversity of readings reflect the values of the broader global community defined in chapter 2. A corollary of this is that concerns, content and approaches *not* engaged by the Pentecostal readers will *not* be reflected in the description of their readings. For example, if the Pentecostal reading community does not exhibit interest in textual issues, concern for the original language and Hebrew text or demonstrate an interest in the comparison of English translations, then this lack of interest will be reflected in the description of their readings. In this way the "voice" of the community can be heard through the practice of reading Old Testament texts.

The readings of *Isaiah* by the Pentecostal community reflect a diversity of responses and interpretations of the biblical texts. However, the process of gathering readings elicited a tendency by Pentecostal readers to be drawn to particular texts within *Isaiah*. For some sections of *Isaiah* there is a proliferation of material (sermons and articles) while for others the sources are scarce. It is clear that only certain sections of *Isaiah* circulate widely in the Pentecostal community. Therefore the texts discussed in this study are the texts discussed by the Pentecostal reading community; it reflects their interests, their choice and their reading practices. Their interest in particular texts will be discussed in

---

4. Archer, *A Pentecostal Hermeneutic for the Twenty-first Century*, 168.

the next three chapters of the book. In this way, the study of Pentecostal readings can offer alternative reading approaches to Old Testament texts to benefit the wider reading community. While this chapter will discuss how the Pentecostal community has interpreted Isa 6, 9, and 53 in the light of the specific dialogue with Old Testament studies, the following two chapters will discuss Isa 25 and 40, then Isa 54 and 61 respectively in the light of hermeneutical issues and theories.

This selection process by the community also provides insight into the values of the community. Why is it that certain *Isaiah* texts (6, 9, 25, 40, 53, 54, and 61 in particular) are most commonly discussed in the Pentecostal community, while other texts are not? The community has assigned importance to these texts and, by default, not assigned importance to other texts. This selection of texts for sermons and articles is particularly significant as Pentecostal preachers do not follow a lectionary, but are "led by the spirit" in their choice of texts to discuss. Why is it, then, that the "Spirit has led" most preachers and writers on *Isaiah* to the same texts? Does the Spirit have favorite passages as well, or is there something about these particular passages that resonate with the values and practices of the Pentecostal community? As Bird notes, communities read the Bible selectively, giving attention to what is most congenial to their own faith.[5] In a largely oral tradition, what are the implicit rules for selection and (self) reflection? Perhaps these implicit criteria represent some of the fears of the community as well as hopes? The specific selection and focus on texts by Pentecostal readings that witness to transformational encounters of God highlight this concern as an important value of the Pentecostal reading community. It is in response to such questions that this book will seek to excavate an outline of the readings from the Pentecostal community on these texts from *Isaiah* as it engages in the three-fold discussion with hermeneutics and the Old Testament. The aim of this approach is to reflect the reading process of the Pentecostal community. Therefore the concerns, content, and approach of the Pentecostal readers are described.

PENTECOSTALISM AND THE OLD TESTAMENT

This same quest for definition and uniqueness of "voice" is also a concern in recent developments of Old Testament Studies. As the previous chapter noted there is a consistent tendency in current proposals of a unique Pentecostal hermeneutic to emphasize the role of New Testament narrative, particularly the book of *Acts*. These approaches suggested by scholars of the academic community clearly raise the question of the role of the Old Testament for the Pentecostal community. While recognizing the importance of oral testimony and storytelling to the Pentecostal community, it does not necessitate that this value mandates or prioritizes New Testament narrative. However it is not just particular genres within the New Testament that are prioritized in these proposals, but the New Testament becomes the lens through which the Old Testament is read. In this approach, the Old Testament becomes absorbed into the New Testament reading.[6]

---

5. Bird, *The Bible as the Church's Book*, 82.

6. Brueggemann's critique of some biblical theologians such as Brevard Childs includes this charge that a two-stage reading simply absorbs the OT into the reading of the NT. (Brueggemann, *Old Testament Theology*, 732).

In particular many Pentecostal readers tend to not only look for the pre-shadowing or prediction of Christ in Old Testament texts, but to also read the text in the light of the resurrected Christ. While this can be appropriate for a *Christian* reading of the text, as a one-dimensional reading it does not allow the uniqueness of the "voice" of the Old Testament testimony and witness to be heard.

The absorption of the Old Testament witness into the New is not unique to the Pentecostal community. This approach is exemplified in biblical scholarship by the work of canonical critics, particularly Brevard Childs of the Yale Divinity School. While emphasizing the theological unity of the canonical union(s) of the Old and New Testaments, Childs highlights the christological priority in its interpretation inherited from the early church.[7] While Childs theorizes that "The Old Testament is understood by its relation to the New, but the New is incomprehensible apart from the Old,"[8] his actual practice of a two-step biblical theology tends to dissolve the Old Testament witness into the interests of the New Testament. While this priority is crucial to a Christian reading, this approach does not recognize that the connections between the New Testament and the Old Testament are made on the side of the former by reading *back* into the latter. While the New Testament writers boldly announce that the Scriptures have been fulfilled, their affirmation is made from the side of the fulfillment (and not from the side of the Old Testament).[9] Yet there is a concern within Old Testament studies, led by scholars such as Walter Brueggemann, that this approach undermines the unique witness of the Old Testament. This is particularly highlighted by the fact that the Old Testament does not always obviously and cleanly point to the New Testament.[10] Yet the work of Childs does offer some important insights for the Pentecostal community who share a similar adoption of the "final" or "received" forms of the Christian canon. Childs notes that the shape and theology of the Jewish canon was basically left unchanged by the early church (apart from the expansion of the number of books). The early church also resisted the attempt to Christianize or insert commentary within the earlier text. This respect for the uniqueness of the Jewish Scriptures and their separation from the writings collected by the post-apostolic community suggests that their distinct witness was valued. As Brueggemann writes, "Since the church rejected the views of Marcion in the second century C.E., it has been impossible in Christian theology to dissolve the Old Testament into to the New. The church, in a programmatic decision, held on to the Old Testament as Scripture because the Old Testament affirmed something definitional for Christianity that was not elsewhere affirmed and that Christians dared not lose."[11]

Yet biblical scholars have struggled to pinpoint exactly how this unique affirmation of the Old Testament can be defined. Some scholars, such as Longman, suggest it can be found in the representation of the continuity and discontinuity of the Testaments. The Jewish Scriptures were not read as an unbroken, historical extension of the nation of

---

7. Childs, *Biblical Theology of the Old and New Testaments*, 64.

8. Ibid., 77.

9. Brueggemann, *Old Testament Theology*, 732.

10. Ibid., 731.

11. Ibid., 730.

Israel, but as a theological or prophetic extension. The continuity of faith between the two testaments is not political or historical. Yet, neither is there a complete discontinuity. The earlier Testament is not designated as "Old" as a testimony to its failure (in the order of Bultmann).[12] The Old Testament community was not an interim group until the New Testament community could be formed.[13] Instead both communities must be valued while recognizing both continuity and discontinuity of their voices. Yet the determination of what is continuous and what is discontinuous is a difficult and often intuitive task. This determination also differs according to community values, experience, and critical reflection. For example, the controversial prosperity doctrine has been adopted by some Pentecostal groups as a continuation of the deuteronomic blessing without reflection on how this integrates with their twin value of being a discontinuation of the socio-geographic extension of ancient Israel.

However, the concerns of Old Testament scholarship to preserve the uniqueness of the former writings cannot be overlooked. It must be questioned as to whether a Christian reading can uphold the distinctive voice of the Old Testament. Must a Christian reading priorities the voice of the New Testament? This is a conundrum similarly reflected within the Pentecostal community. Within the Pentecostal community there tends to be a dual approach to understanding the role of the Old Testament. For some, there is a christocentric emphasis whereby the role of the Old Testament is to primarily bear witness to Jesus Christ. The second role identified, is the approach that understands the Old Testament as an exemplar of life and faith. In this approach, readers discover through the examples and moral dilemmas of its characters models for contemporary Christian living. Yet, as Clark notes, not all experiences of Old Testament characters are to be applied to the contemporary Christian life, such as the separation of the special class of anointed people (such as kings and prophets) from the general community—a value democratized in Acts 2.[14]

The former christocentric approach is reflected in a recent sermon by the former national Australian AG President, Pastor Brian Houston at the 2004 Hillsong Conference, a key focusing event in Australian Pentecostalism. Houston commented, "Some pastors should be banned from preaching from the Old Testament, until they've put their Jesus-colored glasses on. Because the Old Testament is full of life, full of power, full of authority. Oh, I tell you the Old Testament is full of great stories, great prophecy, great examples. The Old Testament's powerful. But I can't stand up on a Sunday morning and preach the Old Testament from being positioned in the Old Testament; I have to preach it as a New Testament, a new covenant believer."[15] He continued to encourage the conference by referring to Rom 10:6, "If you're going to ignore the work of Jesus when it comes to

---

12. Childs, *Biblical Theology of the Old and New Testaments*, 77.

13. Brueggemann, *Old Testament Theology*, 730.

14. Clark, "An Investigation into the Nature of a Viable Pentecostal Hermeneutic," 155.

15. The Hillsong Conference 2004 was attended by over 20,000 delegates, the majority of whom were non-clergy, which makes his emphasis even more poignant; Houston is exhorting non-clergy to teach the Old Testament through the resurrected Christ. Yet while many would not be a position to "preach," Houston models a Bible-reading practice.

the way you speak the Old Testament or the way you teach people, you may as well do exactly what that verse says. You may as well reach into heaven and pull Christ from his resurrected position and bring him back to where we're at. And live your life rigid and inflexible and legalistic and full of bondage and full of judgments and harshness."[16] For Houston, the Old Testament is an important authority but is considered insufficient in itself as a Christian witness for the Pentecostal community. The Pentecostal community appeals to *both* the newer Testament and the older for instruction in faith and living as the "whole counsel of God." However, as Houston suggests, the New Testament provides the interpretive lens through which many Pentecostal readers view the Old Testament. It is the perspective or "position" from which the Old Testament is read by the Pentecostal community.

One does not have to look far to find how common this value is within the Pentecostal community. This approach is also reflected in the writing of Ronald Greaves in the 1936 *Australian Evangel*:

> Open the Bible where you will, and beginning at that Scripture you can preach "Christ" . . . So that the Divine purpose is that the Scriptures in various ways and divers manners should bear abundant testimony to the Eternal Son (John 5:39). The literary perfection of this "priceless gem" should not arrest us in our pursuit of the truth, for as the astronomer finds in his lens a channel of vision which enables him to explore the magnificent splendor of the heavens, so the earnest student should learn to handle the Bible as a visible telescope, through which the invisible glory of Jesus is discerned with enraptured eyes.

This is an important feature in the *description* of a Pentecostal reading as it emphasizes the christological nature of their approach. Christ, and the newer covenant he inaugurated, is considered the interpretive starting point of any reading from the older covenant text.

Yet for other Pentecostal readers, the moral stories and testimonies of the pre-New Testament community are heard and appreciated for their direct resonance with the experience of the believer in the post-New Testament community. Pentecostal readers identify in the text an experience that resonates with their world or context, and so find comfort, guidance and counsel in the text. In this sense the voice of the Old Testament witness acts as a guide to the Christian believer through the sharing of experience. The testimony or experience of the Old Testament, like in the Pentecostal community and liturgy, become paradigmatic. The stories and experiences represented in the text become normative for all believers to emulate, such as the calling of the prophet Isaiah. While there might be aspects of the Old Testament witness that are identified as discontinuous with the values of the Pentecostal community, its testimony is valued for the faith it presents and encourages. The experience of the Pentecostal reader informs their reading and understanding of the text. For some readers, the testimony of the Old Testament not only helps verbalize their personal encounters with God but also directs their encounter into the presence of God, as the following Pentecostal readings of *Isaiah* will demonstrate. However, these dual approaches are often mixed and tend to lead to an

16. Ibid.

inconsistency in the understanding of the role and place of the Old Testament within the Pentecostal community. It is the analysis of these varied approaches to the "voice" of the Old Testament within Pentecostalism that the dialogue of the three-fold fellowship now turns—in particular through readings of Isa 6, 9, and 53.

READINGS OF ISAIAH 6

The various readings of Isa 6 by the Pentecostal community, including pastors, lay people, and songwriters, emphasize the experiential nature of both their own spirituality and what they see reflected in the text. Isaiah 6 is often used by Pentecostal readers to either make explicit through analogy the nature of an immediate encounter with God or to anticipate a future spiritual experience. The experience of the Pentecostal reader resonates with the vision and encounter of Isaiah with the "Holy one of Israel" as they reconstruct their own encounter through the verbalized experience of the prophet. Yet, while the prophet identifies the object of the vision as the "Holy one of Israel," most Pentecostal readers tend to identify the concealed figure in the text as the person of Jesus Christ. They associate their experience of Christ with the experience of the "Holy one of Israel" by Isaiah and so equate the two identities. When Pastor Ken Legg[17] questioned his Bible class: "Who did he [Isaiah] see?" The class unanimously responded: "Jesus." Legg continues, "We know that from John 12:38–41. Where did he say that in Isaiah chapter 6? These things Isaiah said when he saw His glory and spoke of Him." This association with Christ tends to originate from an intuitive association with the Pentecostal experience of salvation in Christ rather than specific study of the theophany.

However for other Pentecostal readers, the figure presented in the pre-New Testament *Isaiah* text maintains its sense of mystery. This is exemplified by an article in the 1985 *Australian Evangel* by Charismatic minister Ron Hoffmann,[18] which begins, "I awakened suddenly at 5a.m., dressed quickly and went to my study. As I knelt by my chair, I was overwhelmed by the presence of God. My thoughts were directed to Isa 6. I was caught up in the awesome majesty and holiness of God. I began to think about the greatness of God. Like Isaiah, I too was aware of my uncleanness and unworthiness."[19] Hoffmann begins with an experience he describes as being overwhelming in nature, which he identifies as the presence of God. In an attempt to turn this encounter into narrative he adopts the text of Isa 6. His experience resonates with the description in the text as he, like Isaiah, encounters the immediacy of God's presence and holy nature. Hoffmann continues to identify with the text of Isa 6 as he follows the narrative from describing the greatness of God to realizing his own unworthiness or "uncleanness."

Once Hoffmann identifies with the text and engages with it, his experience is then directed and transformed by that text. The text directs the thoughts of Hoffmann as he moves from the initial overwhelming encounter of God to the realization of his own unworthiness. However, no sooner has Hoffmann been directed by the text to reflect on

17. See Appendix 1, Ref E.

18. See Appendix 1, Ref G.

19. Ibid., 14.

his own unworthiness but he deviates from the directive of Isaiah as he continues his tale, "Then I began to think about the perfect sacrifice of Jesus, that the 'blood of Jesus cleanses us from all sin' (1 John 1:7). I was forgiven, cleansed, accepted, and caught up in all the wonder of the presence of God."[20] Hoffmann's narrative demonstrates a shift from the strict pattern of Isa 6 to introduce a christological emphasis. The experience of "unworthiness" associated with the prophet Isaiah is redefined as the writer begins to reflect on the cross of Jesus Christ. Hoffmann reads the forgiveness in the Old Testament text through the message of the New Testament. The redemption of the prophet is associated with the process of redemption presented in the New Testament, rather than recognition of the conceptualization of redemption for the world of the Old Testament. The process of forgiveness does not come to Hoffmann via the burning coal, but through the "perfect sacrifice of Jesus." The cleansing and forgiveness he receives has already been realized through Christ (he "was" forgiven); a reminder of the past acceptance he has received. Pentecostal readers view the message of Isa 6 through christological glasses. Christ is more than an occasional actor within Old Testament texts, but is the means of salvation and the very message which the Old Testament anticipates. This combination of the person, experience and message of Christ through which Pentecostal readers view the Isaiah texts, underlines the christological approach of their interpretation.

Reading the passage with christological emphasis, Hoffmann then returns to the Isaiah text, "Then God spoke to me with a *rhema* word through the Scripture 'Whom shall I send, and who will go for us?' I had read those words many times before, now they were charged with a new personal challenge. How would I answer? Here am I, but send someone else! God was challenging me to a new adventure, to another step in ministry. Was I willing to be available, to be obedient? To say like Isaiah of old, 'Here am I, SEND ME.'"[21] Initially, for Hoffmann, the passage of Isa 6 came to him because it resonated with his experience of the "presence of God." His thoughts were directed to the passage to make intelligible (and tell-able) his immediate encounter with God. However, having been directed to the concept of unworthiness and available forgiveness, Hoffmann became the director (rather than the text) and deviated from the passage to transform Isaiah's presentation of forgiveness into a christological understanding. But now, in this section of his account, Hoffmann is once again directed and challenged by the Isaian passage. The process of challenge is described by Hoffmann as being a "rhema" word. This concept is common in Pentecostal preaching and writing, and particularly so in the Charismatic section of the movement. The "rhema" word refers to a text (Scripture passage, concept, word, song lyric, etc.) that "jumps out" at the person through the presumed action of the Holy Spirit to enliven the text with revelatory impact and personal immediacy. This concept of the "rhema word" will be discussed in chapter 6. However Hoffmann's description does highlight this immediacy of effect of the Old Testament as he is newly challenged by a familiar text that is suddenly quickened in his heart and mind. His response to this challenge involves a deep self-questioning; it cannot be lightly

20. Ibid.
21. Ibid.

dismissed. The directive of the text also challenges the reader to respond positively to the call of ministry as exemplified by the prophet. Hoffmann follows the direction of the prophet and accepts the challenge (in this written re-telling of his encounter) with a willingness and obedience that mirrors the passage he is challenged by. His experience is directed and informed by the text, as well as informed by his christological reading.

The importance of the revelatory impact of Scripture for the Pentecostal community is also highlighted by an earlier British Pentecostal writer, Donald Gee,[22] in the 1939 *Australian Evangel* and *Glad Tidings Messenger*. In response to the topic of "The prime need of the hour for Pentecostal young people," he suggests the answer comes from "that inexhaustible mine of inspiration" of Isa 6. He identifies this primary need as "greater depth" as he writes,

> Isaiah had already been engaged in prophetic ministry, probably for about two years, when he received this memorable vision. Yet the death of King Uzziah marked a new and deeper personal experience for the young prophet. It was a time of national crisis, and such times are opportune for driving spiritual life deeper.
>
> The curse of so much that dares to call itself "Pentecostal" today is its shallowness: as if anything really Pentecostal could ever be shallow! To each of us personally comes the temptation to rest upon some first touch or taste of the Spirit's power, and we become wretchedly satisfied with what should have only been regarded as a first installment.
>
> The result is an attempt to live on the momentum of some past height of spiritual emotion that becomes less and less powerful as it recedes into the background. We need a fresh visit to the throne of the Lord of Hosts continually, made possible by the blood of Christ. There we shall find greater depth where Isaiah found it.

Gee goes on to emphasize the personal nature of Isaiah's vision which he describes as "vividly personal rather than 'second-hand.'" The importance of the passage for Gee's reading is its power as a model for Pentecostal believers. The historical context of the passage is only important as it provides the emotional context of the prophet; a time of crisis. The experience of Isaiah is understood by Gee to be a "vision"; a literal rather than symbolic event. Likewise Gee understands the location of the call narrative to be chronological (he approximates two years after the initiation of his prophetic activity); it is the re-affirmation of an already engaged prophet. For Gee, this may further validate his reading of Isaiah's testimony as an ongoing experience, as the prophet has already been the recipient of revelation. Rather than this vision being unique to the prophet, Gee encourages all Pentecostal believers to seek and desire a similar encounter that will produce (according to his article) "greater depth." The experience of the prophet is normative for all believers to emulate. Even for Pentecostal teachers such as Gee, spirituality is deepened by experience, rather than by education or reflection.

Imperative for Pentecostal readers is a "fresh visit to the throne of the Lord of Hosts"; it is both necessary and continual. Like Hoffmann, Gee reads this Old Testament text through christological glasses: the experience is only available through the "blood of Jesus Christ." What is presented for Isaiah as a unique experience becomes the prototype

22. See Appendix 1, Ref F.

for expected and ongoing encounters by Pentecostal believers in Jesus Christ. Gee expects similar Isaianic experiences as only a "first installment." Through Christ, he anticipates an Isaian experience to be normative and ongoing. The vision necessary for Pentecostal believers is identified by Gee as an experience of the Spirit: "a taste of the Spirit's power," which he assumes was one of many such similar experiences. Considering there is no mention of the Spirit in the Isaiah passage, this association of the vision of the prophet with the work of the Spirit by Gee is indicative of the Pentecostal worldview that tends to highlight any activity of God as the work of the Spirit. It pairs the present vision with past narratives of vision to demonstrate "this is that." This concept from their worldview is read *into* the Isaiah text by Gee, rather than being drawn from it. The experience of the Pentecostal reader has informed their reading and theologizing of the text.

The theme particularly highlighted from Isaiah 6 by this early prominent Pentecostal is the need for "greater depth." This deepening of the spiritual life is not an intellectual deepening, but a revelatory encounter—or in the later charismatic vocabulary adopted by Hoffmann, a "rhema word." This concern for personal revelation is particularly reflected in Pentecostal worship songs that encourage the personalization of biblical texts and identification with their message. As noted in the quest to define Pentecostalism (chapter 2), music plays a central role in the liturgy and theology of the community. As Brett Knowles[23] notes, even the furnishings of most Pentecostal churches reflect the importance of music. While the "sacred space" of many evangelical churches is dominated by the pulpit, in most Pentecostal churches the drum kit and copious amplifiers overshadow their furnishings.[24] As Knowles notes, a recent study by Mandy Miller on religious experience in New Zealand Pentecostalism notes that, "The music performed at a Pentecostal church is designed to emotionally charge and elicit certain feelings. Its stated function is to prepare congregants for worship and to be open before God, with the expectation of leading to religious experience."[25] The central role of music in the Pentecostal community would suggest the importance of considering the theology and reading methods modeled in the community's songs.

This is particularly emphasized in a popular song, "Lift Up Your Eyes," that has emerged from one of the major Australian Pentecostal youth ministries, Planet Shakers:[26]

"Lift Up Your Eyes"
Written by Henry Seeley & Nathan Rowe
©2002 Planet Shakers Min.

I see Heaven before me
Angels passing around me
Here I stand in awe of Your beauty
Captured by Your Holiness

---

23. Knowles, "From the Ends of the Earth We Hear Songs," 3.

24. Ibid., 3.

25. Ibid., 4.

26. See Appendix 1, Ref J.

Lift up your eyes, all of Heaven's in Worship
Angels rejoice and the clouds will be filled
With the wonder of Your Name
With the wonder of Your Name
The train of His robe fills the Temple with Glory
Heavenly hosts fall before Him in worship
Crying Holy Holy Holy is the Lord God Almighty

Holy Holy Holy is the Lord God Almighty

For the Pentecostal songwriters, the context is certainly a spiritual or mystical setting as the writers describe their vision of heaven. This song describes a vision of the transcendent God enthroned. In the transference from text to song, there are some interesting changes in tense from the vision of Isaiah. The historical setting of Isaiah's vision is removed; in Isaiah 6 the prophet *saw* the Lord in the year that King Uzziah died whereas in the song the songwriter now *sees* (present continuant) the Lord, emphasizing a direct and on-going experience of God. To continue the immediacy of the song, the train of the Lord's robe *fills* (present continuant) the Temple, whereas Isaiah testified to the train having *filled* the Temple. It becomes clear as the song progresses that this is the very Temple of Heaven that they envision. The song echoes the vision of Isaiah in chapter 6 through the vision of God in the Temple surrounded by the enraptured cry of worshippers: "Holy, holy, holy is the Lord Almighty; the whole earth is full of his glory" (6:3 NIV). These changes in tense from the Isaiah passage suggest the importance of an on—going experience of God to the Pentecostal worldview, as well as the use of literalism as a reading practice. It also presents a sense of the eternal now—the throne room is eternal and unchanging. The association of the "train of the robe" with God's glory suggests the spiritualization of the vision and its definite removal from any physical or temporal setting. This gives the song a mystical influence as it describes a spiritual experience through the image of the physical temple. The exact meaning of the "glory" is undefined; is it the presence of God? Creation? Or is it a community of believers who embody this glory? The christological reading here is implicit as the Pentecostal songwriter approaches the throne-room through the Christ. Musically, the repetition of "holy" builds to a climax in the affirmation of "Holy is the Lord God Almighty." However, by deleting any response by the singer through an Isaiah—like self realization, the singer does not engage with the object of the worship, they only observe. Neither are they responsible for those around them, as Isaiah was, but remain individuals separated from the community of believers and wider society. The transcendence of God is highlighted and maintained as God is untouched by the human witness, and the human untouched by the vision.

While recognizing the glory and holiness of God, the singer does not respond in the pattern of Isaiah. Unlike Hoffmann, this reading does not focus on the repentance or acknowledgment of "uncleanness" of the prophet; rather, it affirms the beauty of God. This ahistorical nature of the interpretation is most prevalent. The vision is removed from the temporal setting of Isaiah's encounter with the Lord to an abstract or ahistorical setting. The tense changes from Isaiah's "saw" to the current "see" as the vision is appropriated into the experience of the contemporary worshipper. This invites the worshipper to join the heavenly hosts in their adoration of the holiness of God; in both song and posture. While Isaiah 6 presents a missionary call and sending from the vision (the prophet is to leave the vision and "go" to his society), the singer invites the people to leave their society and join them in the vision. The participation of worship does not seem to require cleansing, only recognition of the holiness of God. While Isaiah's vision results in a missionary call, the song presents no altar, coal or commission. The only response required of the participant is demonstrative worship. This may be reflective of Pentecostal theology that emphasizes the priesthood of all believers; it is no longer special, anointed people who receive visions or prophetic encounters, but rather the spirit is available to all.

Rather than being repelled by self—loathing, as the Isaiah 6 text suggests, the writers are enticed by the vision as they focus on the beauty of God, rather than the glory or terror. This beauteous glory, emanating from the throne of God, remains captured in the heavenly realms as "Angels rejoice and the clouds will be filled with the wonder of Your Name," and does not seem to extend to the "whole earth" as it does in Isaiah 6. While the shift from the seraphim of Isaiah's vision to "angels" may reflect the mystery of the identity of seraphs, the prominence of heavenly beings in worship in Pentecostal songs emphasizes the importance of music and demonstrative worship in their community. These heavenly hosts "fall" before the Lord in worship, a feature not uncommon in Pentecostal liturgy and worship, within which demonstrative acts are encouraged to reflect the adoration of the worshipping community. The emphasis is on creating continuity between the temporal "now" of the Pentecostal worship and the eternal "now" of angelic worship.

As in the Planet Shakers' song, it is the holiness of the Lord described in this passage that was most prominent in the discussion of a Pentecostal youth cell,[27] comprising mainly female and male high school students. Of the entire chapter, this aspect dominated their dialogue and interest when asked what they thought the passage was about. One participant commented: "I suppose it comes back to the might and glory of God—how powerful he is. How powerful he is, definitely, and how he's the centre of the universe." Another young participant continued the thought: "Everything exists because of him; he's the creator of the universe. He's the supreme one." It was interesting to note that the group of young people identified the figure on the throne as the Creator, rather than directly identifying the figure as Christ. In contrast, a study group of older women from an independent Charismatic fellowship[28] immediately identified the figure of the "Lord of Hosts" (v. 5) with Christ. They justified this reading not only because of the concept that 'no eye has seen God' but also due to the sense of uncleanness that the prophet felt and the removal of his iniquity which is achieved for Christians only through Christ. They identified the purging of the prophet as the work of "God" in the Old Testament. One participant noted: "Because it was a continual sacrifice, it was never a once-for-all. So there would always be that sense of iniquity in their life." Another continued the point:

27. See Appendix 1, Ref I.
28. See Appendix 1, Ref H1.

"This is Old Testament and the law was different then to what we would experience." While identifying the figure with Christ, the ladies, like other Pentecostal readers, differentiated the process of forgiveness of the prophet from their New Testament experience of forgiveness found in Christ.

The discussion of these older women was also centered on the impact of this vision for the prophet in his memorable calling. One participant commented, "It was such an amazing way that God called him to stand in that role of the prophet. He would have needed that, what he would have went through and the call that was on his life. He needed to know beyond a shadow of a doubt that this is what I'm meant to be doing and that God is real." While they emphasized the majesty and glory of the vision, they also recognized the prophet's sense of terror, particularly in the literary style and rhetorical impact, "When we compare the Old Testament to the New Testament and what's written in them: Isaiah says 'woe is me for I am ruined' and John just says I fell at his feet as dead. We relate to what is written with John, when Jesus said: 'Don't be afraid.' Then that would have been exactly what Isaiah was going through. But it's just 'woe is me'—but he would have been terrified. We see the awe of it but not the terror that would have been in his heart—the fear." One of the ladies continued, "For me, the first half of the passage is just beautiful—the majesty of seeing the Lord, of that vision, that insight that he had."

While the youth group ignored the second half of the chapter to concentrate on the call, the older ladies attempted to incorporate the message of the prophet in the latter section of the chapter into their discussion. One lady noted, "Whenever the passage is read it's the first half—during the worship service or wherever. You don't want to hear of the doom—the impending [doom] that's to come." The response of some of the ladies during the discussion was that the second half had left them "stumped." One participant confessed: "I don't understand the bottom part!" While they wrestled with the passage, they looked to the final element of the message for their inspiration: "There's always the hope that there would always be a remnant." While they expressed confusion over the identity of the remnant—which they suggested could be either God's people generally or a remnant from Israel—their focus was on the glimmer of hope offered by the passage and the willingness of Isaiah to be sent to his own people. When asked what the second section is about, one of the ladies responded, "I think it's what's going to happen; the people's hearts are hard and their eyes are dull and their ears are dim and there's going to be devastation, but a remnant will remain. It's God's telling Isaiah: 'this is the big picture of what's going to happen over the next so many years.' He doesn't give the details, but there's to be a captivity. It's like the ball-park picture." This reading emphasizes the Pentecostal understanding of the nature of prophecy and the role of the prophet in foretelling future events. Yet, the prophetic word was not just for the original hearers but also considered relevant for the ladies in their own lives. They identified this section as a warning not to have a hardened heart against the Lord: "So that you don't become that people that have insensitive hearts and dull ears and dim eyes."

This attempt to assimilate the message of Isaiah with "the call" is similarly expressed in another song that has emerged from Pentecostal youth culture entitled "Send Me."[29] The focus from the Isaian passage is on the vision of Isaiah and invisible glory of God as the singer responds as a volunteer to an unspoken question:

"Send Me"

Written by Sam Evans and Henry Seeley
© 2001 Planet Shakers Min.

Send me I will go
Send me I will go
To this city, to this nation
And to the nations of the world

Send me I will go
Send me I will go
I will proclaim the truth
That Jesus Christ is Lord
I stand before You pleading from my heart
That by Your Spirit, You would set me apart
To bring good news and liberty
To see this nation on its knees

I cry out for every family
You'd open blind eyes, and set people free
That as a nation we would turn back to You
And see revival sweep this land

As we humble ourselves
And seek Your face
Fall on our knees
Turn from our ways
You will hear our cry
Wipe our sins away
Come and heal our land we pray

The song "Send Me" begins with Isaiah's voluntary response to the missionary call of the Divine council: "Here I am. Send me!" (6:8). The willingness of Isaiah to bring the prophetic word of Yahweh as an individual to the nation or corporate body is mirrored in this first line of the song. In fact, the song echoes the volunteering of Isaiah even without a vision of God to elicit this response. In contrast to the *Isaiah* passage, the singer appears to request the commission and eagerly volunteers a christological message. Like Isaiah's call, this song has a missiological focus directly related to the revelatory experience of the worshipper.

29. See Appendix 1, Ref M.

According to Oswalt, almost all sermons on Isa 6 conclude with verse 8;[30] as do the Pentecostal songs. When it is pointed out to them, the message of Isaiah that follows verse 8 is perceived by many readers to be problematic as the discussion of the older ladies' study group[31] highlighted. The fact that it has to be pointed out to them identifies the action of selective processes informing the reading process. These problematic verses anticipate that Isaiah's message will have the ironic effect of dulling vision and hearts (6:9–10). In contrast, the writers of "Send Me" anticipate the opening of blind eyes, preaching of good news and liberation of people, reflective of the later text of Isa 61 and its christological application in the New Testament. They do not ask "How long, O Lord?" but anticipate continual repentance until the "land" is healed (1 Chr 7:14) and revival has swept the "land." It is not clear if the "land" refers to the physical terrain or the secular community (city, nation, and nations of the world), or both. The numerous echoes of Old Testament scripture reflected in the song, particularly Isa 6, Isa 61, and 1 Chr 7:14, emphasize the thematizing reading method of the Pentecostal community as the verses and theology of different Bible verses and contexts are strung together. The writers have linked Old Testament passages addressing corporate repentance and consequent restoration.

While the experience of Old Testament prophets in fulfilling their calls were fraught with dangers, risks, and rejection (for example, the life and ministry of Jeremiah), the writers demonstrate an expectation of a favorable response to their message. For Pentecostal songwriters and singers, viewing the text through christological lenses, the latter half of Isa 6 is no longer problematic. They expect an overwhelming positive response to their message that results in revival, humility, and healing as God hears (rather than the Judean community, as in the case of Isaiah) and responds. That message is not one of judgment as in the experience of Isaiah, but the christological message of the gospel that "Jesus is Lord." Neither is there any reluctance or dilemma on the part of the respondent to the call or message. Instead, the Pentecostal singer anticipates and pleads for the commission: "pleading from my heart/That by Your Spirit, You would set me apart." The Pentecostal singer, like Gee, identifies this activity of God with the work of the Spirit who continues the ministry of Christ in the world.

These readings highlight that the testimony of Isa 6 is readily identified by Pentecostal readers as a spiritual encounter that is reflective of the values and normative experience of the Pentecostal community. The various readings of Isa 6 by Pentecostal pastors, lay people, and songwriters tends to remove the vision from its historical context, in order to emphasize the immediacy of the prophet's vision and availability of the experience for all believers.[32] While focusing on the call and experience of the prophet, they displayed little interest in the social or historical context behind the call. The passage was read at face-value with no interest in either textual issues of even comparing translations. This feature highlights the immediacy of the reading for the Pentecostal community—God

30. Oswalt, *Isaiah*, 187.

31. See Appendix 1, Ref H1.

32. This issue of the ahistorical and acontextual nature of Pentecostal readings will be discussed in the next chapter.

speaks through whatever English translation is used. However, as will be discussed below, this potentially leads to an absolutizing of a translation as "God's Word." Many of these features are also evident in readings of Isa 9:1–7.

READINGS OF ISAIAH 9:1–7

For many Pentecostal readers, the text of Isa 9:6 is associated with the coming of Christ, particularly with the Christmas message. The use of this passage to bring hope and consolation during the Christmas period is presented in an article by missionary Jenny Complin[33] in the 1993 *Australian Evangel.* While Complin identifies the Isaiah passage as being fulfilled in Christ, she identifies it as the fulfillment of a distinctly Jewish promise. She writes, "Is Christmas a Jewish festival? Yes, *in the sense* that we celebrate the birth of the Jewish Messiah, sent for the salvation of all mankind. Isaiah 9:6 says, 'For to us a child is born, to us a son is given, and the government will be on his shoulders. And he will be called Wonderful, Counselor, Mighty God, Everlasting Father, Prince of Peace.' The birth of Jesus is rooted in the promises and hopes of Israel that are at the core its very existence and history."[34] While Complin acknowledges the Jewish origins of the promise, she identifies it to be fulfilled solely in the person and ministry of Jesus Christ. What began as a national promise has become infused with international significance, as the Christ-child born at "Christmas" is the means of salvation for all nations. The coming of Christ has given new hope through the salvation and spiritual peace established on the cross.

In the Christmas edition of the 1970 *Australian Evangel,* W. G. Hathaway[35] presents this passage as a message of hope in the return of Jesus Christ to establish an earthly kingdom in the "last dispensation of this turbulent world's history."[36] He begins his discussion on Isa 9:6, 7 with the expectation that "Like the chimes of Christmas bells this message rings out its peals of joyful expectation that this divine Prince of the house of David will, according to His promise, come again and introduce to our troubled world His own blessed peace."[37] Hathaway anticipates the fulfillment of this passage in the second coming of Christ who will "hold the reins of all governments in His own nail-pierced hands"[38] in an eschatological vision. It is a reality also anticipated by Harvey[39] in the 1944 *Australian Evangel and Glad Tidings Messenger* as he acknowledges that this text of Isa 9:6 "has never yet been completely fulfilled."[40] Harvey laments concerning the urgency this realization should evoke among believers, who instead: "We are mostly lukewarm, if not indifferent, to the teaching, the exhortations, the warnings of Scripture relative to His personal return." Harvey warns his readers of the reality of this expectation that

---

33. See Appendix 1, Ref Q.

34. Ibid., 5.

35. See Appendix 1, Ref P.

36. Ibid.

37. Ibid.

38. Ibid.

39. See Appendix 1, Ref R.

40. Ibid., 16.

"This world is coming rapidly nearer to the time when the present order of things will be broken up and pass away." [41] Rather than being a message for the contemporary community of the eighth century Isaiah, Harvey considers it a message for his contemporary community in 1944 of a promise yet to be realized in return of Christ.

Similarly, L. A. Wiggins[42] begins with Isa 9:6 as part of her Christmas message on the coming government of Christ in the 1965 *Australian Evangel*. She begins, "The other day, I heard this well-known verse read, and, as usual, associated it with Christmas."[43] On hearing this text, Wiggins immediately understands it as referring directly to Christ in a manner that suggests a pattern of interpretation ("as usual"). As Wiggins continues, "We hear it so often at the festive season and take pleasure in the thought that 'a child is born . . . a son is given . . . his name shall be called Wonderful, Counselor, The mighty God, The Everlasting Father, The Prince of Peace.'"[44] She sees a direct association of Isa 9:6 (and the attributes of this ideal ruler) with Christ. However it is the following verse that particularly captivates the attention of Wiggins: "the government shall be upon his shoulder." In this statement, she expresses comfort:

> As a general rule, women are not particularly interested in politics, as such, but present-day events, both national and international, intrude their significance into the home as never before. Our newspapers carry headlines—"Vietnam"—"Pakistan"—"Indonesia" and there follow accounts of hostilities in these lands. "Where will it end?" is the query which tugs at the heart-strings of every wife and mother . . . What comfort it brings to us to realize that a time is coming when the world government will be such that all these things will be suppressed. When He is King, righteousness will reign and all other forces be brought into subjection.[45]

Wiggins identifies Isa 9 as containing a direct reference to the second coming of Christ. While she suggests that women (of her generation in the 1960s) were not interested in politics, the uncertain nature of the global political context of the 1960s invaded even the domestic situation of Australia. Wiggins looks to the passage to find comfort. But this comfort is not in the established reign of Christ, who has not inaugurated an earthly kingdom, but the coming reign of Christ in the eschaton. Her interest is in the eschatological government yet to be established by Christ. She sees this passage as a promise still to be fulfilled in which Christ will reign supreme, bringing peace to the earth. In this Wiggins finds solace from the uncertainty of the political climate of 1965 and the instability of society.

While the expectation of the coming rulership of Christ is also expressed in the poem "His Name" by Francis Burg[46] in the 1976 *Australian Evangel*, the poet emphasizes the fulfillment of the names from Isa 9:6 in the earthly ministry of Christ:

41. Ibid., 17.
42. See Appendix 1, Ref N.
43. Ibid., 6.
44. Ibid.
45. Ibid.
46. See Appendix 1, Ref T.

Wonderful

Because He took the sinner's place
And died to save a guilty race;
Because He stooped to bear the shame:
For ever WONDERFUL His name.

Counsellor

Because He bids me come and ask
For guidance in my daily task,
In Him alone all wisdom's found;
So be His name with honour crowned.

The Mighty God

Because, though veiled in lowly guise,
He came from far beyond the skies,
To all the world the tidings tell,
His name is blest Immanuel.

The Everlasting Father

Because He lived a life below
That man might thus His Father know;
The Spirit thence bears witness plain—
Now, "Abba, Father", born again.

The Prince of Peace

Because, as once by shepherds heard,
"Good will to men". This blessed word,
Proclaimed while angel chorus sang
Till all the hills of Judah rang,
Will be proclaimed the world around
Till He as King of Kings is crowned.
Then all the earth's wars and strife shall cease;
Then the world shall own Him PRINCE OF PEACE.

Burg understands each name to be a direct reference to the person and work of Jesus Christ. While scholars recognize that the names have significance in their immediate Isaian and Old Testament contexts,[47] these references are overlooked in Burg's christo-

47. For example, the first two names of Isa 9:6 have significance in their *Isaiah* and Old Testament context. The term *Wonderful counsellor* has significance in its immediate context of chapters 7–9. While under siege during the Syro-Ephraimite war, Isaiah advises Ahaz "stand firm" in trust of Yahweh's plans. According to the text, Isaiah confirms God's plan by the "sign" of a child being born to the royal court called Immanuel. Isaiah counsels Ahaz to trust God's plan that the siege would fail and that Assyria would punish Israel and Syria, which of course, Ahaz does not accept. The name "Wonderful counsellor" reflects this specific time that God is indeed wonderful in counsel, even though humans fail and lack faith. This child-king prophesied in Isa 9 is pictured as faithfully governing Judah unlike Ahaz who lacks faith in God. This is recognised by scholars such as Brueggemann as fulfilled in the son of Ahaz, Hezekiah, who later accepts

centric reading. Burg emphasizes the humility and suffering of Christ with the use of words such as "stooped," "bear," "shame," "veiled in lowly guise," and "below." Yet Burg also acknowledges that through this suffering, Christ has secured present and future glory. "Because" Christ suffered the humiliation of the cross, he has secured a wonderful name, crowned with honor. Burg emphasizes the present and future ministry of Christ who not only reconciles believers to the Father but who guides believers in the "daily task." This work will continue until the future age of peace is established.

The immediate application of the names from Isa 9:6 to the person of Jesus Christ, rather than the eschatological vision of the previous readings, is reflected in the writing of Gerald Stewart.[48] Stewart introduces his discussion on the "wonder" of Christ in the 1970 *Australian Evangel* with reference to Isa 9:6. By focusing on the translated term "wonderful" from the Isaiah text, Stewart plays with contemporary verbal associations and uses of the word throughout his reading. While his contemporaries (c. 1970) used the term "wonder" to refer to admirable but soon out—dated scientific developments, Stewart contrasts this colloquial reference with the eternal "wonder" of Jesus Christ. He writes,

> The theme of wonder in the human mind usually subdues after a period of time [*sic*]. The thing that once amazed is accepted as part of our adventurous and scientific age.
>
> The Christmas season presents us with a sense of "*wonder*" that has never lost its grip upon the human race. There is a resurgence and renewal of "*wonder*" that covers the entire earth when the month of December rolls around in its annual orbit. Happiness, gaiety and Liberality stalk abroad, and it seems as if the world has thrown off a straight-jacket of restraint to don the glad-rags of joy and jubilation. Cards, telegrams, presents and verbal greetings of goodwill are part of the lavish joy of Christmastime . . . All this, because God Himself did a wonderful thing. The giving of His only Son as Saviour to the world. Everything appertaining to Jesus Christ is *wrapped in wonder*" (author's emphasis).[49]

---

the wise counsel of Yahweh (Brueggemann, *Isaiah 1–39*, 82. It is similarly fulfilled in Christ as well, as God has a master plan for salvation that is truly a wonderful plan, as acknowledge by Christ.

The second name is *Mighty God*. This is a name or presents an image of God going out to battle like a champion fighter on behalf of his people—God as a warrior. It is important in the history of the people of Israel that God is their captain of war and fights their battles with them and for them, as the books of *Exodus* and *Joshua* particularly emphasise. This name is significant to Isa 7–9 as the city of Jerusalem has been besieged and the people exist in the context of war. To highlight Yahweh as "Mighty God" is important because it is God who not only plans and orchestrates history, but who fights with and for Judah at this time. Ahaz however did not believe this, and called on Assyria to fight for him. The passage suggests, therefore, that God has rejected Ahaz and is looking to another ruler who will accept the wonderful counsel of God, and will acknowledge God as their strength in battle, not Assyria or another champion. Again, many scholars suggest that this promise is fulfilled in Hezekiah who allows through his faithfulness in Yahweh, the demonstration of this name in Isa 36–37. This name is also recognised by the New Testament writers as fulfilled in Christ who not only acknowledges God as the wonderful counsellor and divine warrior, but reveals his divinity by being the divine warrior himself.

48. See Appendix 1, Ref O.

49. Ibid., 21.

Stewart continues to describe the "wonder" of Christ, beginning with his birth and incarnation and extending to his victorious death on the cross. For Stewart, the passage of Isa 9:6 refers exclusively and obviously to Christ without explanation of how it functions in the context or historical occasion of the Old Testament. The Isaiah passage is taken to be a direct reference to Christ and the wonder of salvation experienced by his contemporary Pentecostal community, rather than the eschatological hope of Wiggins or Hathaway.

What is interesting in Stewart's reading, is the verbal associations he makes between the biblical text of Isa 9:6 (specifically the reference to the title of Christ as "wonderful") and the contemporary use of the translated word in his social context. The various nuances of the English term "wonder" are presented through adjective, noun, verb, and adverb, to highlight the significance of the singular term from the biblical text. This makes the single use of the term "wonder" appear more prevalent than perhaps what the text expresses. And yet, through the playful use of the English word, Stewart expresses the delightful anticipation of a spiritual encounter with this "wonderful" person of Jesus Christ. His description builds in intensity, inviting the reader to similarly experience the wonder of Christ, as he writes, "OH! THE WONDER OF IT ALL (sic). His incarnation, His spotless character, His Spirit-filled ministry, His dynamic verbal authority and the crowning victory of the cross—all combine to exalt Christ to the highest station. He far surpasses all who have ever lived. He produces a heavenly wonder in the soul that compels us to fall prostrate at His feet and crown Him Lord of all."[50] Stewart encourages the reader to respond to the immediacy of the wonder, ministry and authority of Christ in a physical manifestation (prostration as often described as "slain in the spirit") common to the Pentecostal community.

This association of the child of promise in Isa 9:1-7 with the earthly work and ministry of Christ was also reflected in the discussions of a Pentecostal cell church meeting,[51] observed for the purposes of this study. The names of Isa 9:6 were applied by the group intrinsically to Christ, blurring the distinction between present fulfillment and eschatological expectation. One participant commented: "I only read this as predicting Jesus' birth." Another participant expanded, "The kingdom of God rests on his shoulders; he's the new covenant." The government of this promised ruler was considered to be the ruling of Christ in the expanding kingdom of God, identified in the new covenant as being located in the hearts of women and men. Yet, they also associated the bringing of light to the darkness (Isa 9:2) with their own mandate for the need to evangelize their contemporary society.

What is common in these readings is that the Pentecostal community tended to understand the passage to be a direct reference to the person and ministry of Christ. While historically earlier readings emphasized the imminent return of Christ to complete the fulfillment of the passage regarding government and future peace, more recent readings tended to highlight the fulfillment of the passage in Christ's first, earthly mission. Yet, while there is a shift from eschatological expectation to the focus on the

50. Ibid., 21.
51. See Appendix 1, Ref S.

present achievements of Christ, there is still a christocentric focus in both approaches. Whether Pentecostal readers considered the "promise" of Isa 9:6–7 fulfilled in the first or second missions of Christ, the focus is still on Jesus Christ as the fulfillment of messianic expectations of the Old Testament. It is quite remarkable, therefore that the Pentecostal community—which highly prizes the prophetic ministry and immediacy of God's word (forth-telling)—have tended to see the prophetic activity of the Old Testament as only christologically driven (foretelling).[52] The Pentecostal readings ignore the potentiality of the prophetic voice in Isaiah providing a message relevant to their contemporary community, perceiving instead the prophet as a predictor of the coming(s) of Jesus Christ. This tendency is even more pronounced in readings of Isa 52:13—53:12 (for convenience herein after referred to as Isa 53).

READINGS OF ISAIAH 53

Like the readings of Isa 6, there was little dispute among Pentecostal readers regarding the identity of the servant of Isa 53; almost all identified the servant exclusively as Jesus Christ. The Pentecostal readers perceived Isa 53 as a prophetic announcement concerning the person, character, and actions of Jesus Christ, fulfilled in the New Testament. However, for many readers, while they considered the identity of the servant to be secure, they differed in their appropriation of the text. Many, particularly preachers and pastors, discussed the text only in relation to the theological impact of the passage in the formation of their Christology and doctrine of healing in the atonement. Those readers that developed the passage for theological purposes tended to consider the presentation of the servant-Jesus as unique, so rendering his actions as *not* normative for the Christian life. However some readers, particularly in the group discussions observed for this study, perceived several different issues in the text as it related to both the presentation of the servant-Jesus and their spiritual life.

Most Pentecostal readers of Isa 53 tended to associate the servant of Isa 53 with Jesus Christ. This view is exemplified by the testimony of Moshe Elijah,[53] a former follower of Judaism, who describes his experience of salvation through a reading of Isa 53 in the 1993 *Australian Evangel:*

> Most Gentile Christians do not know about the Old Testament messianic prophecies. However, some years back, before I believed in Messiah Yeshua, two Christian colleagues discussed religion with me. I decided to challenge them with a seeming impossible task.
>
> I asked them to prove to me logically and objectively, without any emotionalism or faith in the New Testament, but using only the Jewish Old Testament, that Jesus (Yeshua) is the Jewish Messiah of Israel as foretold by the Jewish prophets. I chuckled to myself with an attitude of arrogance and skepticism, as I thought I had given them an impossible mission.

52. This distinction in the role of prophecy is highlighted in Fee and Stuart, *How to Read the Bible for All Its Worth*, 150.

53. See Appendix1, Ref HA.

> To my amazement, they opened the Old Testament to Isaiah 53 and asked me to read it. I read it three times. The first time I noticed a mist before my eyes hindering me from seeing the words properly. The second time, as I began to understand the meaning of the scripture, holes started to appear in this hindering mist. The third time, when I fully understood the scripture, the mist disappeared.
>
> I was shocked by what I read. This scripture stated the gospel story! Here, before my eyes, was a passage by one of the great servants of God, the prophet Isaiah, pointing to the death of Yeshua, the "arm of the Lord," as a human sacrifice for the atonement of the sins of others—the sacrificial Passover lamb of God . . .
>
> The enlightenment I received from these Old Testament prophecies created in me a burning desire to search for the truth, the whole truth and nothing but the truth about Messiah Yeshua . . . I then read the New Testament with great interest. I soon became aware that this was not a dead book of symbols, but alive and powerful, with a ring of truth and sincerity. The words appeared to come alive and penetrate into me with a supernatural power.[54]

There are several important aspects to the reading of Isa 53 by Moshe Elijah to be highlighted. As consistent with most other Pentecostal interpretations of this text, he identifies the servant to be a prophetic pronouncement of the person and work of Jesus Christ. In his testimony of conversion from Judaism, he sees in the Hebrew Scriptures the "messianic prophecies" foretelling the sacrificial death of Christ as a means of atonement. Elijah displays no previous acquaintance with the passage (although he seems familiar with the prophet Isaiah generally) neither does he offer any previous assessment of the identity of the servant from Judaism, yet still recognizes the correlation of Jesus' death within the symbolism of Judaism (via the New Testament) as the sacrificial lamb.

Another important feature of Elijah's reading concerns the transformative power of Scripture highlighted in his testimony. As he read and re-read the passage, he describes an experience of transformation through the words of the text. Each successive reading led to an increased revelation and clarity of understanding that Elijah describes using the imagery of mist. The transformative power of the text overcame the "hindering mist" which disappeared with the full revelation and comprehension of the meaning of the passage. Elijah goes on to describe his experience of reading Scripture as being "alive and powerful." Just as Hoffman (reading Isa 6) identified the ability of the text to "jump out" at the reader to enliven the text with revelatory impact and personal immediacy, so also Elijah emphasizes the capacity of the text (which he describes as "supernatural power") to transform. From this significant moment of revelation, he reads Scripture, particularly the New Testament, with the expectation of continued revelatory impact. The text was not "dead" or a container of lifeless symbols, but alive with truth and "sincerity." The purpose of the reading was to comprehend the person and work (the "truth") of Christ and to be transformed by the encounter.

Participants in a Pentecostal youth cell[55] of mainly students, also immediately associated the figure in Isa 53 with the person and work of Jesus Christ. When asked to respond to the passage, the first participant to speak up noted: "I don't know the exact

54. See Appendix 1, Ref HA, 30–31.

55. See Appendix 1, Ref I.

words but the pain that he went through. Saying what he went through and how because of that everyone can be free. His blood that he shed is our salvation, for our sins." When asked to identify the servant, the group simultaneously and exclusively nominated Jesus Christ as the figure described. They understood the passage to be prophetic of the atoning sacrifice of Jesus on the cross. One of the youth noted "Verse 4 is special to me as it reminds us of how we have all turned our back on God and all turned our own way. And its only because of what Jesus did on the cross, its only that price he paid, laying down his life, paying our penalty for sin which is death, so that we can now have a relationship with God." The young people perceived the passage to speak of salvation in Christ and the restoration of relationship to God without reference to physical healing (a feature of most other Pentecostal readings). For the youth, the text of Isa 53 presents the gospel of Jesus Christ.

The group identified the work and person of Christ portrayed not only in the actions of the servant, but also through the various images presented in the text. In particular, the group resonated with the image of the sheep. One of the youth commented: "The lamb part is [that] he went gracefully, he didn't put up a fight. A lamb just goes, it knows it's going to be killed but just goes anyway. That's what I think Jesus did, he didn't put up a fight, he just went for us." Another continued the discussion: "Lambs are really cute, and why would you want to kill a lamb?—so it seems a bit stupid to kill a lamb, but then you do it and you can imagine how innocent the lamb would look up at you and you're sort of punishing it and the lamb won't do anything about it." While identifying Jesus' passion with the lamb, the young people saw the lamb as symbolic of his submissive attitude rather than a reference to the sacrificial system presented in the Old Testament. The lamb was perceived by the youth as innocent, submissive, silent, graceful, obedient, and vicariously suffering; the same attitude they identified in Christ. This attitude of servant-Jesus perceived by the youth in Isa 53 is not just a theological truth, but an attitude which they, as Christians, should emulate: "In Philippians (I think it's in Philippians) it says to have a Christ-like attitude and in Ephesians it says to be an imitator of God—they're really verses that I've been living off this year. Just to die daily on the cross is a lot like [our pastors] Marilyn and Nathan say in their sermons. And seeing "The Passion of the Christ" I just realize—yeah—that I have to, I have to die daily, I have to live every second of the day for Jesus because that's what my life is about basically." The attitude and suffering of the servant-Jesus, according to the youth cell, is normative. The youth considered the vicarious suffering of the servant-Jesus not to be unique, but the exemplar for the Christian life. The passage is applicable to the youth as they also identify with the servant-Jesus; they must each symbolically die to themselves (their own will and desires) on their own cross.

The possibility of the appropriation of the text is also evident in other group discussions. Like the youth study group, most participants identified the servant exclusively with Christ. However, once identifying the person, attitudes, and actions of Christ, they also applied the message to their own lives and situation. Interestingly, for a cell group of

Pentecostal young professionals[56] reflecting on the passage, it was not the submissive attitude of Christ that they noted but rather the nature of his appearance. Both women and men highlighted the offensive appearance of the servant. One participant commented on 53:2:

> He had no beauty or majesty to attract us to him, nothing that we should desire him. You know, despised, rejected . . . the whole; God's way is not the way of this world. It's just so different. It's hard to explain. God is just so much . . . I think God is more long-term, whereas this world is more short-term. You know—short-term preservation, but God is more lasting. Things just aren't what they seem to be in this world . . . He was Jewish, so he would have had a big nose . . . He was probably bald . . . Yeah, whatever, but he probably wasn't Brad Pitt, he was more Danny Devito. This whole thing about exterior, it's just not what it's about.

The group emphasized the counter-cultural nature of the servant's exterior (who they equated with Christ). Yet, it was an understanding of culture based on their own experience. They equated being judged by their appearance and professionalism as being the opposite of what the servant-Christ represented. Their experience in the professional workforce meant that they felt an expectation to act, look, and appear a certain way. In the persona of the servant-Christ (as representative of the ways of God) they saw the opposite values to those that the "world" lived by. This reading emphasizes the uniqueness of Christ, who is considered counter-cultural to the experience of the Pentecostal reader.

This expression of the uniqueness of Christ (as a counter-cultural force) is similarly expressed in a sermon entitled "A Joyful Jesus" by Evangelist William Booth-Clibborn[57] in his 1931 campaigns. Unlike the young professionals, he encounters a different culture. The Pentecostal culture of Booth-Clibborn was the austere Pentecostal-holiness culture of the 1930s, living on the fringes of society. For this outcast group, the dejected and rejected Jesus was a comforting image that Clifford-Booth challenges. He says:

> The picture given us of the saviour in Isaiah fifty-third is not so much of the Ministering Master as of the Sacrificed Christ—of the Lamb of God at the time of His being offered up. It was then there was . . . no form nor comeliness . . . no beauty that we should desire Him and so forth. But Christ in his life and looks was altogether lovely. His figure was tall and His features fair, His face was full of warmth and kindness, his body beautiful and strong, His person radiating virtue and the Glory of God . . . No! The Son of God was not dejected and depressed.

Booth-Clibborn presents a reading of Jesus that is counter-cultural to the 1930s Pentecostals; a joyful and beautiful Jesus. In contrast, the beautiful Jesus is culturally consistent with the circumstances of the young successful business people;[58] they instead read the counter-cultural elements of servant-Jesus to speak prophetically to their situation. So while both readings maintain divergent descriptions of the servant-Jesus, they both

56. Appendix 1, Ref S.

57. See Appendix 1, Ref IA.

58. See Appendix 1, Ref S.

reflect an inherent attempt by Pentecostals to relate Scripture to their contemporary context as a prophetic text. No matter what the circumstance, Pentecostal readers maintain that Scripture can speak prophetically to their particular situation.

Pastor Chris Mulhearn[59] in his sermon entitled, "The Gospel of Healing" (2003) similarly discusses the appearance of Jesus in his reading of Isa 53. However, unlike the cell group of young professionals or Clifford-Booth, he doesn't use the appearance of Jesus to emphasize difference. Instead, he associates both Jesus and the congregation with plainness in order to draw parallels between the two groups. Mulhearn emphasizes the immanence of Jesus in the healing process as he notes, "He's not that feature picture in the Christian bookshop wall—the blond haired, blue-eyed beautiful Jesus. The Bible actually says the opposite of him—you'd walk past him in the street you wouldn't recognize him! He was as plain as anyone of us. And that's one of the most powerful things about him. Because he was just like us, he knows just what it's like to be just like us." Mulhearn emphasizes the compassion of Christ who desires relationship and communion with his creation. He goes on to say, "Some people see God as distant, unmoving, uncaring, detached. Yet the Bible teaches God is looking for an opportunity to be involved with your life—with you!" Like the young professionals and Booth-Clibborn, Mulhearn's reading of Isa 53:2 is highly appropriated to the cultural context and situation of his audience, and identifies the figure to exclusively be Jesus Christ. Of these three contrasting readings of Isa 53:2, they share a common focus on personal experience and christological emphasis.

However the chief interest of Pentecostal readers in Isa 53 is not the identity of the servant or the ambiguity of speakers (which are chiefly critical issues)—these are all assumed to be pointers to Jesus Christ. Rather, their chief interest in Isa 53 is in the achievements of the servant. The focus of Pentecostal readings of Isa 53 is to determine the achievements of the servant (Christ) as prefigured by the prophet. For Pentecostal readers, one of the most important achievements of the servant of Isa 53, apart from salvation, is the achievement of healing. The important role of Isa 53 in the formation of the Pentecostal doctrine of healing lends itself to an extended analysis. In early Pentecostal missions, healing was even more central than the charismatic gift of "tongues." The christological reading of Isa 53 is also the basis for the current theology of the Australian AG that asserts the availability of healing through the atonement explicitly within its articles of faith: "We believe the redemptive work of Christ on the cross provides healing of the human body in answer to believing prayer (Isa 53:4–5; Matt 8:17)." The current statement also reflects the importance of faith by the believer and the traditional Pentecostal preference for Matthew's reading of Isa 53, both of which will be discussed below.

When asked to give an initial response to a reading of Isa 53, a participant from the Bible study group of older ladies from an independent charismatic church[60] commented: "He bore our griefs, he carried our sorrows—we don't need to have them anymore. And, you know, he was wounded for us and bruised for our iniquities to have our sins forgiven.

---

59. See Appendix 1, Ref I.A.

60. See Appendix 1, Ref H1.

You look at it and see—and we're healed by his stripes. We just have to have the faith to believe the word of God instead of the symptoms sometimes of our bodies. That always stands out to me." Physical healing is perceived to be available for all believers through the work of Jesus Christ on the cross; it is seen as a past victory that must be appropriated by the believer. Through the physical bruises and wounds of Christ on the cross, the believer can now receive freedom from physical bondage. The ladies highlight a common feature of Pentecostal theology of healing in the atonement, that is, its nature as a past event. Physical healing of believers is already achieved, therefore to receive physical healing the believer must simply appropriate the promise from Isa 53 by believing in faith. This is in tension with Jas 5, where the focus is ecclesial rather than individual.

The passage from *Isaiah* is also seen as a promise to be appropriated by the Pentecostal reader in the numerous articles and sermons by leaders in the various Pentecostal groups. As the General Superintendent of the Australian AG, Andrew Evans[61] writes in the 1992 *Australian Evangel* concerning faith, "God has already given us some 7,000 scripture promises to meet every need in our lives, therefore every need can be overcome by exercising faith in these promises. For example, if we are sick, we meditate on the healing promises of Ex 15:26; Ps 103:3; Isa 53:5; Mk 16:18 and the like. As revelation comes we can have faith and thus overcome sickness by the power of faith. So too when we need financial blessings, guidance or whatever."[62] To appropriate the promise, Evans suggests the believer needs to exercise faith. He suggests meditating on appropriate Scripture passages relating to the issue until revelation (and presumably, the awaited healing) comes. This reading highlights the important revelatory function of Scripture for Pentecostal readers to actualize a theological truth. A doctrine is not realized (or actualized) until the believer has a revelation of its truth. Faith and revelation are tightly intertwined in the Pentecostal understanding of appropriating promises from the bible.

The writing of Harriet Bainbridge[63] in a 1935 *Australian Evangel* similarly emphasizes the role of faith in the development of the doctrine of healing in the atonement. Bainbridge's article incorporates both scriptural citation and personal testimony in appealing to the validity of healing ministry in the contemporary post-Apostolic context. She writes, "We need to learn to believe in Christ in the way appointed for us in Scripture." For Bainbridge, that way is through believing in Jesus Christ as Physician. She writes, "When we have learned to know, and to believe, this statement of Holy Writ, we are enabled, by the teaching and enlightenment of the Spirit of God, to pray in faith for physical healing."[64] Healing was considered one of four focal points of the gospel, particularly highlighted in the "four-square" creed of Jesus as Savior, Healer, Baptizer, and Coming King. According to Bainbridge, the experience of healing only comes as a result of the reading of Scripture. However, she anticipates the act of reading will be Spirit-inspired and revelatory in nature. Therefore, for Bainbridge at least, Scripture informs the experience rather than the experience informing the reading of Scripture. However

61. See Appendix 1, Ref MA.

62. Ibid., 50.

63. See Appendix 1, Ref NA.

64. Ibid., 1.

the impetus of personal experience as the motivation for reading Scripture and the particular selection of texts must be questioned. The testimony incorporated into Harriet Bainbridge's teaching also emphasizes the experiential nature of a Pentecostal theology of healing in the atonement:

> The Holy Spirit whispered to a believing woman of my acquaintance, who was earnestly looking to the Lord for deliverance for her daughter, who was ill with diphtheria: "Where do you see this diphtheria? Do you see it in Annie's throat, or do you see it in the body of Christ crucified?"
>
> Rays of light emanated from these words, and entered into the mother's heart and mind. She realized anew the declaration of God through the Prophet Isaiah that sin and disease were crucified in the body of Christ on the cross, and she was enabled to praise Him that Diphtheria had no power to hurt her daughter, because they truly believed His Word and Work of Redemption.
>
> In a moment this mother's heart was completely set at rest. She knew all would be well with Annie, for she had exercised faith to the acceptance of her child's healing by the power of God. It came to pass as she believed. Annie came downstairs a few days later, the disease having departed from her.[65]

The words of Isa 53 were "realized anew" as the revelatory effect of Scripture is highlighted in the testimony. The declaration of Isaiah was perceived in the testimony to concern the vicarious suffering of Christ to gain salvation and healing for all believers. However, this doctrine was not actualized until the revelation was received in the mother's "heart and mind."

As noted above, Pastor Chris Mulhearn[66] presented a message that, like Bainbridge, intersperses teaching and testimonies of healing. He said: "The gospel and healing are intertwined in the Scriptures. You cannot separate the two—because it's a gospel, remember, of completeness." Mulhearn presents three levels of healing that were achieved through the atoning death of Christ on the cross. The first level is the spiritual healing identified as salvation. For most Pentecostal readers, this level is the most important. As Mulhearn comments: "We've come here for a healing meeting tonight, and definitely we're gonna be praying for the sick. But what point is that for someone to receive a physical healing in their body so that they can then perish in eternity? What is the point to that?" The second level discussed by Mulhearn was the mental-emotional area, in which Christ's work on the cross brings healing to the emotional element of our being including freedom from fear and shame. The third area of healing achieved by Christ's death on the cross, presented by Mulhearn, is the physical level. He preaches:

> If you've got faith to be saved, you've got faith to be healed. It's that same faith . . . The last phrase of this verse says this: "By his wounds we are healed." Friends, if you have come tonight and you have come in seeking healing, I want you to look at the cross, and I want you to look at your savior. I want you to look at that one that was bruised, I want you to look at that one that was crushed, I want you to look at that one who was pierced, I want you to look at that one whose back they whipped,

---

65. See Appendix 1, Ref NA, 1.

66. Appendix 1, Ref LA.

> because 1 Peter 2:24 literally says that by the stripes that they laid on his back it brought your healing; as the blood of the son of God ran to the ground it purchased your healing every bit as much as it purchased your salvation.

Faith and revelation are intertwined as the believer directs their faith for both salvation and physical healing to the atoning work of Christ. While reading and "believing" healing in the atonement from Isa 53, do these Pentecostal readers suggest that everyone is healed automatically at their salvation or that every prayer for healing is actualized? The Pentecostal readers do not suggest that God heals every sick believer. Neither do they suggest that God is incapable of hearing and healing every prayer request. Instead, the reason why prayers for healing may remain unresolved is because of lack of faith. Hoover[67] in the 1930 *Australian Evangel* writes, "Healing is an evidence of faith, and where there is no faith there is no healing." Though the prayer may be instantaneous or delayed in its actualization, the program of God for healing is unchanged.

As noted previously, there is a tendency for Pentecostal readers of Isa 53 to understand the passage exclusively through the New Testament. The Pentecostal readings emphasize the vicarious suffering of Christ to gain salvation and healing for all believers. Reading through their christological lenses, Pentecostal readers unanimously identify the servant as a prophetic description of Christ, and Christ alone. The possibility of a contemporary figure to the writer of Isa 53 suffering vicariously for the exiled nation is generally not considered. This implies that for Pentecostal readers, prophetic texts do not necessarily speak to the contemporary community of the prophet, but are given for the benefit of the eschatological community to understand the nature of Christ's mission as well as their own. This perspective is exemplified in a sermon by Harold Harvey[68] entitled "The Unfair exchange" which notes, "The prophetic word from Isa 53, some 600 years before Jesus was born, stated that God's righteous servant would take the place of sinner [sic] and would suffer in their stead." The pronouncement of Isaiah was not considered to be a forth-telling message to his community, but a fore-telling message proclaiming Christ. This reading of Old Testament prophecy will obviously have implications in their understanding of the function of prophecy within the contemporary Christian community. Yet, even the use of New Testament texts to read the Isaiah passage was specific to passages consistent with the Pentecostal experience, namely the discussion of the healing ministry of Jesus in Matthew.

Most Pentecostal readers emphasizing healing in the atonement, tended to emphasize the references of Isa 53 in Christ's ministry of physical healing in Matt 8:16–17 rather than the spiritual achievements of the atonement reflected in 1 Pet 2:24–25. Through this reading of Matthew, they see the mission of Christ in the world to be the removal of physical sickness as well as sin. One Pentecostal pastor[69] who formerly did not hold to the doctrine of healing in the atonement wrote of his change in theology, "In regards to Matthew 8:17 the simple reason I changed my view is that if the Isaiah passage was not

---

67. See Appendix 1, Ref OA.

68. See Appendix 1, Ref KA.

69. See Appendix 1, Ref PA.

related to physical healing then it wouldn't be referred to here in Matthew. The scripture says that when Jesus healed all the sick, 'this fulfilled the word of the Lord through Isaiah who said, "He took our sicknesses and removed our diseases."' If it fulfilled the Isaiah 53 scripture, it means that the OT prophet was referring to actual physical sickness not just 'spiritual infirmity' (sin)."[70] The ministry of Christ is identified by the pastor as more than just the mission of salvation, but for healing as well. However, the question must be raised whether the healing ministry of Jesus Christ was unique or paradigmatic for all believers to emulate. Pentecostal readers generally agree on the latter.

The basis of this paradigmatic view, according to early American Pentecostal Thomas Attebery,[71] is the commission of Christ for his disciples to continue his ministry. For Attebery, who wrote in the 1930 *Australian Evangel*, this follows that because Christ's mission was to heal the sick and Christ only did the will of the Father (John 6:38), it is therefore God's will for people to be healed as well as forgiven for their sins. Because God is unchanging, it must remain God's will for people to be healed today.[72] This theology is also confirmed by the experience of the writer as Attebery concludes, "From my experience I can testify that God is just as willing to heal all that are sick to-day as he was nineteen hundred years ago."[73] It is interesting that while both Matthew and Peter can appeal to Isa 53:4 for support in reference to either physical or spiritual healing without compromising Isaiah's words, it is the Matthew interpretation that is preferred by Pentecostal readers. Isaiah 53 tends to function as a proof-text for the ministry of physical healing by Jesus as described in Matt 8. Christ's ministry of healing emphasized in Matthew is perceived as paradigmatic for Pentecostal readers, whereas Christ's ministry of salvation (emphasized in Peter) is perceived as unique (Christ died once for all). It is also important to note the influence of the New Testament writers as models for exegesis among Pentecostal readers. This influence is not just demonstrated by the adoption of christological lenses by which to read the Old Testament, but by the method of appropriating the Old Testament into the experience of the reader (discussed in chapter 5). The use of Isa 53:4 as a proof-text in Matt 8 provides a model of exegesis that Pentecostal readers have adopted. Using these same methods of the New Testament writers, biblical texts are applied to the ministry and experiences of Pentecostal readers to validate their own experience, such as their contemporary experience of healing. As noted above, the continuation of the ministry of Christ in healing, according to Attebery, is to be actuated by believers according to Mark 16:15–18. As Attebery writes "The promises given in this passage were not for the Apostles alone, but for 'they that believe,' and that includes Christ's faithful followers in the nineteenth century as well as those in the first century."[74] The biblical text is used to validate the ministry and experience of the reader and offer a paradigm for the contemporary church.

---

70. Personal correspondence.

71. See Appendix 1, Ref QA.

72. Ibid., 2–3.

73. Ibid., 3.

74. See Appendix 1, Ref QA, 2.

The Matthean interpretation of Isa 53 was used by early Pentecostals such as Hoover[75] not only to define their experience, but also to defend their theology of healing. Hoover also writes of Isa 53:5 in the 1930 *Australian Evangel*, "But some who have not come into the light of this Scripture will say it refers to the sin-sick soul and not to the healing of the body. But is this true? Let us see. If you will turn to the book of Matthew, the eight chapter and the 16th and 17th verses, you will find an inspired and therefore a correct interpretation of Isaiah's prophecy . . . To the reasonable mind this is final proof that provision was made in the divine atonement for every infirmity and sickness of man."[76] The use of Isa 53 in Matt 8 to describe the healing ministry of Jesus is perceived and assumed by Pentecostal readers to be paradigmatic for all believers and not simply unique to the ministry of Jesus.

Of the various groups studied, only one Pentecostal pastor (Ref RA) from Western NSW (formerly a Baptist minister)[77] viewed the Isa 53 passage as an inappropriate basis for a doctrine of healing (while still upholding the doctrine from other Scriptures). He writes:

> The context of the Isaiah passage, relates to the Nation of Israel. The Nation was in anguish, in pain and had turned from God—in short, Israel was sick, spiritually sick. There is no doubt that chapter 53 is Messianic/prophetic, however it is difficult to mount a strong theological argument that makes verse 5 relate exclusively to the physical healing of the individual. Isaiah here is seeing the healing of the Nation. I submit that Peter's quote from this passage (1 Pet 2:24), likewise has a broader base than the physical healing of the individual; again the implication is National, contextually he is not speaking of the individual's physical health. Let me repeat, there is much provision in Scripture for the healing of the individual from physical, emotional and demonic oppression and/or sickness, I simply submit that this Isaiah passage is not one of them. I submit that it is read in the context of personal physical healing because it is convenient and, in a non-contextual quick read of the verse, it appears to bolster a strongly held doctrine.

His claim is insightful. While he later suggests that this is reflective of the limited education and theological training of most Pentecostal pastors and leaders, it also represents a deeper hermeneutical issue. The complete disinterest and ignorance of the historical context of the passage by Pentecostal readers points to an approach that reads texts for pragmatic purposes—a purpose which is aimed at the transformation of the contemporary reader. And yet, Pentecostal readers would claim to have adopted this approach from the biblical writers, such as Matthew (chapter 8) who also utilizes the text with seemingly little consideration for the historical context. The appropriateness of this use of Scripture will be discussed in the next chapter.

Overall, it has been observed that the Pentecostal readers perceived Isa 53 as a prophetic announcement concerning the person, character and actions of Jesus Christ, fulfilled in the New Testament. In this sense, the passage was read christologically as

75. See Appendix 1, Ref OA.

76. Ibid., 1.

77. Personal correspondence.

the Pentecostal readers adopted the New Testament (particularly Matt 8) interpretation of the text. The prolific writing and preaching on this passage in particular, highlights the keen interest of the Pentecostal community in the issues it raises. In this sense, the text was not understood as addressing the Isaian community, but as fore-telling the person and ministry of Christ for the benefit of the future people of God, including the Pentecostal community. Yet, in the various readings surveyed, Pentecostal readers generally demonstrated a concern to apply the text of Isa 53 to their contemporary context. They maintained that Scripture can speak prophetically to their particular situation, no matter what the circumstance, even if that produced contradictory interpretations of the passage, (with regard, for instance to the physical appearance of the servant-Jesus). Most Pentecostal readers who emphasize healing in the atonement, tended to emphasize the references to Isa 53 in Christ's ministry of physical healing in Matt 8:16–17 (rather than the spiritually salvific achievements of the atonement reflected in 1 Pet 2:24–25). The text of Isa 53 thus tends to function as a proof-text for the ministry of physical healing by Jesus. Through this reading of Matt 8, Pentecostal readers identify the mission of Christ in the world to be the removal of physical sickness as well as sin. This ministry is paradigmatic, rather than unique, and therefore to be continued by the disciples of Christ.

PROBLEMATIC USES OF CHRISTOCENTRIC READINGS

This practice of reading Christ as the centre of the Old Testament is not unique to Pentecostal readers, but has been evident in many Christian communities (including the New Testament writing community against which Pentecostal communities define themselves through the Acts 2 narrative). Following the lead of New Testament writers, Pentecostal readers look for ways in which the Old Testament testifies to Christ as the "fulfillment" of these texts. As Holmgren notes, one of the features of the New Testament writers is their explicit intent to portray Jesus as the "fulfillment" of the Old Testament.[78] Holmgren highlights the importance of demonstrating Jesus as the "Messiah" of the Old Testament; a reading that is "permitted" by such passages such as 1 Cor 15:3–5 that highlight the person and ministry of Jesus as the "fulfillment" of the Old Testament or Scripture, "For what I received I passed on to you as of first importance: that Christ died for our sins according to the Scriptures, that he was buried, that he was raised on the third day, according to the Scriptures." The New Testament interpretation of the Old Testament understands it against the background of faith in Jesus. When a Christian believer confronts the plain sense of an Old Testament text, the ambiguities disappear—the text seems to lean or lead toward Jesus.

According to Peterson, "the New Testament shows how the earliest Christians explored the Christological significance of a great range of Old Testament texts"[79] Peterson suggests, therefore, that readers should be encouraged by the example of the New Testament writers to similarly interpret the Old Testament in the light of its fulfillment, in a way that leads people to Jesus as Savior and Lord. For a Christian restorationist

78. Holmgren, *The Old Testament and the Significance of Jesus*, 13.

79. Peterson, *Christ and His People in the Book of Isaiah*, 12.

community, the Old Testament cannot simply be considered in isolation, in a purely historical sense. Readers need to be challenged by Jesus and his apostles to discover its Christian significance.[80] Hagner describes the New Testament exegetical process as "a deeper, more significant meaning or a fuller sense contained within and alongside the primary or contemporary meaning"[81] hence the more common terminology of the *sensus plenior* of Scripture.[82] In this deeper meaning, the New Testament writers saw Christ as the "fulfillment" of Old Testament "promise," even when that fulfillment did not always have a direct relationship to the context of the original passage.

Richard Longenecker notes that the New Testament writers did not always adhere to the original context of the Old Testament text being employed, especially when appealing to its christological significance.[83] He writes, "There are also times when the New Testament quotes the Old Testament in ways that appear quite out of context yet claims fulfillment by Christ or in Christian experience for those passages."[84] He comments that the use of Isa 9:1–2 in Matt 4:14–16 uses certain events of the nation's history to prefigure Jesus' life and ministry, specifically his preaching ministry in Capernaum. So, rather than direct prediction, Longenecker identifies many New Testament fulfillment passages as being more to do with what he describes as a "corporate solidarity" and a "typological correspondence in history."[85] For example, when Matt 4:14–16 quotes Isa 9:1–2 (a great light appearing to the people of Zebulun and Naphtali), the writer uses certain events from the nation's history to prefigure Jesus' preaching in Capernaum.[86] The example overflows any simple prediction-verification formula to emphasize the solidarity or resonance between the two events. This is not to say that all allusions to the Old Testament in the New are for christological purposes, or that all citations of Old Testament texts in the New abandon all awareness of context, but that a *correspondence* is often drawn by the writers between the events of Israel's history and the events of the life and ministry

---

80. Ibid.

81. Hagner, "When the Time had Fully Come."

82. The midrash approach is developed by Hagner who writes, "The midrashic technique involved an atomistic approach, wherein a single word or phrase, regardless of its meaning in its own context, could become the source of fresh meaning by the use of free association of ideas and wordplay. Therefore, even what seemed a most trivial item in the sacred text could become, through the ingenuity of the interpreter, the bearer of new significance and meaning" (ibid., 97). The atomistic approach is described by Longenecker as an approach which "interprets sentences, clauses, phrases, and even single words, independently of the context or the historical occasion, as divine oracles; combines them with other similarly detached utterances; and makes large use of analogy of expressions, often by purely verbal association" (Longenecker, "Who is the Prophet Talking About?" 381). Its purpose is to contemporize the revelation of God given to an earlier community for those living in a different situation. It is characterised by the maxim: "That has relevance for This." What is written in Scripture has relevance for our present situation (ibid., 381).

83. Ibid., 375–86.

84. Ibid., 377.

85. Ibid.

86. Ibid., 377–78.

of Jesus Christ.[87] Hays describes this as "intertextual reflection" by the New Testament writers (such as Paul).[88]

However, Barnabas Lindars[89] suggests that the New Testament writers did not take an Old Testament book or passage, and sit down and ask, "What does this mean?" Instead their concern, like the Pentecostal community, was more pragmatic. They were interested with the kerygma; the need to teach and to defend and to understand their new faith for themselves. He writes, "Believing that Christ is the fulfillment of the promises of God, and that they are living in the age to which all the Scriptures refer, they employ the Old Testament in an *ad hoc* way, making recourse to it just when and how they find it helpful for their purposes. But they do this in a highly creative situation, because the Christ-event breaks through conventional expectations, and demands new patterns of exegesis for its elucidation."[90] This pragmatic concern for kerygma is similarly emphasized in the contemporary Pentecostal community as Houston's comments (noted earlier) with regard to Pentecostal styles of preaching and teaching of the Old Testament emphasizes. Again, this highlights the purpose of Pentecostal readings—the reader desires to be transformed. The purpose for which one reads determines what and how one reads. What troubles many scholars is the exegetical process by which the New Testament writers (and perhaps Pentecostal readers) arrived at their christocentric conclusions.[91] The identification of a christocentric approach with a prediction-verification formula also questions the role and purpose of Old Testament prophecy. Is it primarily to forth-tell or fore-tell? As Fee notes, "It often happens, therefore, that many Christians refer to the Prophets *only* for predictions about the coming of Jesus and/or certain features of the New Covenant age—as though prediction of events far distant from their own day was the main concern of the Prophets."[92]

The fact that too few Pentecostal readers are concerned to understand the original context of Old Testament prophecies is not something isolated to the Pentecostal community. Commenting on early Christian use of the Old Testament, Snodgrass notes their lack of historical sensitivity or treatment of extended texts. He writes, "Instead, the

---

87. According to Dyck, not only were modern biblical scholars finding that their historically particular interpretations were different from those reached by the New Testament writers, but that "we had reached one conclusion, but the New Testament writer argued another. Our theological sensibilities about the oneness of Scripture were especially under attack at this point. Put directly, history was in conflict with canon" (Dyck, "Canon as Context for Interpretation," 36).

88. Hays, *Echoes of Scripture in the Letters of Paul*, 182.

89. Lindars, "The Place of the Old Testament in the Formation of New Testament Theology," 143.

90. Ibid., 143.

91. Although the New Testament writers begin with their experience of the resurrected Christ then move to the text, Childs does not condone the adoption of this approach for the contemporary church. He writes, "the hermeneutical practice of the New Testament does not in itself provide a theological warrant for the church's imitation of this approach. We are neither prophets nor Apostles. The function of the church's canon is to recognize this distinction. The Christian church does not have the same unmediated access to God's revelation as did Apostles, but rather God's revelation is mediated through their authoritative witness, namely through Scripture. This crucial difference calls into question any direct imitation of the New Testament's hermeneutical practice" (Childs, *Biblical Theology of the Old and New Testaments*, 381).

92. Fee and Stuart, *How to Read the Bible for All Its Worth*, 150.

Old Testament was viewed as prophecy about Christ, as providing types of Christ, or as holding hidden ideas and symbols that may be spiritually understood through allegory."[93] Yet, the Pentecostal community emphasizes the spiritual gift of prophecy, consistent with the Old Testament, as the ability to forth-tell a message of encouragement to their community. The concern to understand the original context of an Old Testament text by Pentecostal readers would also reinforce this function of prophecy as a message relevant to the contemporary generation. As Pentecostal readers appreciate the importance of the prophetic message to the prophet's own contemporaries, the Pentecostal community can find confidence in the purposes and function of prophecy in their own context.

This particular christocentric approach not only impedes the understanding of the function of prophecy, but it supports the potential toward extreme interpretations by readers who feel obliged to extract christological significance from every Old Testament text. As Snodgrass asserts, "We must resist superimposing Christian theology on Old Testament texts and should feel no compulsion to give every Old Testament text, or even most of them, a christological conclusion."[94] Scholars such as Johnston and Brueggemann[95] suggest that readers should actually resist a christocentric reading approach to the Old Testament. They suggest this would avoid not only the subjectivism of *sensus plenior*[96] but also avoid violation of the text.[97] As noted above, Brueggemann highlights the value of the Old Testament for its unique contribution. With regard to christological readings of *Isaiah*, Brueggemann writes:

> It is a matter of considerable importance, in my judgment, that Christians should not preempt the book of Isaiah. It is legitimate to see how the book of Isaiah fed, nurtured, and evoked Christian imagination with reference to Jesus. But that is very different from any claim that the book of Isaiah predicts or specifically anticipates Jesus. Such a preemption, as has often occurred in the reading of the church, constitutes not only a failure to respect Jewish readers, but is a distortion of the book itself. It is strongly preferable, I suggest, that Jews and Christians together recognize that the book of Isaiah is enormously and generatively open in more than one direction. No interpretive tradition is able to monopolize and close interpretation. This is a difficult and important question to which respectful attention must be paid.[98]

---

93. Snodgrass, "The Use of the Old Testament in the New," 33. Snodgrass continues in his discussion to highlight the diverse treatment of the early church in its treatment of Old Testament texts, emphasizing the dominance of allegorical exegesis, as promoted by the Alexandrian School (represented by Origen and Augustine), until the Reformation (ibid., 33). Post-Reformation readers tended to focus on the plain meaning of the text rather than engage in allegorical exegesis. However, Snodgrass does note its continued use in the contemporary church as "pastors read into texts spiritual meanings that have nothing to do with the original purposes of the authors" (ibid.).

94. Ibid., 49.

95. Johnston, "Pentecostalism and Theological Hermeneutics"; Brueggemann, *Theology of the Old Testament*.

96. Johnston, "Pentecostalism and Theological Hermeneutics," 60.

97. Brueggemann, *Theology of the Old Testament*, 6.

98. Ibid.

Yet, if Christ is not the central anticipation of the Old Testament, how did the New Testament writers understand him as the fulfillment? Should the past distortion of the text by previous communities inhibit the Pentecostal community from embracing a *christo*-logical approach as part of their reading approach?

THE READING EVENT AS FULFILLMENT OF CHRIST IN PENTECOSTAL READINGS OF THE OLD TESTAMENT

The language of promise-fulfillment is important to the New Testament writings. However, as Zimmerli notes, it would be a sharp criticism of the New Testament use of the language of promise-fulfillment if such language were something foreign or not current in the Old Testament itself.[99] Instead we find that the language of promise and fulfillment corresponds to authentic Old Testament forms. Zimmerli cites the example of the Exodus narratives, which involve progressive fulfillment of the promise to the earlier patriarchs.[100] He also notes the didactic story of Jonah as an example of a recalcitrant prophet (who would have enjoyed being proved correct in the word which he proclaimed, a word understood as a kind of fortune-teller's prediction) who turns scoldingly against Yahweh because the promised event moved in a direction different to that expected. He writes, "Only Yahweh himself can legitimately interpret his promise through his fulfillment, and the interpretation can be full of surprises even for the prophet himself."[101] In conclusion, Zimmerli asserts, "When we survey the entire Old Testament, we find ourselves involved in a great history of movement from promise toward fulfillment."[102] The language of fulfillment in the New Testament thus stands over and against this situation in the Old; as Paul formulates it, all the promises are "yes and amen" in Christ.[103] The promises of the Old Testament, according to Zimmerli, are not fulfilled in the literal sense of the coming to pass of a prediction that can be documented after the manner of a fortune-teller, but are fulfilled in the promise of the divine person (Jesus) as the fulfillment personified.[104] This fulfillment of the Old Testament promises by Jesus Christ is a central act of reflection by the New Testament writers. Holmgren asserts, "Clearly, the New Testament writers did not first consult the Old Testament and then form their opinion about Jesus. On the contrary, they moved from Jesus to the Old Testament scripture. Viewed in the light of Christ, certain texts took on new meaning which gave early Christians fuller insight into this figure in whom they experienced the

---

99. Zimmerli, "Promise and Fulfillment." In particular, see Clines, *The Theme of the Pentateuch*, for discussion on the connection between promise and fulfillment within and between Old Testament texts.

100. Zimmerli, "Promise and Fulfillment," 92–93. Similarly, the royal history of Judah presented in the book of Kings is shaped in terms of the fulfilment of the promise of Nathan to David (ibid., 98). The language of promise and fulfilment is not foreign to but evident within the writings of the Old Testament. Yet, as the prophetic writings demonstrate, the announcement of promise is dynamic and free from predetermination.

101. Ibid., 106.

102. Ibid., 111–12.

103. Ibid., 113.

104. Ibid., 121.

presence of God."[105] He writes, "from their meeting with Jesus, Christians looked back to the Old Testament, their Scripture, in order to gain understating of what took place."[106]

The movement whereby Christ is identified as the "fulfillment" of the Old Testament is noted by Holmgren as a "looking back" or reflection by the New Testament community. The early Christians were engaged in relating the two most important realities of their lives—the Scriptures and Jesus Christ.[107] The New Testament writers first experienced Christ then searched the scriptures to understand this new reality. As Snodgrass writes, "The conviction about his [Jesus'] identity did *not* derive from the Old Testament. They did not find texts and then find Jesus. They found Jesus and then saw how the Scriptures fit with him. They were not *proving* his identity in the technical sense so much as they were demonstrating how the Scriptures fit with him."[108]

As the New Testament writers moved from their experience of Christ to Scripture, select Old Testament texts such as Isa 53 took on new meaning and were transformed as they read through the glasses of their Christ-experience. Christ is therefore understood to be the fulfillment of these Old Testament passages, not because these texts had him specifically in mind, but because what happened earlier was somehow analogous to what happened to him.[109] Passages from the older scripture corroborated their faith in Jesus.[110] There is correspondence between the acts of God in the writings of Israel with the life and ministry of Christ. Climatic events in the history of Israel became paradigms by which new events were explained.[111] Writing of Isa 9, Brueggemann comments: "According to Matthew, Jesus relocates so that 'what had been spoken through the prophet Isaiah might be fulfilled.' This claim of course does not mean that the poet in Isaiah 9:1–7 had Jesus in mind or 'predicted' Jesus. It means rather that the text, powerful and generative as it is, surges beyond its 'original setting' to illuminate and redescribe new situations. The text is 'reheard' in the Matthew community as a disclosure of Jesus' ministry."[112] In the attempt to articulate their Christ-experience, the New Testament writers looked to Scripture.[113] Jesus was the faith hypothesis which provided one answer to Isaiah's questioning about Israel's relationship with its God.

---

105. Holmgren, *The Old Testament and the Significance of Jesus,* 53.

106. Ibid., 13.

107. Snodgrass, "The Use of the Old Testament in the New," 29.

108. Ibid., 40.

109. Holmgren, *The Old Testament and the Significance of Jesus,* 41–42. Childs in particular argues against an exclusivity of a reading that locates the only legitimate reading of Isa 9 as referring to a contemporary historical figure (namely Hezekiah). Instead, he highlights "the messianic shaping of the larger Isaianic narrative context within the eschatological framework" (Childs, *Biblical Theology of the Old and New Testaments,* 11).

110. Holmgren, *The Old Testament and the Significance of Jesus,* 53.

111. Snodgrass, "The Use of the Old Testament in the New," 38.

112. Brueggemann, *Old Testament Theology,* 85.

113. For discussion on the handling of "Messianic" prophecies in both conservative Christian communities and the New Testament writings, see the chapter "The Best Story in the Old Testament: the Messiah." in Thompson, *Who's Afraid of the Old Testament God?* 130–57.

The older testament provided the words and imagery that enabled the early church to understand and articulate to others the significance and identity of Jesus.[114] According to Holmgren, "Christians 'knew' by experience who Jesus was, but they needed the words and imagery of the Scripture common to both Jews and Christians to articulate this 'knowing.'"[115] Basic to almost all speech about Jesus, is the language and imagery of the Old Testament. As Roger Nicole writes, "Thus certain Old Testament prophecies may have conveyed to the original hearers a meaning more restricted than the perspective opened in the New Testament pages. The original understanding was a legitimate interpretation of the prophecy, yet one which does not preclude the propriety of the larger vistas, authoritatively revealed in the New Testament."[116] Yet, this kind of analogous reasoning is not limited to Jesus in the New Testament; in some cases early Christians saw themselves or their situation addressed in ancient Scripture. Snodgrass asserts, "Often words that find their climax in Jesus find further correspondence in his followers. If Jesus is the fulfillment of Isaiah 49:6 as the light to the Gentiles (Luke 2:32), the words can still be applied to Paul (Acts 13:47)."[117] This is consistent with those experiential and dynamic readings by the Pentecostal community explored above—they too identify themselves in the text. The contemporary Pentecostal community has adopted the methods of the New Testament writers in the sense that they too utilize Scripture to articulate their experiential encounter with God and His ongoing mission.

Pentecostals see themselves as the restored early church. In ways similar to those of their forebears, Pentecostal readers also look back to scripture (Old & New Testaments) for an understanding and articulation of their experience. The adoption of Old Testament imagery not only helped early Christians articulate their experience of Christ, but it established continuity between their witness and the Old Testament scripture.[118] In this same way, Pentecostal readings tend to lead or lean towards their pneumatic experience and to find in Old Testament scripture the words and imagery to enable them to articulate to others the significance of their encounter. The Pentecostal community "knows"[119] the blessing of God's presence but requires the words and images of scripture to bring this knowing to expression. The Old Testament provides the imagery for the Christian proclamation of the Pentecostal community. The Pentecostal community identifies itself in continuity with the people of God of the Old Testament as they look back to the older text to articulate their Christian life and pneumatic experience through the symbols, events and figures found in its pages.[120]

114. Holmgren, *The Old Testament and the Significance of Jesus,* 13.

115. Nicole, "The New Testament Use of the Old Testament," 13.

116. Ibid., 27.

117. Snodgrass, "The Use of the Old Testament in the New," 38.

118. Holmgren, *The Old Testament and the Significance of Jesus,* 104.

119. This "knowing" of the Pentecostal community is not just metal assent but the knowledge or "yada'" of Johns and Johns (Bridges-Johns and Johns, "Yielding to the Spirit").

120. As Coulter suggests, "Although early Pentecostals used a typological approach common to fundamentalist hermeneutics, the typologies Pentecostals found were not simply Christological but reflective of the whole spiritual life" (Coulter, "What Meaneth This? Pentecostals and Theological Enquiry," 59).

Recognizing the role of re-interpretation of the Isaiah text by New Testament writers and contemporary communities, Melugin questions whether the tendency of biblical scholars to focus on original meaning is too narrow a conceptualization for the task of biblical interpretation. He writes, "Has modern biblical scholarship too readily jettisoned intellectual reflection about the work of the Spirit in the interpretation and use of scripture in the present-day church?"[121] If the New Testament writers considered the words of the Old Testament to be alive with meaning and meanings,[122] is it appropriate for Pentecostal readers to adopt a similar approach? Can Houston "stand up on a Sunday morning" and preach the Old Testament as a "new covenant believer"? The resounding response of Pentecostal tradition is: "yes and amen." However, the challenge for the Pentecostal community is to develop a christological approach as part of their reading practice that hears the concerns of Old Testament scholarship and is responsible to the older testament. This requires an appreciation of both the original context and the analogous experience that situation represents to the Christian community. As Holmgren writes, "Every text has its historical, religious and cultural context and is therefore, to a greater or lesser extent, bound by this context. In order to 'live,' the text must be interpreted and brought into the world of those who are looking to the text for guidance."[123]

It is crucial that to be consistent with the tradition of the Pentecostal community—the reader, their experience of God and spirituality are allowed to "speak" with the Old Testament text. It is likewise crucial for the theological consistency of the Pentecostal community that the Old Testament texts be allowed to "speak" to the reader their own message, one both relevant to their historical context and part of the redemptive story of the people of God. This does not deny the belief of the Pentecostal community in the *ability* of God to predict the future, but recognizes the role of the prophetic message as a communication from God relevant to its community, even if it may concern future events. It also emphasizes the responsibility of the reader to come to the biblical text seeking a fresh knowledge of God's will under the guidance of the Spirit.[124]

FROM PRINCIPLE TO PRACTICE

According to LaSor the principle of *sensus plenior* can provide helpful keys in developing a Christian reading of the Old Testament, "In one sense, it [the *sensus plenior* or fuller meaning] lies outside and beyond the historical situation of the prophet, and therefore it cannot be derived by grammatico-historical exegesis. But in another sense, it is part of the history of redemption, and therefore it can be controlled by the study of Scripture taken in its entirety."[125] LaSor continues to give an illustration of how these controls of a *sensus plenior* reading may function. He asserts that "An ordinary seed contains in itself

---

121. Melugin, "Texts to Transform Life: Reading Isaiah as Christians," 110.

122. Holmgren, *The Old Testament and the Significance of Jesus,* 21.

123. Ibid., 29.

124. Thompson, *Who's Afraid of the Old Testament God,* 24.

125. Quoted in Beale, "Did Jesus and His Followers Preach the Right Doctrine from the Wrong Texts?" 393, Grand Rapids: Baker Books, 1994.

everything that will develop in the plant or tree to which it is organically related: every branch, every leaf, every flower. Yet no amount of examination by available scientific methods will disclose to us what is in that seed. However, once the seed has developed to its fullness we can see how the seed has been fulfilled . . . [and] we have sufficient revelation in the Scriptures to keep our interpretations of *sensus plenior* from becoming totally subjective."[126] Adopting a *sensus plenior* approach can be appropriate if the Pentecostal reader places it within the wider framework of the redemptive-historical perspective of the two testaments.[127] Following the example of the New Testament writers, the redemptive-historical context provides the wider context for reading Old Testament (and New Testament) texts. By identifying the meaning of the Old Testament text for the audience contemporary to the prophet, the Pentecostal reader can appreciate the wider redemptive significance of the text and place it within the framework of God's activities among his covenant people. The patterns and activity of God in Israel's history can now apply to Christ and the church as inclusive of the people of God in the New Testament, but it requires the recognition of God's actions among ancient Israel first.[128] The Pentecostal reader, from this place, can then locate their Christian life and pneumatic experience in the text as part of their reading of the Old Testament to make it christo-*logical*.

However, does this principle of *sensus plenior* justify experiential and acontextual readings within the Pentecostal community? Some features of the Pentecostal readings of *Isaiah* described above would be considered by scholars such as Hagner to be allegorical in nature, as the readings depart from historical patterns. According to his definition, an allegorical reading extracts timeless or "spiritual" truths from documents that on the surface are time-conditioned and "earthly."[129] For Hagner, these readings are illegitimate appeals to the concept of *sensus plenior* (deeper meaning). His contention with this type of reading is the seeming lack of control or boundaries of responsibility. He writes, "In allegory there are no controls. One produces from the Old Testament what one has predetermined to produce, and the product bears no necessary relationship to the source from which it is derived."[130] Hagner denies that there is any real example of allegorical readings (by his definition) of the Old Testament in the New Testament,[131] suggesting instead that any violation of historical contexts of the Old Testament is avoided by these

---

126. Beale, "Did Jesus and His Followers Preach the Right Doctrine from the Wrong Texts?" 393.

127. The political implication of this view will be discussed in the next chapter.

128. Beale, "Did Jesus and His Followers Preach the Right Doctrine from the Wrong Texts?" 396. Beale notes that while readers can employ the exegetical methods of the New Testament writers, contemporary readers cannot reproduce the inspired certainty of their interpretations (ibid., 402).

129. Hagner, "When the Time Had Fully Come," 95.

130. Ibid., 94–95.

131. The only concession that Hagner acknowledges is the reference of Paul in Gal 4:24 to "speaking allegorically" as he compares Hagar and Sarah as representatives of the two covenants. He writes, "although Paul suggests that he is speaking 'allegorically,' we may with some justification see in this material a moderate extension of the principles of typology" (ibid., 95). Hagner claims the use by Paul to be akin to typology since he preserves the historicity of the two women, yet concedes that if it is allegory then it is a severely "controlled" use (ibid., 95).

writers.[132] He suggests that the adoption of allegorical or atomistic readings is inappropriate and should also be avoided by contemporary Christian communities.[133] However, to suggest that the New Testament writers are always considerate of the original historical context of Old Testament texts is a deliberate hermeneutical sleight of hand, to justify the sole employment of the grammatical-historical approach based on supposed New Testament models of reading. As discussed above, scholars such as Longenecker have demonstrated occasional abandonment of the original context of Old Testament passages by New Testament writers as they appeal to the christological significance of the texts that exist beyond the original motivation or context. The denial of the "creative" genius of New Testament writers by scholars such as Hagner is a political attempt to control readings of the text within the contemporary Christian community by delegitimizing any reading outside the boundary of grammatical-historical rules.

Longenecker also suggests that the exegetical practices of the New Testament writers should not be adopted by contemporary Christian readers. Instead, he proposes that the present task is to "contextualize the gospel in our own day and for our own circumstances, speaking meaningfully to people as they are and think today."[134] According to Hays, Longenecker's approach forces contemporary readers into a kind of "intellectual schizophrenia" to which readers "grant privileged status to past interpretations that we deem unjustifiable with regard to normal, sober hermeneutical canons."[135] Longenecker also assumes, then, that all "people" in the contemporary age "think" in categories of grammatical-historical exegesis. The idea that all Christian communities are dominated by the sort of Modernist thinkers assumed by Longenecker is clearly not demonstrated in the examples of Pentecostal readings of *Isaiah*. The Pentecostal community resists the scientific approach of grammatical-historical exegesis, instead opting for a more theological interpretation reflective of their confessional interests. As Poythress writes of this intra-Evangelical debate: "We are not to despise laypeople's understanding of the Bible. We are not to reject it just because on the surface it appears to 'read in' too much. Of course, laypeople may sometimes have overworked imaginations. But sometimes their conclusions are may be the result of a synthesis of Bible knowledge due to the work of the Holy Spirit. Scholars cannot reject such a possibility without having achieved a profound synthetic and even practical knowledge of the Bible for themselves."[136] The individual Pentecostal reader is informed by the Pentecostal community, which is (in turn) informed by the wider Christian dialogue.

---

132. Ibid., 98.

133. Ibid.

134. Ibid., 385.

135. Hays, *Echoes of Scripture in the Letters of Paul*, 181. As Hays suggests, Paul would fail any contemporary exegesis course! Hays continues to critique this approach of Longenecker that places Paul's writings in the New Testament on a pedestal which contemporary readers are to believe and reproduce his teachings, "but not to emulate the freedom with which he reads Scripture" (ibid., 181). Hays goes on to suggest that the hermeneutical methods adopted by Paul and the New Testament writers can and should be adopted by the contemporary Christian community as they share the vision of Scripture and read the Bible under the guidance of the Spirit as primarily a narrative of election and promise (ibid., 183).

136. Poythress, "Divine Meaning of Scripture," 112.

This engagement with the concerns of biblical scholars, challenges the Pentecostal community to not reject the historical-cultural context of Old Testament texts in the development of a unique Pentecostal reading model. Yet neither should this concern for the historical witness of the text dissolve or undermine the dynamic nature of their readings. This model must also take seriously the concerns raised by biblical scholars to validate the uniqueness and contribution of the Old Testament for its own witness to the Pentecostal community. By hearing its unique voice, it values the wider redemptive significance of the text as it places it within the framework of God's activities among the covenant people of all ages and all times. Instead, the development of a reading model must include recognition of values and practices of the Pentecostal community. This includes recognition of both the significance of the life and ministry of Christ identified in the matrix of the text, as well as the identification of the Pentecostal community as part of the on-going ministry of Christ.

5

Common Interests with Hermeneutics

In the attempt to verbalize their experience with God and the reality of Christian living, Pentecostal readers turn to the stories and imagery of the Bible. This is where the dialogue between Pentecostals, hermeneutics, and the Old Testament finds interests common to the three conversation partners. The Old Testament text provides a pool of language and experience which Pentecostal readers draw from and identify with, regardless of the context or historical distance. This dynamic approach emphasizes the purpose of Pentecostal readings (and indeed Christian allegorical readings back to Clement and Origen); to encounter God. The Pentecostal reader aims to understand God and the world in which they live by reading the text as a universal snapshot of God's operations in the world. However, this often means dismissal of the distance between their own horizon and that of the text. While Pentecostal readings embrace a dynamic nature, the cost is a lack of recognition of the historical and literary context of the passage. This is represented in the readings of Isaiah 25 and 40. The meanings and applications from the text highlighted by the grassroots community tended to be developed acontextually. This dynamic nature of Pentecostal readings exemplifies their tendency for multiple meanings and applications drawn by readers from identical texts of *Isaiah*. As Croatto writes, "The text contains a reservoir of meaning, ever exploited and never exhausted."[1]

This raises the question of the importance of context for reading communities. Should the Pentecostal community find meaning only within their dynamic response to the text and maintain the authority of the reader, or should the text have an authority within this process? How can a reading approach maintain the value of devotional readings without sacrificing a commitment to the prophetic independence of the text to, in turn, speak and challenge the community of readers? Context is important as the text is produced within a specific cultural framework, and so must be understood as a product of that framework. Yet, conversely, limiting a responsible reading approach to

---

1. Croatto, *Biblical Hermeneutics*, 30.

the strictures of historical criticism denies the role (and subjectivity) of the reader, and the possibilities for multiple meanings as highlighted by postmodernism. Pentecostal readings share a presupposition with postmodernity that the text is autonomous and meanings are multivocal. However, unlike many postmodern readings, the Pentecostal community has not dismissed meta-narrative.

The Pentecostal community identifies Scripture as providing *the* authoritative description of reality through which they can understand their own experience. The text is autonomous from the historical context as the divine author is also autonomous, operating outside the domain of historical criticism. For the Pentecostal community, because it is autonomous from the historical context it presents specific universal truths about God and the Christian life, and is therefore authoritative. Instead of acting as a repository of historical information, the biblical passage in Pentecostal readings serves as a symbol for the reader. The use of the hermeneutical theory of semiotics can assist them in identifying the role of Scripture in the readings of the Pentecostal community. Through the adoption of this theory to understand their own reading practices, Pentecostalism finds a common interest with Hermeneutics. Using this theory, the symbol (text) acts as a sign that points to God's interaction with and laws governing the world. The Pentecostal reader identifies in this symbol a particular universal truth or experience. As Coulter writes, "For both Pentecostal and medieval interpreters Scripture possesses different levels of meaning that can be unlocked by an experience of the Spirit. Scripture supplies truths not only by reference to its historical context but also by understanding how it symbolically reflects the truth encountered through an experience."[2] By using the text as a symbol[3] independent of the historical and cultural context of the passage, Pentecostal readings can continue to invite the possibility of multiple readings of the text.[4] In this way, the conversation of the triune dialogue partners uncovers this common interest for Pentecostalism and Hermeneutics as they explore the use of this theory in readings of the Old Testament.

READINGS OF ISAIAH 25

The *dynamic* approach to texts by the Pentecostal community is demonstrated by the readings of Isaiah 25. Using an identical passage, Pentecostal readers identified multiple meanings in the text that related to their experience of God and Christian living. These readings focused on the text as symbolic experience. The reader enters this symbolic experience or text encounter through their associated contemporary experience. For example, the symbol (text) of Isaiah 25:6 is used by Williams to discuss the concept of "An Open Heaven" in the 1985 *Australian Evangel*. He writes, "In this remarkable verse we are shown that nations of this world can have a 'vail' [*sic*] spread over them . . . I have visited some of these countries and talked with missionaries from there. They have told me that

---

2. Coulter, "What Meaneth This? Pentecostals and Theological Enquiry," 61.

3. For Pentecostals, the "sign" is never merely nominal, but a "real" projection attached to the signified.

4. Ironically, Pentecostals—while affirming "sola scriptura" with Luther—also affirm the philosophical realism which informs Catholic sacramental theology, against which Luther revolted.

at times the heavens seemed so dark and heavy over them, that they could hardly pray."[5] Williams links this passage to the importance of prayer as a weapon in spiritual warfare. For Williams, prayer breaks the veil of darkness that prevents people from receiving the gospel of Jesus Christ. He continues, "So beloved, if you are in a situation which grieves you [sic]. A situation of darkness over a town or a church or a country, you can break through by using spiritual warfare and intercession."[6]

Once this open heaven is achieved, the gospel will spread and salvation will be received. The invitation to the salvation feast can be accepted. Williams' reading adopts the Isaian text as a symbol for his contemporary experience in evangelism and church life. For Williams, death is represented as a veil or covering that has produced universal suffering, soon to be swallowed completely by the Lord. The banquet provides not only salvation but also consolation through this act.[7] Williams, the Pentecostal reader, associates the richness of the salvation feast offered in the Isaiah text with the salvation offered by Christ. However the veil oppressing the nations is not death itself (like the Isaian text) but the blanket of spiritual oppression. For Williams, this produces spiritual death. Once this veil is lifted the gospel can be spread and the invitation to the salvation feast accepted.

This same concept of spiritual blindness is developed in a different way by John E. Ollis in a later article of the 1992 *Australian Evangel*. Ollis reflects throughout his article on an "excellent sermon" on Isa 25:7 he had heard recently, "particularly emphasizing that through the death of Jesus the veil has been taken away from people's faces and the scars of sin are removed when a person receives Christ as Savior. Positionally it was done at Calvary, but experientially it becomes actual when a person appropriates this in his or her individual life."[8] It is interesting to note that while both Williams and Ollis identify the "veil" of the Isaian text to be a "veil of spiritual blindness," the means of removal is different. The experience of the Isaiah text anticipates the removal of the veil as the Lord will "swallow up on this mountain the covering that is cast over all people" (25:7). Exactly how this veil is swallowed is ambiguous. For Ollis the spiritual blindness (or spiritual death) is swallowed at the event of Calvary and actuated in a person's life in their experience of conversion. As a missiologist, Ollis identifies the removal of the "veil" in Isa 25:7 with his own experience of the expansion of Christianity as he continues: "around our world statistically more than at any other time men and women from every nation and religion are turning to the Lord." The event of the removal of a veil that covers the nations in Isa 25:7 becomes a symbol for Ollis' experience of missionary activity. In comparison, pastor-evangelist Williams associates the veil of death with the spiritual principalities of evil working within creation that blind unbelievers from the truth of salvation offered in Christ. This spiritual blindness is "swallowed" by the participation of believers in spiritual warfare.

---

5. See Appendix 1, Ref W, 3.

6. See Appendix 1, Ref W, 4.

7. Goldingay, *Isaiah*, 143.

8. See Appendix 1, Ref WV, 31.

Ollis and Williams both identify in this text the delay of the feast of salvation for the nations that they have experienced in their own ministry. For Ollis, the removal of the delay is immediate ("now") as the veil is lifted in the event of conversion or, as the Isaian text symbolizes it, in the feast of salvation. The veil has already been removed at Calvary but only realized through conversion. In comparison, the delay of salvation according to Williams is the result of the spiritual forces that hinder the work of evangelism. Presumably, the veil cannot be removed until the source of death, God's adversaries, are destroyed in the eschaton. Yet, the two readers not only differ with regard to their *raison d'être* for the delay of salvation, but also with regard to the process by which the veil is removed; the metaphoric "swallowing." According to Ollis the veil will be lifted as believers pray and preach salvation to the unreached nations. Williams, by contrast, suggests the spiritual blindness is removed through the denouncement of the satanic forces over the city as the devil is bound by using the name of Jesus as part of "intercession and confession."[9] Both readings by Williams and Ollis adopt the Isaian text as a symbol for his contemporary experience in evangelism, church life, and spiritual warfare to demonstrate the difficulties of Evangelists within some nations.[10] The text provides the symbol by which they understand or view their world; this world is illuminated as a battlefield of spiritual forces. The experience of the text is associated, regardless of the historical and cultural context of the prophetic utterance to Judah, with the contemporary experience of Williams. The experience of the text and the reader (Williams and Ollis) are not identical but parallel, as Williams views the spiritual battle through the victory of Christ's passion. The event of the text is not simply transposed onto the situation of the reader (Biblicism), but rather the event of the text becomes a symbol (through its resonance with Williams' and Ollis' own experience of spiritual warfare) for the eschatological realization of Christ's salvation feast. Therefore Isa 25:6 is not only read christologically, but also as a symbol for the readers experience in evangelism. The veil covering the nations will be removed by the Lord at the eschatological salvation feast offered by Christ.

While Ollis and Williams focus on the actualization of Isaiah 25 in spiritual warfare, the concept of the salvation feast of verse 6 is developed by Ps Ashleigh McKenzie in the 1981 *Australian Evangel* to represent "God's desire during the millennium to give, 'wine on the lees well refined.'"[11] The image of matured wine provides a vehicle for McKenzie's reflection on the Christian life as he writes, "The wine was allowed to settle just long enough to mature; then came the unsettling as it was poured from one vessel to another. [Ever found this occurring in your life?]"[12] For McKenzie, the preference for the "mature wine" of the Isaian text, points to the preferred maturity of character in believers. The event of the "feast of salvation" is representative of the importance of maturation in the Christian life. He writes, "Being conformed to the image of Jesus is to be our highest goal,

---

9. See Appendix 1, Ref W, 5.

10. As my colleague, Associate Professor Mark Hutchinson noted, in this sense the reading is ecclesiological rather than theological. It is a means for writing evangelists back into the larger story of a church dominated by pastors, and perhaps in danger of losing its evangelistic edge.

11. See Appendix 1, Ref X, 12.

12. Ibid.

and a large proportion of that conformity occurs in our character."[13] For McKenzie, the event of the Old Testament feast of salvation thus becomes a symbol for the importance of Christian maturation. The historical and cultural context of the text is subordinated by the resonance between a moral meaning and the reader's contemporary experience. The event of the Isaian salvation feast is read as the symbol for the process of salvation through sanctification. He writes, "Being conformed to the image of Jesus is to be our highest goal, and a large proportion of that conformity occurs in our character."[14] While Williams, Ollis and McKenzie identify the event of the Isaiah text with their own experience, the text inspires multiple meanings according to the context of the reader as they identify their experience of the Christian life in the text, rather than the historical or cultural context.

Similarly, in a 2002 sermon by David Mead,[15] the preacher identifies Isaiah's salvation feast of verse 6 with his own experience. However, for Mead, it is the experience of feasting with which he resonates. He says, "Well, there is one verse in here that speaks volumes to me and that verse is 6 where Isaiah tells us 'On this mountain the Lord Almighty will prepare a feast of rich food for all peoples, a banquet of aged wine—the best of meats and the finest of wines.' Now when I look at this verse it stirs my heart because one thing in my life that I am absolutely passionate about and that is fine food and fine wine. I love fine food and fine wines." However, Mead identifies a "greater wine" available for Christian believers—the Holy Spirit. The full feast of wine in the Isaian text represents, for Mead, the fullness of intimacy with the Holy Spirit. He goes on to say, "I interpret this as the Holy Spirit being poured out without holding back, I see it as an end-time anointing, that is evangelistic and mission orientated."

The metaphoric use of wine frequently adopted in the New Testament is similarly applied to this Old Testament text. The experience of Mead with the "wine" of the Spirit resonates with the rich feast described by the Isaian text. Rather than discussing the literal meaning of the text, Mead reads the text as representative of his desire and self-identifying experience of the Holy Spirit. From this point, Mead's sermon associates the feasting event of Isaiah with communion (the Eucharist). He describes this feast as "the fullness of Christ's body, not just a meager portion of God's grace in our lives but the absolute completeness of the work that Christ did on the cross for us." For Mead, the wine of the Isaian text points not only to the fullness of experience of the Holy Spirit, but also the blood of Christ "that was shed on the cross for us so that we too can participate in eternal life with the Father, with Jesus, with the Holy Spirit and all those who accept Jesus as their Lord and Savior." Like the acontextual readings above, Mead similarly identifies the experience of the feast with his own experience, albeit the experience of feasting with which he resonates. As a former caterer, Mead understands the salvation feast to be a gastronomic event of flavor and pleasure. However, while Mead resonates with a literal reading of the text, he identifies a "greater wine" available for Christian believers—the Holy Spirit. The full feast of wine in the Isaiah text becomes a symbol not for salvation,

13. See Appendix 1, Ref X, 13.

14. See ibid.

15. See Appendix 1, Ref Y.

but for the fullness of intimacy with the Holy Spirit. The symbolic use of wine, particularly as a reference to the Holy Spirit (and as frequently adopted in the New Testament) is similarly applied to this Old Testament text. Mead's experience with the "wine" of the Spirit resonates with the rich feast described by the Isaiah text, which thereby becomes a *symbol* for his (desired) experience of the Holy Spirit. Mead associates the gastronomic experience of flavor and pleasure in the text with the outpouring of the Holy Spirit reflective of Acts 2 and identified in the Pentecostal value of Spirit baptism. The symbolism is thus double layered through two biblical texts being caused to point at an evidential personal experience—each element reflexively reinforcing the other. Mead then goes on to associate the feasting event of Isaiah 25 with communion. For Mead, the wine of the Isaiah text symbolizes not just the fullness of experience of the Holy Spirit but also the blood of Christ. This single sermon from Isa 25:6 presents layered and multiple readings of the Isaian feast.

For some of the members of the girls youth group Bible study from a Pentecostal church in Western Sydney in 2004,[16] comprised of mostly later teenage girls, it was this concept of death being swallowed that also stood out to them from the passage. One participant commented: "It's the Lord's compassion, I suppose: that he has swallowed up death and that he's gonna wipe the tears away from all faces—His compassion and salvation power." The salvation presented in the passage was perceived by the girls to refer to the salvation offered by Christ. Commenting particularly on verse 9, another member offered: "It's a verse of confirmation that you will be saved by Jesus if you have faith and believe." The salvation of Isaiah 25 was linked by the group to the protection of God perceived in the passage. In particular it was the image of the fortified city and God being a defense for the needy that they highlighted. One member commented, "It just reinforces that God will never walk away from us. He's always there anytime, and for any person to turn to. When most people do turn to the Lord it's in a time of need, and it stands out to me because during the week this has happened to me. A total nonbeliever has just turned around and asked if they could pray with me because they were in a complete time of need." Her reading flowed out of her experience. She linked the salvation and protection desired by the non-believer to the implied promise of the text. Another member commented: "The thing that stood out to me was the fortified city . . . that God is the powerful one, God is the one that's gonna take over even people that seem strong. Even people in my life that seem as though they're gonna have their way with me, or they're gonna win in whatever battles are going on in work, or job—even though they seem strong . . . God is above all of that. He's safe and he's gonna take care of me." The image of the fortified city points to the character and actions of a God who protects his covenant people, as experienced and anticipated by these youth group members.

These four examples highlight the tendency of Pentecostal readings to interpret the Isaian text acontextually. They offer a variety of interpretation and meanings of the text as they adopt the Isaian event as a symbol for their own experience. While some Pentecostal readings may demonstrate a level of interest in the historical-cultural context or authorial intention of a passage, this is usually minimal and selective. Often it

16. See Appendix 1, Ref Z.

seems to be merely an apology to either the text or to an imaginary guild of biblical scholars. None of the four examples from Isa 25:6 highlighted the historical or cultural context of the passage, suggesting the value of meaning over context in Pentecostal hermeneutics. The readings demonstrated a tendency to not just appropriate the Isaian text to the situation of the reader, but to read it through an external event or experience; as a symbol. Generally that symbol will be a particular *event* in the New Testament, such as Calvary or Pentecost, or an *experience*, such as salvation or Baptism of the Holy Spirit. So Mead does not just appropriate the Isaian feast to the enjoyment of literal food and wine, but reads the text through the symbol of his Christian experience, namely the Spirit and the cross. The pleasure of rich feasting in the Isaiah text becomes a symbol for the richness of his experience of the Christian life in the Spirit and communion with Christ. The fact that he elsewhere notes that his hearers know of his secular experience as a chef, introduces other, more extended experiential references as *his* hearers are invited to the allegorical feast.

READINGS OF ISAIAH 40

Similarly, the readings of Isaiah 40 highlight the dynamic feature of Pentecostal readings as they presented multiple meanings from the identical text developed from their experience of Christian life. These readings generally display no interest in the historical or literary context as they focus on the "meaning" of the text. There were two main motifs highlighted by the grassroots Pentecostal readers: the "voice in the wilderness" (Isa 40:1–5) and "waiting on the Lord" (Isa 40:28–31). The presentation of the prophetic "voice in the wilderness" is an important motif developed by Pentecostal readers. Pentecostal minister, P. B. Duncan[17] identifies the voice to be the New Testament figure of John the Baptist. In his article in the 1972 *Australian Evangel*, Duncan highlights the preparatory role of the prophet as presented in Isa 40:1–5, and associates that person and role with this forerunner of Christ. He writes, "Realising at last that this was the revelation that had been foretold in the Scriptures, stating that before Messiah was manifest, He was to be preceded by one sent as a herald to prepare the way of the Lord."[18] According to Duncan, John the Baptist was the herald of a new dispensation in the plan of God, as "foretold" in the Old Testament Scriptures. In a similar way, he then applies this text of Isa 40:1 and the preparatory role of John the Baptist to his contemporary Pentecostal community. He identifies his community as a herald of the second coming of Christ, just as John the Baptist was the herald of his first coming. He concludes, "We, born at this time are the people of destiny—the Elijahs—the John the Baptists of the last days . . . So let us face our responsibilities and see our similarity to the Herald of Christ's first coming."[19] Duncan identifies the fulfillment of this Isaiah passage not only in the life and ministry of John the Baptist, but by extension (and the logic of analogies) as a passage to be fulfilled by the Pentecostal community as they prepare the way for the *second* coming of Christ.

17. See Appendix 1, Ref BA.

18. Ibid., 6.

19. Ibid.

The appropriation of this passage to the Pentecostal community and ministry is also emphasized in the writing of A. T. Davidson.[20] Reflecting upon over fifty years of ministry in the 1980 *Australian Evangel*, he suggests "if I were to begin again . . . I WOULD do it all again—for Jesus!"[21] While he would not change his life or call, Davidson continues to reflect upon the areas of ministry he would redress. He presents seven suggested changes, the third of which concerns the nature of his ministry: "My ministry would be one of comfort (Isa 40:1) "'Comfort ye, comfort ye My people,' saith the Lord." Davidson identifies this passage from Isaiah as a mandate to give comfort to his generation. He considers this passage to be speaking directly to his role as a representative of God and subsequent message of comfort. Davidson does not consider the passage for its significance to the Isaianic community, or even New Testament readings of this passage (as fulfilled in the person of John the Baptist). Instead, he reads the verse as directly applicable to his ministry and message to the contemporary Pentecostal community. It represents a shift from the harsh millennial prophetic voice of early Pentecostalism—which emphasized repentance—to a nurturing emphasis suited to a permanent, self-replicating community.

While the presentation of the prophetic voice in the wilderness is an important motif in Isaiah 40, perhaps the most widely discussed section of the chapter concerns the themes of "waiting on God" identified by numerous Pentecostal readers. The theme of "waiting on the Lord" for the purposes of strength and direction was discussed in the various readings. The concept of God's provision and strength is developed from Isa 40 in an article by Michael C. Smith[22] in the 1988 *Australian Evangel*. He begins by describing a vision he received as a new Christian in which a carpenter is working the rough timber into a beautiful design. However the carpenter's work with the timber was hindered by the blunting of the saw, so he had to re-sharpen the saw for it to be useful to his purposes. Smith interprets this vision for the reader as the need of Christians for renewal and re-sharpening.[23] Smith then turns to Isa 40:28–31 as an example of this teaching in the Bible. He writes: "This is a most powerful truth and yet is seldom heeded. Whether we are a pastor, a homemaker, or a laborer there will be times when we need the power of God renewed in our lives because, as Isaiah clearly states, even if we are one of the fittest and strongest young men, we *will* grow weary and faint."[24] Smith emphasizes the opportunity for believers to draw their strength from God, and "tap into the abundant supply of His mighty power."[25] This is done by the believer taking time in a daily basis to "wait on God." Smith cites the example of Christ in Luke 6:12–13 withdrawing for prayer and renewal. By waiting on God, Smith encourages his readers "Then we will truly renew our strength and soar like an eagle."[26]

---

20. See Appendix 1, Ref AA.

21. Ibid., 3.

22. See Appendix 1, Ref DA.

23. Ibid., 15.

24. Ibid.

25. Ibid.

26. Ibid., 17.

The editorial of the March 1985 *Australian Evangel* presents Isa 40:31 as a message of hope by emphasizing the four "shalls" of the verse. The editor, Harold Bartholomew, writes: "The context makes crystal clear that something more is needed to face and conquer the stresses and pressures of modern day life, than physical stamina."[27] Instead he presents the key to stamina as "waiting upon the Lord." This is possible not through the greatness of humanity, but through the greatness of God. He emphasizes the opportunity of waiting in expectant faith for God to move in the believer's life. Highlighting the importance of oral testimony and preaching in Pentecostalism, Bartholomew particularly emphasizes the imagery of the eagle as he recalls the story of another preacher:

> Walter Beuttler, a preacher and teacher, spoke of being in the North of India and witnessing an approaching storm. As the dark clouds gathered and the wind increased, the small birds scurried for cover to escape the approaching fury. Walter Beuttler observed an eagle in the sky. The eagle took advantage of the increasing velocity of the wind. It set its wings so that it went up and up, mounting higher and higher on the increasing strength of the air currents. The same wind that sent the smaller birds scurrying for cover, carried the eagle higher and higher.[28]

Through the imagery, Bartholomew reminds readers of the opportunity for God "to minister himself to the needy soul" and meet the believer with stamina and strength in the midst of storms. While these images of the eagle (objective symbol) and renewed strength (experiential bridge to the symbol) in the Isaiah passage draw on the covenantal metaphors and experience from the Exodus to assure the exiled people of a second exodus, this literary context is absent in Pentecostal readings.

Pastor Fred Evans[29] encourages readers of the 1985 *Australian Evangel* to apply the principle of "waiting on God" from Isa 40:31 to their Christian walk. Evans highlights the conditional nature of the verse for those looking for strength, renewal and blessing. He writes: "The key to the unlocking of this Scripture is in the first few words, 'They that wait upon the Lord.' This is the one condition upon which the four resultant blessings rest."[30] Evans then describes what the condition of "waiting on the Lord" means. Firstly, he identifies it not as prayer and the making of requests, but "silence."[31] In this state of silence, Evans suggests that God is able to speak to the believer as they stop and listen. For Evans, this carries the thought of expectation and hope as waiting produces "a steady, optimistic, confident expectation that God is in control and He will meet your need."[32] The third element of "waiting" he describes is being "alert, vigilant, watchful, alive and expectant." He writes: "In my experience, it is only when I have waited upon God that I have heard from Him." In the state of silence and expectation, God speaks. However, as Evans highlights in the final element of the meaning of the word, the task of the believer is not only to hear the voice of God, but to also do it. He asserts, "Friends, when we wait

27. See Appendix 1, Ref EA.

28. Ibid., 2.

29. See Appendix 1, Ref FA.

30. Ibid., 5.

31. Ibid.

32. Ibid., 6.

upon the Lord with quiet expectancy and watchful purpose, it is then that the sensitivity of our spirit will pick up the wishes and desires of our God whom we serve. His wish will become our command." However, it is clear that Evans defines the condition of "waiting on the Lord" through his own experience. His definition is not a conclusion from the text, which does not identify the term, but is drawn from his experience of Christian living. For Evans, this produces a life with unmeasured possibilities in God as the believer is finally promised the ability to "run and not be weary."

In the second article of his series, Evans[33] outlines the resultant blessings of those who fulfill the condition of waiting on the Lord. He identifies four blessings "promised" in this passage from Isaiah 40, the first being the renewal of strength. He teaches, "This very expressive term really means to exchange strength. It is the same term used when speaking of a change of garments."[34] Evans suggests that believers need to renew or change the "garments of our experience in God to receive a fuller revelation of His Spirit."[35] Secondly, the believer receives the promise of mounting up with wings as eagles. Evans understands this to be a spiritual blessing as he writes, "I think of seeing as God sees and of discovering the unknown: of reaching the highest and of meeting God."[36] This includes dreaming of a life with unmeasured possibilities in God as the believer is finally promised the ability to "run and not be weary." After the believer has had their strength renewed in flight, they are able to run and walk without fainting. According to Evans, the resultant blessing of Isaiah 40 can be actualized in the life of the contemporary Christian believer.

As part of a Pentecostal church in Western Sydney, the girls youth group Bible study[37] immediately fixed upon the concept that "glory of the Lord shall be revealed." One of the girls said: "It stood out to me, because I believe it to be true, every word of it. The glory of the Lord *will* be revealed." According to the group, this passage points to Christ—not as a direct or specific reference to a promise fulfilled, but it is generally through the salvation offered by Christ that the believer can experience these truths. Like Evans, they considered the blessings of Isaiah 40 to be readily available to the believer through salvation in Christ. One of the girls highlighted verse 28 with the comment: "Basically if you give your faith to the Lord Jesus, just have faith in him and everything, he won't let you fall, he won't let you stumble, and he will give you all that you need. Umm, if you just have the faith in him then he'll give you what you need to get through life. He won't allow you to fall and to stumble and to become tired and weary and things like that. It's just through faith and through his guidance that you gain that strength and ability to persevere." While this passage is not a direct prediction to the life and ministry of Christ, it is seen to somehow resonate with the experience of the believer in their Christian walk. It is interesting to note that (as in the Pentecostal writings discussed above) the girls in the youth group Bible study highlighted the *latter* part of the chapter 40—the same section

33. See Appendix 1, Ref GA.

34. Ibid., 20.

35. Ibid.

36. Ibid.

37. See Appendix 1, Ref Z.

discussed in the articles. This suggests that there is something about the latter section of the chapter that resonates with the experience or worldview of the Pentecostal community. This emphasis on the experience of the reader is highlighted in the closing comment of the Bible study discussion. One of the participants noted, "I like the point that he is sovereign, he's creator, he's so almighty, he's so beautiful, he so wants to lift us up from wherever we are. Like, to allow us to rise upon the wings as eagles. But, you know, up to those places where he wants us to be." The passage was seen as directly applicable to the Christian experience of the Pentecostal reader and appropriated by the contemporary reading community.

In a 2003 sermon on evangelism, Andrew Mina[38] presents Isa 40:28–31 as a challenge to the congregation on their "Missions Sunday": "What is the message that we are to bring to situations of life that you find yourself in?" He identifies Isaiah 40 as the answer. His notes summarize his message that: "These Scriptures are an anthology of encouraging, hope-inspired confidence-giving loving messages, and it is these very messages that we need to take the people of our world." In the midst of the problems and difficulties of life that lame or hinder believers, God is able to give strength to the faint-hearted and to carry his people on wings like eagles. Mina continues, "First God is able to help everyone, whether life feels like you are constantly running or even less energetic walking. The message for us to share from this passage is that God can sustain you!" Mina then links this concept to Matt 11:28–30, inviting his hearers to enter the rest offered by Jesus Christ. For Mina, the text emphasizes the principle that in the midst of the problems and difficulties of life God is able to give strength and stamina to the faint-hearted. These Pentecostal readers have identified their experiences of prayer and silence in the text of Isa 40 without regard to the historical and literary context of the passage.

These dynamic readings of *Isaiah* highlight the use of the text by Pentecostal readers as a symbol for their experience or current spiritual state.[39] The event or experience presented in the text resonates with the experience of the Pentecostal reader in that particular stage—whether individually or corporately. In this way the meaning is not found exclusively in the significance of the historical event but also in the spiritual insight that the symbolic event reveals concerning the Pentecostal reader's own situation. As Coulter asserts, "Insight into the text does not depend solely upon historical exegesis of the original meaning and authorial intention, but on the meaning consigned to the text as it is experienced through the Holy Spirit."[40] The Pentecostal reader recognizes in the event or experience of the text a similarity or resonance with their own present experience which they can appropriate for themselves. The "pay off" for such an appropriation may include comfort for the reader in the similarity of experience; a new direction which the symbolic text reveals through the example of the historical situation; or, new insights into the reader's own personal development. This reading act divorces the event in the text from its historical-cultural context which is no longer exclusively necessary for the creation of meaning.

38. See Appendix 1, Ref CA.

39. Coulter, "What Meaneth This?" 56.

40. Ibid., 57.

THE DYNAMIC READING EXPERIENCE

The dynamic reading experience of the Pentecostal community presents the opportunity to encounter God in the text event. This is both the beginning and ending point of a Pentecostal reading approach. The Pentecostal reader begins with their experience of encountering God, or experience in Christian living. The pneumatic experience of the Pentecostal community includes not only a revelation of the nature or character of God, but includes a transformation of the self through the spiritual experience.[41] The Pentecostal reading experience is made relational and dynamic through the reader's desire to meet with the divine "author" and be transformed through encounter. Pentecostals bring a presupposition of spiritual experience to their reading of the text. They then look for resonances between the text and previous personal experiences of divine encounter.[42] The text helps verbalize their pneumatic experience through its imagery, experience or events. Pentecostal readers recognize something of their own lives in the text. As Evans notes (commenting on the reading methods employed by the early church), "The community's experiences are found in Scripture and, at the same time, Scripture explains more fully to the community its experience."[43]

Since the Pentecostal community (by definition) espouses an experience that borders on the ineffable,[44] the adoption of biblical language is necessary to verbalize this experience. Encountering God is also the end point of the reading experience as the Pentecostal community anticipates transformation and renewal from the encounter. The insight drawn from the text does not depend on the historical context or authorial intention, but on the meaning consigned to the text as it is revealed through the Holy Spirit.[45] As Bridges-Johns and Johns write, "the study of Scripture must always be approached as sacred encounter with God."[46] However it is not just the experience of the individual that influences their reading, but also the expectation and tradition of the Pentecostal community. In reading the Old Testament out of the "Pentecost experience," it is the worldview of the Pentecostal community as the newer covenant people of God (rather than the older covenant Scripture) that provides the parameters for understanding and experiencing the text. The book of *Isaiah* is re-interpreted by the Pentecostal community

41. While this concept of "experience" is encapsulated in the doctrine of Spirit baptism, it is not exclusive to it. This is reflected in the writings of Coulter who asserts, "Spirit baptism came to symbolize an experience or encounter with the divine that had radical implications for the individual Pentecostal. Although a Lukan construct, for Pentecostals it came to embody more than its Lukan meaning, pointing to a fundamental transformation of self through a spiritual experience" (ibid., 42).

42. This concept does raise important questions for the PC community which are beyond the range of this study. For example, if a PC value is to "experience God," in the contemporary cultural setting of postmodernism, what does "God" when they speak of encountering the "postmodern God"? What is the "desire" that energises this quest mean? Questions raised by Caputo and Wyschogrod in their *Cross Currents* exchange. See Caputo and Wyschogrod, "Postmodernism and the Desire for God," 293.

43. Evans, *To See and Not Perceive*. 14.

44. Coulter, "What Meaneth This?" 46.

45. Ibid., 57.

46. Bridges-Johns and Johns, "Yielding to the Spirit," 118.

for the purpose of shaping Christian identity and behavior as a means for community transformation rather than an end in itself.[47]

While the Pentecostal reader brings their pneumatic experience to the reading of the text, they also acknowledge the role of the text in personal transformation. The dynamic nature of the Pentecostal readings include both an inductive (experience read into the text from community's expectations) and deductive (experience read from the text) text encounter. The Pentecostal readings appreciate the transformative power of the text, as the experience of the reader and text interact. Pentecostal readers are not just interested in understanding, but in action and change resulting from their reading experience. As Arrington notes, "experience informs the process of interpretation and the fruit of interpretation informs experience. So Pentecostals admit that their praxis informs what they find in Scripture, and they go on to acknowledge that what they find in Scripture informs their Pentecostal praxis."[48] In this sense, the Pentecostal readings represent a continual cycle (or spiral) as the experience (and desire for experience) drives the reading and the reading drives the experience. The determining of what came first: the Pentecostal experience or reading is as mysterious as the question of the proverbial chicken or the egg. It can only be recognized that there is a dynamic interaction between the individual experience, corporate worldview and the text within the process of reading. According to Arrington, "We cannot deny that anyone with sufficient rational faculties and skills can glean truths from Scripture, but for Pentecostals real understanding and insight into the truths of Scripture come as a result of faith. They assume that the spiritual and extraordinary experiences of the biblical characters are possible for contemporary believers and that the Scripture can only be interpreted correctly through the eyes of faith."[49] The dynamic of the reading experience is the desire of pneumatic experience identified in the text; it resonates with the Pentecostal experience informing the lives of the Pentecostal reader.

The text not only resonates with the Pentecostal experience but potentially transforms the reader as it indicates to them what choices and actions, such as "waiting on the Lord," are "typical" (or rather "topological") of a personal journey of faith.[50] As they "wait on the Lord," and hear direction from the Lord, the Pentecostal reader is guided in their journey of faith and decision-making in life. While the experience of the reader resonates with the symbol of the text and the worldview that symbol points to, the symbol of the text also questions or challenges their theological worldview and experience. This reverses the trajectory of the reading process as the Pentecostal readers allow the principles identified in the symbol of the text to "read" their own experience. For example, the universal assumption of the importance of maturation in the Christian life "reads" the life experience of the Pentecostal reader to challenge them with the necessity of maturity. Whether the reader has experienced this maturation process or not, the text of Isa 25:6

47. This is, in a sense, consistent with the nature of prophetic writings which points beyond itself to invite other uses of the text.

48. Arrington, "The Use of the Bible by Pentecostals," 106.

49. Ibid., 105.

50. Coulter, "What Meaneth This?" 59–60.

presents through the symbol of the mature wine the need for development in Christian understanding and practice.

This process of revelation is often described by the Pentecostal community as a "rhema" word. It is a terminology based on a proposed Greek differentiation between a "logos" (a general or distant word) and a "rhema" (an immediate or personal word) statement. The "rhema" word highlights the expectation among the Pentecostal reading community that the text will "speak" to and transform the reader. Describing this process of reading, Clark asserts, "Divine knowledge of both God and the legitimate meaning of the Bible are thus received by revelation, not by disciplined and critical perusal of the Scriptures."[51] Clark identifies the concept of a "rhema" word specifically with the "Word of Faith" movement as a subgroup within global Pentecostalism.[52] He describes their approach as a simplistic Biblicist method which takes verses out of their literary and historical context.[53] The danger with this approach, identified by Clark, is the dualism it creates in associating human reason and senses with the flesh (negative) and divine knowledge with the (spirit). He writes, "For this reason the words of the faith teachers are riddled with the phrase 'God/the Lord/Jesus told me . . .' What these leaders have received by revelation knowledge may not be rationally tested nor questioned."[54] While Clark highlights the excesses and extremes of the use of a "rhema" word in the wider Pentecostal community, its general use is far more innocuous. For many Pentecostal readers, the "rhema" word represents the moment of understanding spiritual truths. It is also often described colloquially as the "aha" moment of revelation; the Holy Spirit illuminates a truth which is highlighted from the reading or study of the biblical text.

An attempt to circumvent the Word-Faith construction and yet retain the core Pentecostal project can be seen in the term adopted by Pentecostal scholars Bridges-Johns and Johns: *yada'*. Developed from the Hebrew word, *yada'* represents knowing "more by heart than by mind." They describe it as a "knowing that arises not by standing back from in order to look at, but by active and intentional engagement in lived experience."[55] Again, it represents the revelatory knowledge of God and the reader's spiritual life through engagement with the biblical text as revealed by the Holy Spirit. Within this framework, understanding God is linked to encountering God, just as reading about and meeting a person represents two ways of gaining knowledge of that person. The Holy Spirit is the means of the encounter.[56] Where the reader is willing to test their revelation knowledge (i.e., meeting the person) and assimilate it responsibly into the theology of the Pentecostal community (i.e., reading about the person), the "rhema" word can be a useful description of the process of illumination. In this sense, the "rhema" word or revelation should represent more than just the illumination or understanding of

---

51. Clark, "An Investigation into the Nature of a Viable Pentecostal Hermeneutic," 68.

52. Clark notes that the "Word of Faith" movement is particularly associated with contemporary preachers such as Kenneth Copeland (U.S.) and Ray McCauley (South Africa).

53. Clark, "An Investigation into the Nature of a Viable Pentecostal Hermeneutic," 68.

54. Ibid., 68.

55. Bridges-Johns and Johns, "Yielding to the Spirit," 112.

56. Ibid., 119.

a particular truth—it is the reshaping of the worldview and identity of the reader. This process and event, which constitutes "revelation," is described by narrative theologian Stroup[57] through the image of the veil, a metaphor not exclusive to Isaiah 25. "Revelation" is defined by Stroup as an "unveiling."[58] He describes it as "an event in which a veil is dropped or removed, an event in which that which is masked or hidden from view is disclosed and made known . . . in which existing realities previously beyond the reach of human knowledge become accessible and knowable."[59] Pentecostal readers encapsulate the unveiling of reality in this concept of "rhema."

It is interesting to note that the verses which seem to "speak" to Pentecostal readers most clearly, are those which are dominated by poetic imagery.[60] This observation points to the analogical process inherent to Pentecostal hermeneutics. Pentecostal readers understand a spiritual truth from their experience of Christian living, or encounter with God, and in seeking to verbalize that truth, turn to the imagery of the biblical text. The Pentecostal reader verbalizes their world through these biblical categories and images. Through these (new) categories, adopted from the Bible, they can understand and interpret their past, present and future. It makes their experience of God and Christian life coherent by explaining it in terms of *another*.[61] As Lakoff and Johnson write, "Because so many of the concepts that are important to us are either abstract or not clearly delineated in our experience (the emotions, ideas, time, etc.), we need to get a grasp on them by means of other concepts that we understand in clearer terms (spatial orientations, objects, etc.). This need leads to metaphorical definitions in our conceptual system."[62] The very concept of a "rhema" word is an example of this process in the Pentecostal community. What began as the adoption of a metaphor (the Greek word "rhema") to describe an experience, has now become a key part of the Pentecostal conceptual system. Other metaphors and poetic images from the biblical text are adopted into the Pentecostal conceptual system to highlight the nature and emphases of the community.

The adoption of the image of the "veil" from Isa 25:6 by Pentecostal readers to understand their experience of spiritual warfare and Christian community is an example of this use of symbol. For Williams, for instance, the text provides a symbol to verbalize his own experience of spiritual oppression in missionary activity. Through the imagery, Williams can not only verbalize his experience, but also analyze it. The revelation of a

---

57. Stroup, *The Promise of Narrative Theology*.

58. Ibid., 42.

59. Ibid. In describing "revelation" as previously inaccessible knowledge now accessible and knowable, Stroup recognises that it is not an event that can be initiated by the human will (ibid., 43). He writes, "The person who experiences revelation is really only the passive object in this event and the disclosure is initiated by that which is disclosed" (ibid., 43). For further discussion on the theological debate regarding the nature and definition of "revelation" see Stroup (ibid., 39–68).

60. Paul, "Metaphor and Exegesis." As Dr. John Squires noted in personal correspondence, this tendency for poetic passages to "speak" more to Pentecostal/charismatic readers may be due to the explicitly open-ended, flexible nature of poetic writing that allows for interpretation to develop in a variety of directions. Because of this nature, Pentecostal/charismatic readers may feel more free to engage with poetic texts as opposed to narrative or legal texts which (allegedly) present as more prescriptive or fixed in nature.

61. Lakoff and Johnson, *Metaphors We Live By*, 117.

62. Ibid., 115.

"rhema" word in the Pentecostal community is often unveiled through the reading of an image or text as a symbol that represents a theological truth. As Lakoff and Johnson assert, "understanding our experiences in terms of objects and substances allows us to pick out parts of our experience and treat them as discreet entities or substances of a uniform kind. Once we can identify our experiences as entities or substances, we can refer to them, categories them, group them, and quantify them—and, by this means, reason about them."[63] By adopting symbolic language to describe and analyze their pneumatic experience, Pentecostal readers invite the possibility of transformation. The adoption of a symbol is the first step of conceptual abstraction necessary for the transformation or adaptation of the conceptual system it represents. It allows the exploration of the imagery, creating new realities and possibilities that guide future action.[64] For Williams, the adoption of the "veil" image creates new possibilities as he explores his difficulties with spiritual warfare; the symbol directs him to respond in prayer. The text promises the removal of the veil as he identifies his situation in the text. Since the text presents a future hope in the removal of the veil, so also does Williams' situation by extension anticipate the future removal of the veil at the eschatological salvation feast offered by Christ. In this way, the text directs the actions and possibilities of the situation.

The concept of a "veil" is similarly adopted by charismatic scholar, John McKay, to describe the contrast between reading the biblical text as a Spirit-filled Christian and as a person not filled with the Spirit. McKay adopts the analogy of Paul in 2 Cor 3:14–18, referring to the new insight and understanding with which the Bible is read as a believer, to emphasize the enabling of the Spirit in reading Scripture.[65] He writes, "Now charismatics commonly do speak of some disclosure experience similar to Paul's when they read the Bible after baptism in the Spirit. They tell of passages illuminated in new ways, of texts that take on new meaningfulness, of verses that burn themselves in the memory, of completely new appreciations of whole books of the Bible, of a positive urge to read page after page of the text, of exciting new discoveries about God's self-revelation in Scripture, and so forth."[66] Pentecostal readers experience the truth represented in the biblical text through self-involvement; entering its world through engagement with the story and imagery of the text. The initial adoption of the imagery by the Pentecostal reader appears to work against reason. Why does Williams adopt the image of the "veil"?

According to Gadamer, in art, truth is experienced through the work which asserts itself against all reasoning. Art has an abstract quality about it.[67] It is the abstract nature of the biblical language that allows the Pentecostal reader to resonate their experience with the text. For Williams, the lifting of the veil (in the world of the text) creates a new world of expectation for his own experience. However, it must be noted that this possibility is invited through the dynamic interaction of three elements: the text, Williams' experience and the Pentecostal worldview that anticipates the return of Christ and establishment

63. Ibid., 25.

64. Ibid., 156.

65. McKay, "When the Veil is Taken Away," 21.

66. Ibid., 21.

67. Gadamer, *Truth and Method*, xix.

of his kingdom in the eschaton. It is difficult to imagine that Williams would have been guided by the text through exploration of the imagery if the text described an unfavorable outcome such as the permanency of the veil. Because of its non-rational derivation, the adoption of symbolic language invites not only new possibilities of reading, but also new possibilities of inappropriate reading. This challenges the method of "understanding," as Gadamer points out. To understand what a person says is to agree about the object, not to get inside another person and relive their experiences.[68] Therefore, is the Pentecostal assimilation of the experience of the reader with the text a correct pathway to understanding? Can we even speak of a "correct" pathway to understanding? Is this common interest of Pentecostals and Hermeneutics threatened by this potentially problematic use of the biblical text?

PROBLEMATIC USE OF DYNAMIC READINGS

This value of "subjective" religious experience has caused scholars such as David Reed to suggest that Pentecostals have been more vulnerable to faulty interpretations, especially in comparison to the "objective" interpretations of the modernist offspring: historical criticism.[69] While it is this non-rational, subjective, revelatory nature of Pentecostal readings that makes it so dynamic and productive of the positive appropriation of Scripture, it is also problematic. It means that Pentecostal readers do not recognize any distance from the text. Pentecostal readers, as emphasized by the approaches above, tend to put themselves into the picture. By adopting the worldview of the text, they annihilate the distance between their own horizon and that of the text. According to Archer, this is because Pentecostal readers are praxis driven;[70] they look for applications, transformation, and practical action. This approach ignores the reality that language and texts are culturally embedded. Our Pentecostal source readings of Isaiah 25 and 40—explored above—tended to ignore the culture and historical location of the biblical text. Instead, they assumed a continuity of situation; a universality of truth presented in the ancient text. As Pentecostal scholar David Parker notes, "Memorable phrases such as 'to be or not to be,' are used in situations today totally different from how *Hamlet* used them. The Bible becomes the equivalent of Shakespeare's great classic and some sentences meaningful to me *now* bear no resemblance to what they originally meant when written some thousands of years ago."[71] For Pentecostal readers, discovering the original intention of the author or the historical context is subordinate to the significance of the text to the contemporary reader. This issue is not whether the tools of critical scholarship are bankrupt, but as Stroup suggests, whether they can be expected to disclose the full richness and depth of meaning in a text.[72] While the experiences presented in the biblical text

68. Ibid., 345.

69. Archer, "Early Pentecostal Biblical Interpretation," 41.

70. Ibid., 43.

71. Parker, "Studies in Pentecostal Bible Reading," 13. This highlights for us the rootedness of PCs in their own culture, a culture which through its canonization of both Shakespeare and Scripture have made both transparently available to a pragmatic culture.

72. Stroup, *The Promise of Narrative Theology,* 29.

are unique and unrepeatable *in se* (e.g., Isaiah 6), for the Pentecostal reader the person experienced in the text (God) can be encountered and re-experienced by others.

Context is important as the biblical text is produced within a specific cultural framework, and therefore must be understood as a product of that framework. For scholars such as Klein, Blomberg, and Hubbard, a text without a context can be a pretext.[73] Klein *et al.* warns against the dangers of proof-texting—a process that quotes a biblical passage "to prove a doctrine or standard for Christian living without regard for the literary context."[74] They write, "There is nothing wrong with quoting verses to prove a point provided we understand them according to their contextual meaning (under the correct circumstances proof-texting can be valid) . . . Otherwise the text is only a pretext, a passage that seems on the surface to prove some belief but in actuality does not. Such a pretext carries no divine authority."[75] While Pentecostal readers need to recognize the historical context of the text, it is not sufficient to then simply read themselves into that context (Biblicism), but to recognize a "proper" separation. This is what Gadamer calls the "horizons" of the text. He writes, "Understanding of the past, then, undoubtedly requires an historical horizon. But it is not the case that we acquire this horizon by placing ourselves within a historical situation. Rather, we must always already have a horizon in order to be able to place ourselves within a situation."[76] The task of reading for the Pentecostal community is not to abandon their own horizon in favor of the horizon of the text. The worldview(s) of the biblical writers are so fundamentally different to that of the contemporary Western reader that to simply adopt their worldview or transpose the reader's own location onto the text without recognizing the shifts in culture is to be ignorant of the reader's own identity.[77]

If Pentecostal readers do not consider the text on its own terms (culturally and historically) then "a premature fusion of horizons" will occur.[78] This means the reader will have fused their world with the world of the text without respect for the tension between the horizons of the text and the horizon of the reader. The textual horizon will have collapsed into that of the reader's own narrative biography, and is unable to do more than speak back his or her own values and desires.[79] This location of meaning solely on the significance of the text for the individual reader can result in idolatry. Readers can project their own interests, desire, and selfhood onto that which the biblical text proclaims. The text then no longer act as an independent authority, nor does it challenge the reader with prophetic integrity but simply mirrors the reader's own assumptions or misassumptions. Thereby Pentecostal readers can unsuspectingly re-create the text (and God) in their own image.[80] In this way, they can use the text to justify their own ideas,

73. Klein et al., *Introduction to Biblical Interpretation*, 160.

74. Ibid., 160.

75. Ibid., 160–61.

76. Gadamer, *Truth and Method*, 271.

77. Ellington, "Story, and Testimony," 245.

78. Thistleton, *New Horizons in Hermeneutics*, 530.

79. Ibid.

80. Ibid.

concepts, and theology. Pentecostal readers can avoid this "affective fallacy" (whereby meaning lies in the affect of the work upon the reader) by reaffirming the historical-cultural distance between their own horizon and the horizon of the text. This recognizes that the meaning the reader brings to the text may not be reminiscent of the cultural and historical assumptions attached to the words or symbols of the text.

However, the seemingly objective nature of that task, and its association with critical research of historical-critical methods, actually militates against the Pentecostal community adopting this approach. As Gadamer highlights, "The implied prerequisite of the historical method, then, is that the permanent significance of something can first be known objectively only when it belongs within a self-contained context. In other words, when it is dead enough to have only historical interest."[81] This presents a fundamental dilemma for the Pentecostal reader. They do not have a solely historical interest in Scripture, nor do they understand the Bible to be objectively "dead." The Pentecostal readings of *Isaiah* highlight their dynamic and subjective nature. In common with the pietist traditions, from which they spring, Pentecostals tend to delimit the claims of science and western (modern) rationality. The examples of Pentecostal readings explored above demonstrate that they are not objective but influenced by the "horizon" of the knower. By using the text as a symbol separate from the historical and cultural context of the passage, these Pentecostal readings invite multiple readings of the text. The acontextual readings of Isa 25:6 (as above) demonstrate a dynamic ability to create multiple perspectives; the "feast" of the Isaian text resonates with the experience of the Holy Spirit, salvation and the ritual of communion for the Pentecostal readers. As Israel, Albrecht and McNally assert, "the focus of hermeneutics is not what the author intended, but what the text-explained in terms of linguistic science-claims about the world and the appropriation of the message of the text by the interpreter in the direction of the text itself. The text points to a world, the interpreter orients himself or herself toward the claim of the text and that is where appropriation takes place."[82] Similarly, for Ricoeur, the text's meaning is not limited to that which was intended by its author. He terms this process "exteriorization" and concludes that, "what the text means now matters more than what the author meant when he [or she] wrote it."[83] Pentecostal readers do not ask what the text "meant," but what it "means."[84] In this way, their interest is in the world the text points to; the text as a signpost to truth about God and the world in which the Pentecostal community operates.

THE READING EVENT AS SYMBOL IN PENTECOSTAL READINGS

Acontextual readings among the Pentecostal community draw continuities between the events in the text and the life or experience of the believer. As Coulter writes, "The historical event can become a symbol for the spiritual life in which the individual gains

---

81. Gadamer, *Truth and Method,* 265.

82. Israel, et al., "Pentecostals and Hermeneutics," 143.

83. Ricoeur, *Essays on Biblical Interpretations,* 30.

84. As Croatto notes, to lay claim to fixing the meaning of the Bible once and for all at the moment of its production is to deny its open meaning (Croatto, *Biblical Hermeneutics,* 68).

knowledge of self. As the Spirit reveals how the text symbolizes the persons life at a particular stage, new insights and direction result."[85] The biblical passage in Pentecostal readings, albeit acontextual, serves as a symbol for the reader.[86] The symbol (text) acts as a sign that points to God's interaction with and laws governing the world. The Pentecostal reader identifies in this symbol a particular universal truth or experience. The specific historical event or experience in the text points to a universal truth or worldview that the Pentecostal reader identifies within their own experience or worldview. Again, this approach highlights the aim of a Pentecostal reading. The Pentecostal reader does not approach the text for "information," but to encounter or gain understanding of God, and consequently gain understanding of their interaction with God in the world. The meaning of the text is found in the revelation of God and of the human condition, rather than in historical information.

In such readings, the text as symbol (within its event or experience) points to a universal truth.[87] The text is identified as a symbol rather than a principle which is knowledge orientated. Instead, the text as symbol may represent an experience, principle, emotion, theme, concept, metaphor, or word with which the Pentecostal reader connects and resonates. The symbol points to a principle or universal truth that informs the theology or worldview of the Pentecostal reader (and ultimately, community). As Ricoeur points out, a text is not self-referential; it points to something.[88] A semiotic envisioning of the relationship can be described by the following diagram:

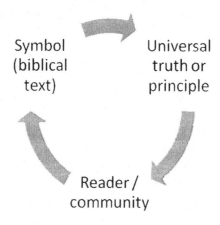

DIAGRAM 1: Text as Symbol

---

85. Coulter, "What Meaneth This?," 60.

86. The symbolic use of the text by PC readers to "point" or refer to a truth outside of its textual world disqualifies the PC reading from being classified under a reader-response approach. As Baker asserts, "Iser views the text as non-referential, in the sense that it does not refer to a hidden meaning" (Baker, "Pentecostal Bible Reading," 47).

87. Droogers, "The Normalization of Religious Experience: Healing, Prophecy, Dreams, and Visions," 46. Droogers notes the use of metonym by Pentecostals to express the totality of experience. In this way, the partial experience of the single subject stands for the immeasurable totality of God's omnipresence.

88. Israel, et al. "Pentecostals and Hermeneutics," 141.

The acontextual readings of the Pentecostal community are thus dynamic and creative, but not illogical. The symbol connects the reality of the reader with the universal truth that the text represents. The symbol provides a model of God's dealings with the world for the Pentecostal reader to connect to their own experience. The Pentecostal experience is understood in the light of God's consistent actions in the world (the Pentecostal worldview assumes consistency) as represented by the biblical texts. These Pentecostal readings discover the universal through the reading of the particular.[89] The role of the imagination is crucial in this process. The imagination, according to Stroup, provides the images that the Pentecostal community uses to bring order and meaning to their experience.[90]

The text becomes a symbol through the mental association of the reader (through their own experience)[91] with the worldview presented in the text. The reader connects the symbol with meaning (universal truth) through the mental association of their recognition of that truth in their lives.[92] For example, Isa 25:6–7 becomes a symbol for Jim Williams to understand his experience of spiritual blindness in the face of (and lack of pragmatic impact) and resistance to the gospel of Christ by unbelievers. The text functions as a symbol as it connects the experience of the reader with the principles or truths of Scripture. The "universal truths" symbolized by this text are diverse: the spiritual forces at war (Williams); the process and need for maturation (MacKenzie) as represented in the mature wine; the need for intimacy in relationship with God is also represented by the symbol of wine (Mead). The adoption of symbols creates a shared world of experience—although the circumstances might be different, the wider "message" or principles the biblical text demonstrates is trans-cultural and trans-historical for the Pentecostal reader. Speaking of the hermeneutical thought of Gadamer and Ricoeur, the authors Israel, Albrecht and McNally write:

> In this model of hermeneutics, texts are understood as autonomous entities which make a claim about the world. The focus of the hermeneutical task is not to delve into the subjectivity of the author, but to *explain* the structural relations and sets of meanings contained in the language of a text and *understand* the claims which the text is making about the world. Understanding here is equivalent to a reve-

---

89. As Roelofs writes, Pentecostal readers "understand their experience of the world to be permeated by divine power. Therefore, they are convinced that their religious language mirrors concrete things" (Roelofs, "Charismatic Christian Thought: Experience, Metonymy, and Routinization," 226).

90. Stroup, *The Promise of Narrative Theology,* 64. Stroup continues his discussion by noting that while in the revelatory event certain images, sparked by the imagination take on an illuminative power, it becomes the task of reason to make sense of what is happening. However, while the imagination provides reason with images by which it can make search the past and examine the present, it does not guarantee that these are the right or appropriate images (ibid., 65). Stroup writes, "The imagination is as susceptible to the powers of evil as is reason" (ibid., 65). Stroup adopts Niebuhr's criteria for distinguishing between a true and false imagination as teleological-imaginations are shown to be evil by their consequences to selves and communities (ibid., 65).

91. It is interesting at this point to note that Albrecht identifies Pentecostal experience with the "rich heritage of Christian mysticism" in which a person has a direct intuition or experience of God (Albrecht, *Rites in the Spirit,* 239).

92. Kristeva, *The Kristeva Reader,* 64.

lation—not in a technical sense—of new insight about the world and oneself. In understanding a text, one does not achieve absolute knowledge of another person; namely, the text's author. Rather, one achieves new insight about his or her own world which opens up new possibilities for living.[93]

This process requires personal engagement with the text—each reader must individually resonate with the text. The results are presented as testimonies or the transmission of the wider principle to which the symbol points.

In semiotics, symbols refer back to one or more unknowable and un-representable universal transcendence(s).[94] For Pentecostal readers, the universal is expressed as the principle of the particular text, which the Pentecostal reader identifies through their own experience (whether that is experience of the principle or lack of experience). The interpreter connects the symbol with its meaning (universal) through the mental association of their experience with the symbol (principle). The event or symbol of the text refers to one or more transcendent truths that correlates with the experience of the reader or challenges their worldview.[95] The symbol from the text illuminates the experience of the reader and makes that experience intelligible;[96] Williams' experience of unsuccessful evangelism is illuminated by the symbol of the "veil" from the text that is identified as a spiritual veil covering the nation. These symbols provide the descriptive language through which the Pentecostal experiences of God (in the text and world) may be interpreted. The symbol induces meaning into the experience. The symbol helps the reader to verbalize their own experience as they see the essence or meaning of their experience reflected in the worldview (or greater principle) of the text. The symbol also provides the vocabulary and imagery for the reader to share their experience. As Avis asserts, "Each image carries with it a host of associations which interact and fertilize each other. Metaphor is not just naming one thing in terms of another, but seeing, experiencing and intellectualizing one thing in the light of another."[97] The symbol provides a common vocabulary with which the community may verbalize their experience. However it must also be recognized that symbols are limited. While they point to an external truth, they do not fully capture either the numinous *or* the experience of the reader. For example, the experience of the Pentecostal readers is explicitly Christian, so the text as a symbol is constrained by this experience of Christian salvation and post-Pentecost

93. Israel, et al. "Pentecostals and Hermeneutics," 138.

94. As Israel, Albrecht and McNally note, "Structuralism can clarify how a text operates, how it functions, but provides no help in understanding or grappling with what the text is about" (ibid., 141). However while the discussion of symbols and metaphors can assist in defining PC reading approaches, it is important to maintain the dynamic nature of its outcome in the discussion of the process. This is affirmed by Ian Paul who writes, "If metaphorical discourse does have the power to engage and transform, analysis of how and why it does this must not be allowed to rob it of the very power that makes it so important" (Paul, "Metaphor and Exegesis," 388).

95. For a discussion on the Pentecostal application of Barthes' concept of the reading of texts as an erotic activity that result in either pleasure (affirming presuppositions) or loss (challenging presuppositions), see Baker, "Pentecostal Bible Reading."

96. Stroup, *The Promise of Narrative Theology,* 62.

97. Avis, *God and the Creative Imagination,* 96–97.

charismatic experience even though the experience of the pre-Christian text *per se* does not reflect these events. Pentecostal readers bring their worldview into the text—reading it as Christians with a pneumatic experience. This does not deny the experience of the Spirit to other communities, but recognizes this as the expected and experienced way of hearing the spirit in the text by the Pentecostal community.

Symbols, like metaphors, create associations. Symbols make association with the text possible, but also allow for future different associations. Pentecostal readers recognize in their reading and experience the ongoing activity of God.[98] They consider themselves in continuity with the community of the text as God is continually active. Avis writes, "the symbols are permanent but the way they are interpreted is constantly evolving . . . the profoundly symbolic character of revelation constantly generates new insights in response to the contemplation of faith."[99] This use of symbols allows the Pentecostal reader to test various possibilities for their lives. They see from the example of the event or experience of the text an indication of what their own decisions or journey might yield. By verbalizing or describing the current Pentecostal experience, the symbol then orients the reader toward the future as they follow the logical conclusions of the text, which is "in-spired" to give birth to new perspectives and possibilities. According to Coulter, "the narrative of the text typifies or symbolizes the Pentecostal journey but it indicates to the Pentecostal what choices should be made in the journey."[100] By entering the world of the text, Pentecostal readers allow themselves to find their place within the text or story. From this place of engagement, their life can be re-shaped by the text.[101] According to feminist critic Lancaster, this is in fact true faithfulness to the text.[102] Therefore, the reading approach of the Pentecostal community is not a linear process, but a dynamic interaction between personal experience, the worldview of the reading community, and the text. The following diagram identifies the inter-relationship of the experience of location of the individual reader, the biblical text, and the value-system they have adopted as part of the Pentecostal community with its unique worldview.

---

98. The transportability of Pentecostalism is noted by Andrew Walls who links it with the ability of the Pentecostals community to translate biblical concepts into symbols which are then re-interpreted locally. In particular, see his work, Walls, *The Missionary Movement in Christian History*.

99. Avis, *God and the Creative Imagination*, 6.

100. Coulter, "What Meaneth This?" 60.

101. Lancaster, *Women and the Authority of Scripture*, 34.

102. Ibid.

Symbol

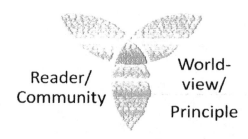

Reader/
Community

World-
view/

Principle

DIAGRAM 2: Inter-relationship of Pentecostal Hermeneutics

This portrays the signification of the biblical text to the Pentecostal reader as a dynamic interaction of personal experience, worldview (or principles identified as scripturally founded), and the text. The text informs the reader, as well as the reader informing the text. These elements are also informing and informed by the value system and worldview of the Pentecostal community in which the reader is placed.

From these Pentecostal readings, the text has a plurality of meanings because there is plurality of experience brought by the reader. However, as the examples from Isa 25:6 cited above suggest, the determination for identifying meaning within a text tends to lie with the reader's worldview (and Holy Spirit working within the reader in the community of faith) rather than in a re-constructed author or even the text itself. Of the examples from Isa 25:6, each of our subjects brought their own Pentecostal experience and tradition into the text and found a meaning that reflected their unique experience. The meaning of the text is produced by its contact with the experience of the reader. And yet, while the meanings presented in the three readings of Isa 25:6 reflect the uniqueness of their experience, it is an experience that resonates with the event or experience in the text. The reader could not bring *any* experience to the text—it had to be one that connected to or could be symbolized by the event in the text *in the mind of the reader*. Each text thus has a constrained plurality of meanings because there is plurality of experience. The acontextual readings of Isa 25:6 demonstrate a dynamic ability to create multiple perspectives; the "feast" of the Isaian text resonates with the experience of the Holy Spirit, salvation and the ritual of communion for the Pentecostal readers. By focusing on the text as a symbol rather than historical-cultural context or authorial intention, the description of Pentecostal readings of *Isaiah* challenges the debate between Pentecostal scholars of the appropriateness of external models of hermeneutics, such as evangelical or postmodern. As Melugin suggests, to try to interpret it only in its ancient contexts would be to fail to use it as Scripture as it is a denial of its transformational intent.[103]

103. Melugin, "Texts to Transform Life: Reading Isaiah as Christians," 115.

The use of text-as-symbol both emphasizes and blurs the distinction of the two horizons of the text. According to Hirsch, "*Meaning* is that which is represented by a text; it is what the author meant by his use of a particular sign sequence; it is what the signs represent. *Significance*, on the other hand, names a relationship between that meaning and a person, or a conception, or a situation, or indeed anything imaginable."[104] Applying these categories to the Pentecostal readings of Isa 25:6, the readings would not be multiple *meanings* but would represent multiple significances. Such an application of Hirsch's categories questions the authoritative role of the Holy Spirit in interpreting biblical texts. The assumption for evangelicals such as Hirsch is that the Holy Spirit has inspired the original author but not necessarily the interpretation. This divorces the Holy Spirit's activity and authority from the interpretative process—a concept Pentecostal readers would be reluctant to accept. However, also inherent within the reading practices of the Pentecostal community is a tendency to present multiple perspectives that appear to have separate meanings. Whether meanings divorced from authorial intention, such as these acontextual Pentecostal readings, are "correct" does not negate their potential existence.

The adoption of this modernist evangelical paradigm (as exemplified by Hirsch) by some Pentecostal scholars (particularly North American Pentecostal scholars such as Menzies) has led to their denial of the recognition of some reading practices of the Pentecostal community. Instead they label any variation as "multiple applications" rather than "multiple meanings" in order to sustain their rejection of postmodern hermeneutics. However, as the examples from Isa 25:6 cited above suggest, the locus for identifying meaning within a text tends to lie with the reader (and Holy Spirit working within the reader) rather than a re-constructed author or even the text itself. Of the three examples noted for Isa 25:6, each reader brought their own Pentecostal experience and tradition into the text and found a meaning that reflected their unique experience. And yet, while the meanings presented in the three readings reflected the uniqueness of the reader's experience, it was an experience that resonated with the event or experience in the text. The reader could not bring any experience to the text—it had to be one that connected to or could be symbolized by the event in the text. Still, it must be questioned: if the tendency of Pentecostal readings to use the text as a symbol in their acontextual readings results in multiple meanings of a passage does this make Pentecostal readings postmodern?

DO MULTIPLE MEANINGS IMPLY A POSTMODERN READING?

There is a growing consensus that, rather than being simply a reaction to the scientific paradigm of the Modern worldview (such seen in postmodernism) the Pentecostal community reflects an alternative worldview. Apart from early classical Pentecostal attempts to engage the Modern scientific worldview using the methods and language of that paradigm (such as the inductive evidentialism in portraying speaking in tongues as the "initial evidence" of baptism in the Spirit)[105] Pentecostalism and the Charismatic movement

---

104. Hirsch, *Validity in Interpretation* 8 [italics author's own].

105. This is exemplified by studies such as Macchia, whose article "Groans Too Deep for Words: Towards

have mostly attempted to exist outside and remain distinct from the scientific paradigm of the Modern world. However the emergence of a postmodern paradigm and the destabilization of the scientific presupposition of Modernism offers Pentecostal scholars an opportunity to connect with the wider cultural mood. According to Johns, Pentecostal scholars must look to their origins to determine their role within and engagement with postmodernity. As he notes, "Pentecostalism was born outside of the dominant theological visions of the Christian world: nineteenth-century liberalism and reactionary fundamentalism."[106] Johns continues to surmise that because of its origins and emphases, Pentecostalism is not the product of a scientific paradigm, and so must be considered outside the domain of this nineteenth century scientific paradigm or worldview. A corollary of this argument is that Pentecostalism must also remain outside the product of self-critical Modernism; postmodernism. In this sense, Bridges-Johns identifies the Pentecostal worldview not as postmodern but as "para-modern,"[107] or perhaps "counter-modern" is a more relative term proper to the historical relations of the developments.[108]

While separate to the Pentecostal worldview, Bridges-Johns identifies postmodernism (particularly Deconstruction) as an appropriate tool for Pentecostal scholars to use in their critique of dominant Modernist ideologies. According to Bridges-Johns, Deconstruction and Pentecostalism "are consummatory, apocalyptic movements which dismantle the 'cathedral of modern intellect' and mock all forms of anthropological reductionism. Both movements mock the modernist conceit that humanity can construct a liveable habitation utilizing the skill of rational analysis and problem solving."[109] Among their shared armamentarium is a common rejection of the modern myth of objectivity where the modern myth of a neutral interpreter is rejected by both.

Many postmodern methods, (in particular feminist criticism) highlight the subjectivity of readers and readings. No reader is objective; each reader brings their own presuppositions to the text and reads the text through their own biases. The experience of baptism or empowerment of the Spirit is the self-identified bias of Pentecostal readers. Pentecostal readers do not limit "truth" to the realm of reason or objective knowledge. Truth also includes affection and behavior as well as cognition,[110] elements bonded together by the revelatory work of the Spirit. As Archer writes, "The truthfulness of Scripture was discovered relationally and experientially, rather than 'scientifically.'"[111] The Holy Spirit, active in both the spiritual and material realms, illuminates the affections, mind, will, and body of the reader in a meaningful encounter with the biblical text. It leads to an expectation of a holistic encounter between the Spirit and the reader when engaging with Scripture.

---

a Theology of Tongues as Initial Evidence" attempts to create a justification for "tongues" through a scientific paradigm representative of the modernist agenda.

106. Johns, "Pentecostalism and the Postmodern Worldview," 84.

107. Bridges-Johns, *Pentecostal Formation*, 47.

108. My thanks to Mark Hutchinson for this insight.

109. Quoted in Archer, "Early Pentecostal Biblical Interpretation," 40.

110. Johns, "Pentecostalism and the Postmodern Worldview," 89.

111. Archer, "Early Pentecostal Biblical Interpretation," 41.

Pentecostal readings presuppose, with postmodernity, both the subjectivity of the reader and the notion that the text is autonomous and its meaning multivocal. The same text is used to support various readings and meanings, demonstrating the importance of the "horizon" of the reader in determining the meaning and significance of the text. Both groups reject the Modernist myth of "objectivity," recognizing instead a valid subjectivity. The concept of the neutral interpreter is a myth as all readers bring their own presuppositions and worldview to the text. The Pentecostal community embraces a more holistic approach in their recognition of the subjectivity of the reader.[112] As Baker suggests, the focus on "objective" readings denies the role of the reader in the text and robs it of its transformational power. He writes, "By committing to read the text objectively from a critical distance, the professional reader subverts the text's evocative power or is at least unable to express the feeling that the text evokes in him or her."[113] However, it is not just the production of multiple meanings that identifies Pentecostal readings with postmodern theories, but also the focus on the role of the reading community. The role of the reader is important in Pentecostal readings-this includes not only the individual reader, but the role of the community in the formation of the meanings of biblical texts.

While different readers will "feel" differently when reading the same text-and even the same reader may feel differently in successive readings,[114] it is the community that guides the formation of meaning. As Lancaster writes, "even though the possible interpretations are endless, a community makes decisions about what to read and how to read it."[115] There is a communal consensus, based on the Pentecostal worldview and theology, evident in Pentecostal readings that determine the boundaries of meaning of a text. These boundaries are acquired through the practice and tradition of the community. It is the "sensus communis," the (shared) common sense of Pentecostal readers that provides the structures and aims of its readings; following the original Roman idea, rather than the later derivation that was essentially *sensus communis*, a form of corrective.[116] For example, while the concept of "waiting on the Lord" from Isa 40 may *mean* different things within the Pentecostal community there is a boundary of possible interpretations. Waiting on the Lord, for instance, would not be expected to refer to intercession to Mary or transcendental meditation. Tanner asserts, "The text appears to have an obvious meaning to the community because the community has tacitly agreed on what that meaning should be."[117] There is a sense that—as well as "this is that"—in other settings: "this is definitely anything but *that*." For the Pentecostal community, that includes their role as a

---

112. Ibid., 38.

113. Baker, "Pentecostal Bible Reading," 35.

114. Ibid., 37.

115. Lancaster, *Women and the Authority of Scripture,* 28. Writing from a more sociological perspective, Droogers notes that experience is shaped by the culture in which it occurs. He writes, "Experience can, therefore, never exist without a cultural framework, and contextualized religious experience can never be isolated from total experience" (Droogers, "The Normalization of Religious Experience," 40). For the Pentecostal reader, it is the Pentecostal community that provides the cultural framework of 'normative' experience.

116. Gadamer, *Truth and Method*, 22.

117. Tanner, "The Bible as a popular text," 32.

prophetic voice to both to the wider community they are trying to reach through evangelism, and the Christian community with whom they share their experience of pneumatic encounter. Both the Pentecostal community and postmodernity identify themselves as prophetic voices, speaking from the fringes of society to challenge the dominant ideologies and previously accepted fallacies. Pentecostalism, from its origins in the Holiness movement of the late nineteenth century, has existed on the fringes of global societies as an expression of counter-culture.[118] Likewise, the charismatic movement among mainstream Australian denominations has generally existed on the fringes of its denominational culture, usually as a loose (and mostly unofficial) network of associated communities. For the Pentecostal community, their prophetic voice is motivated by their evangelistic and renovating mission; for the postmodern community, their prophetic voice is motivated by ethical concerns.

It is this experiential emphasis of Pentecostal community that both links the Pentecostal worldview with the postmodern paradigm and distances it. At the centre of the Pentecostal worldview is the affective experience of God, which generates an apocalyptic horizon for reading reality.[119] For the Pentecostal community, Scripture provides the authoritative description of reality through which Pentecostal readers can understand their own experience. Isaiah 25:6, as symbol, describes equally the core Pentecostal realities of spiritual battle (Williams), maturation and transformation (McKenzie), and desire for intimacy (Mead). Yet, for each of these readers, the biblical text is the authoritative witness to the character and activity of God, which the Pentecostal community attempts to promote. The Pentecostal community upholds the universality of the "truth" found in the Bible. It is essential for Pentecostal readings to communicate this sense of truth and incorporate this reality in their practical application of the text. Unlike postmodernism, the purpose of their reading is not to *deconstruct*,[120] but to *construct* their worldview based on those principles from the biblical text which they have elucidated from their reading. While Pentecostal readers may identify a number of truths in a biblical text, the multiplicity of meanings does not negate the veracity of the various readings or their significance within the Pentecostal worldview.

The use of symbols and images is generated by the drive to understand and articulate the truth identified in the biblical text through the reading event. Pentecostal readings are more than intellectualizing or abstract theory, but are ways of articulating experience and aiding transformation. The biblical text becomes a symbol that points to a principle or truth. In contrast, the postmodern notion of "truth" is more fluid. As Avis asserts, "In postmodernity everything has the potential to become a symbol, but nothing is a symbol of the transcendent. Their pan-symbolism is purely immanent. Symbols, images, and myths interpret one another, interacting immanently, but none of them points

---

118. Johns, "Pentecostalism and the Postmodern Worldview," 85.

119. Ibid., 91.

120. The Pentecostal community does not seek to deconstruct the text in the sense that while they may "pull apart" the text they do not leave their readings open-ended. Instead they pragmatically use it to construct a theology or symbolic universe which points to the character or actions of God.

beyond the symbolic realm. They do not symbolize a reality in which they participate."[121] For the Pentecostal reader, the symbol points to the reality of God's operation in the created world. Therefore the dynamic quality of Pentecostal readings does not make it *postmodern*, even though there are resonances between the two movements.

However, while the Pentecostal reading approach cannot be consumed under the rubric of "postmodern," it can utilize some of the gains of postmodernity in its reading processes. Ideas that can be utilized by Pentecostal readers include the concept of suspicion to critique the self. Like any community, the Pentecostal community is not exempt from the potential for self-delusion. By inviting alternative methods such as the "hermeneutics of suspicion," Pentecostal readers can identify and challenge the unconscious elements of their readings and the various biases it represents. As Thistleton writes, "the nature of the reading-process is governed by horizons of expectation already pre-formed by the community of readers or by the individual. Preachers often draw from texts what they had already decided to say; congregations sometimes look to biblical readings only to affirm the community-identity and life-style which they already enjoy. The biblical writings, in such a situation become assimilated into the function of creeds: they become primarily institutional mechanisms to ensure continuity of corporate belief and identity."[122] The use of postmodern elements can confront the Pentecostal community with their pre-formed biases and comfortability with the biblical texts. Prejudices serve as "conditions of understanding" because the reader's pre-formed assumptions often are revealed in the act of reading.[123] However, while a hermeneutics of suspicion can be helpful, the Pentecostal community is generally critical of endless critique—at some time the process has to embed itself in a statement of belief. The pragmatic value of Pentecostalism will emphasize constructivism over reductionism. Yet, the embracing of tradition and community emphases, such as a dynamic reading approach and pragmatism, should not be used to serve the avoidance of criticism or the stifling of voices different from or outside the tradition.[124]

FROM PRINCIPLE TO PRACTICE

The reading approach of the Pentecostal community identified in the examples from *Isaiah* has a dynamic quality that emphasizes the immediacy and relevance of the text to the reader. The meaningfulness of the text to the immediate reader (as a member of the Pentecostal community) is an important feature of their reading method and should be incorporated into a Pentecostal model for reading the Old Testament. The recognition of the role of the reader in bringing meaning to the text is a crucial element in the development of a Pentecostal reading model. This role is identified through the use of the text as a symbol that points to principles concerning the nature of God as well as God's dealings with the world. In this way, the symbol connects the reality of the reader

121. Avis, *God and the Creative Imagination*, 26.

122. Thistleton, *New Horizons in Hermeneutics*, 8.

123. Gadamer, *Truth and Method*.

124. Moore, "Deuteronomy and the Fire of God," 20.

with a universal truth as represented by the text. This emphasizes the personal nature of the reading event for the Pentecostal community (which will be discussed in the next chapter); the text is alive with relevancy, comfort, and practical application. It is therefore important that the development of a Pentecostal reading model includes recognition of the role of the text as a symbol in the creation of meaning that is personally appropriated to the experience and situation of the individual reader. By using the text as a symbol the Pentecostal reader can identify the relevance of the text to their Christian walk and identify their experience in the text. The dynamic reading approach identified in the Pentecostal community is an important part of the Pentecostal worldview and tradition. However, as noted, the affirming of tradition should not be used to avoid self-critique.

While emphasizing the role and "horizon" of the reader,[125] the development of a Pentecostal model for reading should also incorporate recognition of the separation of the reader-horizon from the text-horizon. As David Parker notes, "The A.O.G. believes the Holy Spirit can use the sentences of the Bible to communicate numerous meanings to anyone. They also believe that the sentences of the Bible had a more specific meaning to the original recipients. It is this more specific meaning, we believe, that sets the boundaries for us today."[126] The identification of the two horizons (of reader and text) may be acknowledged in the *theory* of Pentecostal hermeneutics within the community, but not in their *practice*. The readings of *Isaiah* tend to focus on the significance of the text to the reader without consideration of the context. It presents a challenge to the Pentecostal community to incorporate this horizon into their reading practices and is a significant weakness in the Pentecostal reading practice that needs to be addressed. The historical context can be a means of providing a boundary for personal interpretation by the individual reader. As Wonsuk Ma suggests, "The Pentecostal tradition of participatory reading of Scripture does not have to be entirely reader-orientated. A properly guided historico-literary reading will not only serve as guidance but will also set parameters for 'affective' reading."[127]

This recognition of the historical distance would affirm the reality that the biblical text emerges from a specific historical and cultural context. Rather than dampen the dynamic quality of Pentecostal readings, this recognition can affirm the Pentecostal value of the immediacy of the text as it affirms the immanence of the divine voice in speaking to the people of God in a way that is culturally, linguistically and historically relevant. It would lengthen and deepen the "great narrative" in which Pentecostal readers find themselves as they construct their identities as "the people of God." As Childs notes of earlier allegorical approaches, "To substitute a theological context for the historical caused a major problem for the traditional allegorical approach. Nor does an exegesis which comes to the biblical text from a larger theological grasp of God's reality function

---

125. The issue of the role of the community in which the PC reader is located is discussed will be greater detail below, particularly in regards to the work of Lancaster (Lancaster, *Women and the Authority of Scripture*).

126. Parker, "Studies in Pentecostal Bible Reading," 14.

127. Ma, "Biblical Studies in the Pentecostal Tradition."

apart from the various other historical and literary readings."[128] The revelation of God comes to particular people at particular times and places in a way that is comprehensible to them. This resonates with the Pentecostal worldview of the consistent actions of God; if God can speak to the covenant people in a way relevant to them, God can also speak to the Pentecostal community with relevance and immediacy through the biblical text that will result in transformation and relationship. Therefore the dynamic quality of Pentecostal readings of the Old Testament should be affirmed in the prescription of a reading model without undermining the importance of its older covenant context.

128. Childs, *Biblical Theology of the Old and New Testaments*, 381.

6

When Pentecostalism and Hermeneutics Disagree

Tㅐᴇ ᴅʏɴᴀᴍɪᴄ ɴᴀᴛᴜʀᴇ ᴏꜰ the readings of Isaiah, highlighted in the previous chapter, demonstrate the tendency of the Pentecostal community towards literalist readings. While the conversation between the three dialogue partners of Pentecostalism, hermeneutics, and the Old Testament to this point has evidenced little disagreement, the observation of this inclination is a potential area of conflict within the discussion. The Pentecostal readers tend to appropriate the text according to the reader's own contemporary culture rather than consider its significance in the ancient culture. These readers have demonstrated a limited recognition of the cultural differences between the ancient context and the contemporary context. Instead, the Pentecostal readers were inclined to appropriate the text's imagery without recognizing the differences those images may have had in the original culture. Similarly, the historical veracity of the text is assumed by the Pentecostal reader regardless of the authorial and editorial cues in the text. For example, the Pentecostal readers (both pastor/ teachers and lay readers) generally assumed the eighth century prophet to be the author of the entire book, based on the reference to the name and date of the author in the first chapter (Isa 1:1) and an implicit tradition of interpretation. Within this framework, the eighth century prophet was identified as a forth-seer of the events relating to the Babylonian captivity and eventual restoration of Judah. This affirmation of authorship of the entire Isaiah corpus by the eighth century prophet is not just an issue of scriptural infallibility for the Pentecostal readers, but recognition of the ability of the Spirit to inspire prophetic activity. This literalist tendency highlights the identification of the Pentecostal community with the prophetic ministry of the Old and New Testament and the ability of God to reveal information, including information about future events, to those who seek understanding.

In this sense, Pentecostal readings have a propensity to be Biblicist; a quality associated with Fundamentalism. This is particularly represented in readings of Isaiah 54 and 61. As with the dynamic nature of Pentecostal readings, the literalization of the text questions the responsible use of scripture by Pentecostal readers. While this feature supports a dynamic approach (see the previous chapter) by flattening the text in preparation for symbolization, this comes at the cost of not recognizing the cultural context of the passage. However while the text can serve as a symbol for the reader in pointing to principles and truths consistent with the theological worldview of the Pentecostal community, the literalization of the text is less benign. It does not point to principles so much as it imposes contemporary meanings of words or concepts found in the biblical text onto the interpretation. Pentecostal readers can avoid such irresponsible eisegesis by reaffirming the cultural distance between their horizon and the horizon of the text. While, as Croatto notes, eisegesis is impossible to avoid (since all readers bring their presuppositions to the text)[1] the significance of the text to the original community helps provide boundaries of reasonable interpretation.

LITERALIST FEATURES IN PENTECOSTAL READINGS

The description of Jerusalem/Zion as a forsaken wife who is reclaimed in the marriage relationship, is the primary image presented throughout the passage of Isaiah 54. While the wife (representing Zion/Jerusalem) has been forsaken, she is now promised restoration. As Childs writes, "The exile is portrayed as but a brief moment of being forsaken, which is contrasted with the great gathering in compassion. God's momentary wrath stands opposed to an everlasting love."[2] Now, with enthusiastic exuberance, the new Jerusalem will be built with magnificent splendor. This recurring image and explicit reference to childlessness serves to highlight the irony of calling upon a barren woman, who is suffering the worst fate of her sex, to break into singing.[3] The woman portrayed is desolate, having been deprived of a husband's support and care; therefore completely without chance of future fruitfulness.[4] Baltzer notes the significance of the image of barrenness in the culture of the ancient Near East, "Barrenness is a hard fate in a society where a woman's dignity is bound up with children. Children, especially sons, guarantee the certainty of a legacy for the next generation. Since there is no social insurance, children are necessary as a provision for sickness and old age. Sons can appear for their mothers before a court of law. So when God enables the barren woman to become a mother, the miracle is of particular significance."[5] This image of barrenness is loaded with cultural implications significant to the older testament culture.

However it is not just the image of barrenness that is so culturally loaded within the text, but also the roles of wife and husband. Ackerman reminds readers at the same time, not to impose the egalitarian understandings of modern Western marriage relationships onto the ancient text. She writes, "That culture assigned authority within marriage to the

---

1. Conrad also notes that eisegesis is common to all readings. Every reading is a reading *into*. See Conrad, *Reading Isaiah*, 29.

2. Childs, *Isaiah*, 429.

3. Ibid., 428.

4. Motyer, *The Prophecy of Isaiah*, 445.

5. Baltzer, *Deutero-Isaiah*, 435.

male, including the prerogative of divorce (Deut 24:1–4). A husband, in this case God, was within his rights to abandon his wife without becoming subject to criticism within society."[6] The incongruity of this image in contrast to that of the contemporary wife is also noted by Goldingay. The general solution for a Western woman who has had her husband walk out on her today is to learn to be her own person. Similarly a husband who has left his wife in a fit of anger cannot, in the contemporary situation, simply assume that he can walk back in or expect his wife to accept his reassurances of future non-abusive behavior.[7] Instead the images within the Isaiah text presuppose a patriarchal understanding of marriage roles and relationship, consistent with the culture of the ancient Israelite community. However this incongruity between the culture of the text and the culture of the reader was seldom recognized by the Pentecostal readers.

For many Pentecostal readers, the song of the barren woman presents an image of comfort and encouragement to their immediate context. Ishbel Gunn[8] writes of the concept of God being a "husband" to the widow in an article entitled, "God Takes Special Care of Widows" in the 1984 Australian Evangel. She writes, "You may ask why I became interested in this subject, apart from the fact that I am a widow; well, shortly after I was widowed someone said to me that God is a husband to the widow and a father to the fatherless. I normally want to know Scripture and verse, but this time I took it as a promise to me, and that is exactly what He has been to me in every way."[9] Gunn continues in the article to testify of the varied ways that God has acted as a "husband" to her; from guiding her in money matters to keeping her vehicle free from malfunction. While Gunn was not aware of the Bible passage in which this principle was located, she experienced the concept in action throughout her daily life as a widow. She continues: "Then I got a little worried for I had earlier testified to many people that He is a husband to the widow, and I was guilty of mis-quoting Scripture. Then as I looked up and studied all the references, I thought I would also look up the word 'husband' where it refers to God. I found three references, one in the Old Testament and two in the New. Husband, as it occurs in Isa 54:5, means 'husband, Lord, master, ruler' in the Hebrew."[10] Gunn then gives thanks to God for the "provision, tender care and concern" demonstrated to her. While Gunn adopts the text to testify how God had acted as a "husband" to her through "provision, tender care and concern" she does not recognize the different cultural implications of the image. Her description of God-as-husband was facilitated by use of contemporary terms such as "bread-winner," rather than through an understanding of the role of a husband in the cultural of ancient Israel. Gunn identified the image of "husband" in the biblical text to be identical to her contemporary description (including such functions as guiding her in money matters and keeping her vehicle free from malfunction)—a husband's role hardly conceivable within ancient Israelite society. She appropriated the image to her contemporary context without reference to its significance in the culture of the text.

6. Ackerman, "Isaiah," 167.

7. Goldingay, *Isaiah*, 311.

8. See Appendix 1, Ref UA.

9. Ibid, 7.

10. Ibid.

This trend of appropriating the imagery in the text immediately to the situation of the reader is also perceived in the tendency of other Pentecostal readers to view God as their husband. While most Pentecostal readers identified it as a message for Israel, they did not hesitate to appropriate it for themselves. The initial response of the charismatic Ladies Group,[11] which included two widows, to the reading of Isa 54 was to emphasize the metaphor of enlarging the size of their tent. They highlighted the sense of anticipation and preparation this command implied: "Its like, get ready!" The anticipation of children was identified by the women as a sign of God's blessing for ancient Israel. They then proposed that the concept of barrenness for contemporary readers was to be applied to their life generally, "that sense of fullness in our life that comes from God." The ladies found that, in Jesus, they have fullness of life. One older, unmarried woman spoke of the passage's significance to her with the group: "Isaiah 54 is kind of special to me because it's part of the words that God spoke over me—verse 5. It's very beautiful . . . it really humbles me and I'm awe-inspired. Because God has this infinite patience and reveals his unending love . . . Even to the children of Israel, who turned their back on him continually. But he says that 'I'm your redeemer.' The God of the whole earth has called you." Another older widow similarly described her perception of Jesus as her husband since her earthly husband had died. When asked what that meant, she replied: "He's my all. He's my companion. And for me, I don't need anyone else." They identified in Christ an abundant sense of life and security; not just as a cognitive truth, but as an active experience in their life. The women highlighted the abundance and restoration that overflows in the verse as the people are promised not only restoration, but profusion over and beyond what they had previously known. They emphasized the theme of hope from the passage . . . that God's going to do greater things in the latter than he did in the former." They found encouragement in the willingness of God to fulfill the promised restoration: with God all things are possible. This principle of God's concern for the welfare of the covenant people is also highlighted in a sermon by Pastor Harold Harvey.

While the readers tended to apply the image of God as "husband" directly to their lives as a contemporary concept of provision, companionship and security, they identified other images such as "barrenness" to be symbols for other areas of their lives. The image of barrenness tended to be understood as a symbol for dryness or unfruitfulness (particularly spiritual). Where the Pentecostal readers experienced unfruitfulness, they could transpose that concept onto the image of "barrenness" in the text to then anticipate a reversal of that former state. In his 2003 sermon entitled "Sing, O Barren, Sing," Harvey[12] first introduces the historical context of the passage. He identifies the prophet (noting that Isaiah lived in the eighth century) as prophesying a message of restoration for Judah from captivity in Babylon. His sermon notes highlight the context: "At the time of Judah's restoration to rebuild the temple and city walls, Judah was many times despondent, hassled by enemies, oftentimes discouraged by lack of success and fruitfulness, etc. This caused a great sense of shame and reproach." Isaiah uses the illustration of a childless

11. See Appendix 1, Ref H2.

12. See Appendix 1, Ref SA.

woman as illustrative of Judah's barrenness (barrenness being a matter of shame and reproach for such a woman). Harvey continues to describe the situation of Judah as "barren" in their fruitlessness. Into this situation, the prophet promises a future blessing where this shame and reproach will be reversed.

To prepare for this reversal of situation and promised blessing, Harvey emphasizes the instruction to Judah to sing. From this discussion of the context, Harvey isolates the principle of "preparing for increase." He notes: "In light of pregnancy, preparations are made to accommodate the child: pre-natal checkups, hospital booking, baby clothes bought, nursery furniture acquired and building on an extra room perhaps: all this for the addition of one child to the family. Imagine the preparations needed if planning to receive a dozen orphans. We need to prepare for increase before it happens: (1) To demonstrate our faith, (2) To ensure that new souls will be cared for as soon as they arrive." While the preparation for a child is understood in contemporary terms, Harvey isolates the principle of expansion from the text and applies it to the expansion of the church through evangelism. For Harvey, the text highlights the need of the church to prepare for expansion in practical ways as an act of faith in the anticipated increase in the kingdom of God. Describing the process of preparing his message, Harvey wrote in personal correspondence, "With Isaiah 54, it is a matter of finding the principles or situations the prophet is addressing and looking for similar principles and conditions attaching to the church and then applying the prophet's remedy, advice, exhortation etc. to the church where such is applicable."[13] Harvey begins with the isolation of a theme or principle from the passage, then looks for a suitable application within the life of the congregation. As the example of Harvey highlights, this "barrenness" could refer to a period of unfruitfulness in evangelism and church growth that one might expect to see reversed; mirroring the development of the passage. It is the transposing of one's own situation, culture and context onto the biblical text. For Harvey, this means the church should prepare themselves, like a mother preparing for the birth of a child, for the expected church growth. The text given to the ancient community is appropriated just as if it was given to present-day Christians.[14] This means the text for Pentecostal readers is only trans-historical, but also trans-cultural.

When asked what the passage of Isaiah 54 was about, a new Christian from the Pentecostal women's cell group[15] responded, "Like they must've been naughty, or they've done stuff. They might have been a bit disobedient—the people of Zion. But he's not angry and he's gonna keep his promises, even though, you know, 'cause we disobey sometimes . . . They've done something to upset him and he's like, over it now! God's over it. He's says 'I'm over this, its okay.'" The message of this passage was appropriated by the group as they applied the themes of restoration, forgiveness and compassion from the text and applied them to their Christian walk: "It means he's made a promise with us-us-even us now . . . He's made a covenant of peace, we'll always gonna have that peace in our heart.

13. Personal correspondence.

14. Ma, "Biblical Studies in the Pentecostal Tradition," 55.

15. See Appendix 1, Ref TA.

He'll never take it away, he's made a covenant." Another participant responded: "It's just God—reading that now—He's shared with them some of his forgiveness, and compassion and softness and just understanding. I just see that as a huge wave of forgiveness. It's just encouraging us to not feel guilty, forget about all your humiliations and indignities . . . It's a beautiful image isn't it?—the whole . . . Israel is my bride, I'm the bridegroom. I love you. Isn't that beautiful? He's our husband." Although the group identified the original recipients of these promises as "Israel," they appropriated the promises to their own lives. They applied, and experienced through the reading of the text, the forgiveness offered by God to their own lives. They identified God as being their husband; present and active. In a sense, they became part of spiritual Israel through the salvific/marital analogy imbedded in the story.

A cell group of young, single, professional women from a Pentecostal church[16] in middle-class Sydney highlighted the compassion of God evidenced in the text. One of the group commented: "I guess for me 'cause I often have a picture of God as really angry, so when I hear, you know, 'for a brief moment I forsook you, but with great compassion I will gather you; in an outburst of anger I hid my face from you for a moment, but with everlasting loving kindness I will have compassion on you.' That really speaks to me because it just reminds me, convinces me more, that God isn't about anger; that he's about compassion." They identified the role of God as rebuilding what had been shattered. One participant commented: "I just think: how awesome is that. Even in your own life if you think about that, and apply it to you own life. What has been damaged or pulled down, God will build even better. How cool is that." The Pentecostal readers from this group looked through the imagery to find truths about God.

While some of the Pentecostal readers recognized the original recipients of this message to be "Israel" and identified the cultural significance of the images, they did not necessarily place their reading of the text within its historical context as addressing the exilic community. This meant that the poignancy of the message of restoration was lost to the Pentecostal readers. While they recognized the themes of compassion, restoration and forgiveness, which were the primary concerns of the biblical scholars, the detachment of the passage from the historic context of the exilic community meant that the enormity of the judgment and humiliation on Judah through this definitive event in their history—and the subsequent immensity of their restoration and compassion—was generally lost on these readers. Yet, while some of the poignancy of the historical-cultural context of the passage was lost, the poignancy of the text as a reading experience was not lost. The readers both experienced and applied the themes of forgiveness and compassion offered by God in the text to their own lives.

This experience tended to occur through a literalization of the imagery in the text. Instead of understanding the significance of the text within the social and historical context of the older testament, the Pentecostal readers tended to apply the imagery to their own context directly. For example, they saw in the imagery of God as the bridegroom an image of beauty, wonder and acceptance to be appropriated to their world directly.

---

16. See Appendix 1, Ref VA.

The use of language adopted by the Pentecostal readers to describe this relationship with God however, is interesting—it is the language of a superior-inferior relationship. The Pentecostal readers tended to associate with the culture of the ancient community that assigns authority within marriage to the male. For these (mainly female) readers, they identified the husband as providing security, companionship and provision. This is contrasted with the sober warnings of some biblical scholars noted above, such as Ackerman, who warn against the simplistic appropriation of patriarchal systems by contemporary readers. However, the Pentecostal readers seemed to have no difficulty with the cultural assumptions in the passage, but rather embraced it as further impetus towards the radical submission to God, identified by Fulkerson[17] as a feature of Pentecostal women. This same process of the literalization of imagery in a text was also evidenced in readings of Isaiah 61.

For most Pentecostal readers of Isaiah 61, the text pointed directly to the person and ministry of Jesus Christ in the New Testament. They directly identified the speaker to be Christ as the passage is seen as fulfilled in the New Testament through the life and ministry of Jesus Christ. One of the ladies immediately responded to the text, "It is very plain it is Jesus' ministry: he was anointed to preach good tidings." In particular, it was the anointed nature of Christ's ministry that appealed to them. They continued to discuss the concept of anointing and its connection to the term of "Christ." Another participant commented, "Also, whenever in the Bible it says 'Christ,' it means Jesus Christ, it means the anointed one—the anointed one and his anointing. So, when we have Jesus in us, we have his anointing. It applies to us as well as him." They continued to highlight the "perspicuity" of the text: "It's set out very plain, isn't it? You couldn't read anything else into it, because we are called to preach the good news, we are called to lay hands on the sick." However, while the text pointed to the anointed nature of Christ's ministry, the charismatic ladies group[18] also identified their own Christian ministry as the continuation of that anointing.

The ladies not only identified Christ in the passage, but also perceived it to be a direct mandate of the ministry of the church—including them. They appropriated the passage to their own lives as a directive to continue the ministry of literal preaching and literal healing as described in the text. One commented, "So, this is what we're to do also. It speaks to us that way as well because the Spirit of the Lord is upon us, in us and has anointed us to preach the good tidings to the poor and all the rest of it." While they are the agent of God to complete this mission of preaching and healing, it is only achieved through the direction and empowering of the Holy Spirit. This value of a Pentecostal theology highlights the role of the Holy Spirit in empowering believers for evangelism and charismatic gifting. As one participant commented: "when we have Jesus in us, we have his anointing. It applies to us as well as him." This text was thus appropriated by the contemporary Pentecostal readers through Christ. They continue the ministry and mandate of Christ by appropriating the mission in Isaiah 61. Obedience to the passage

17. Fulkerson, *Changing the Subject*, 253–65.

18. See Appendix 1, Ref H2.

is literalistic for the Pentecostal readers—they are called to literally preach the good news and proclaim the [day of the] Lord's favour. Although there was little emphasis in their readings on the compassionate ministry represented in the text, the focus of the Pentecostal readings was generally on the preaching and healing ministry represented.[19]

The anointed prophet of Isaiah 61 is identified by early Pentecostals as not an ancient Israelite prophet but as referring directly to Jesus Christ in the New Testament. In the "Enquiry Column" of the 1924 *Good News Magazine* (emerging from the early Pentecostal movement in Australia), an anonymous enquirer[20] asked about the "Lord being 'christed' since He was always Christ Jesus, our Lord."[21] The editor responded with reference to the anointing of Christ at his baptism, but then goes on to describe Jesus as God's anointed. The editor wrote "in Isaiah 61:1 we read: 'The Lord hath anointed me to preach good tidings unto the meek.' Yet some 600 years later we find our Lord telling the Nazarenes that this was—on that very day—being fulfilled in their ears. (See Luke 4:16–21)."[22] Like earlier passages, such as Isaiah 6 and 53, this Isaiah passage was read through the lens of the New Testament as the Pentecostal reader identified the speaker's role as being fulfilled in Christ.

For the cell group of young, single, professional women from a Pentecostal church[23] in middle-class Sydney, it was the concept of preaching the good news that stood out from the text of Isaiah 61. They identified this passage to be their own mandate and own task of preaching the gospel. One of the members in particular highlighted the image of the oak tree from verse 3. She commented: "If you picture an oak tree as this huge, solid, enormous tree whose branches go high and roots go down deep—just strong and beautiful." Yet, while recognizing the imagery and resonating with the word-picture, she could not necessarily verbalize how it affected her. The image from the text seemed to "speak" to the group without them necessarily being able to explain how or why. The group identified this as somehow part of "God's favor" that permeated the whole passage as they experienced and applied the passage to their own lives.

The verses that most absorbed the migrant men from the charismatic Bible study group[24] were the first three verses. One participant commented:

> For this, it is literally like God is saying that God is always with the oppressed. He is there to take care of them and he will make justice and make justice prevail in this world . . . Apparently this is to a group of people who are captives, and were prisoners. And they were literally very broken hearted because they know they are God's people and they are being held captive and literally being spitted upon. And their shame was so bad because there was so much disgrace in that situation. So Isaiah's mission seems to be to let them know that God knows what's happening

---

19. The deliverance of prisoners was possibly considered a spiritual image to describe those held captive in the "kingdom of darkness."

20. See Appendix 1, Ref WA.

21. Ibid., 19.

22. Ibid.

23. See Appendix 1, Ref VA.

24. See Appendix 1, Ref XA.

... and he wants to tell his people through Isaiah that there'll be a year of favor from the Lord.

The participant highlighted the comfort and restoration of God promised through the prophet. The issues of justice and restoration of the broken-heart was a theme the participants continually reinforced. They found solace in the passage that just as God brought comfort to the people of Isaiah's time, God would bring solace, comfort, and restoration to them. In this sense, the participants found a measure of healing in the verse as it seemed to speak to their situation through the experiences of the community in the passage.

Throughout the description of these readings there was a general tendency among the Pentecostal-charismatic readers of Isa 61 to apply the passage to both Christ as well as the contemporary Spirit-filled life of the Christian believer. For some groups, such as the charismatic men's group, that meant finding solace and comfort through the text for their own life situation. However, from the readings generally, there was an emphasis on the empowerment of the Holy Spirit to equip believers for the task of healing and evangelism. This represents the focus of a Pentecostal theology and worldview on the activity of the Holy Spirit within the church and the life of the believer. It also highlights the emphasis on mission and evangelism evident in the life of the Pentecostal community. This is priority of evangelism over social issues has led to a separation of the two concerns (i.e., that social justice is not a part of evangelism and the "good news" offered by Christ). Yet, the need for social justice and healing through the addressing of social issues was keenly felt by the charismatic men's group. Yet, the contemporary community continues the ministry of Christ in extending the kingdom of God, and sees itself as a continuum of the mission of the early church as recorded in the book of Acts. Like the previous passages of Isaiah discussed, there was no concern evidenced by the Pentecostal readers in textual issues, translations from the original language or even a comparison of English translations. Instead, the voice of the Pentecostal community has tended to emphasize the values of pneumatic experience and christological perspectives in their readings of *Isaiah*.

From these observations, it seems that Pentecostal readers have searched the book of *Isaiah* in order to find those passages which would corroborate with their faith. Their choice of passages was very selective. Why have they emphasized these texts? This emphasis may be explained by their readings. What resonated with the readers of these passages was their own experience of God reflective of text. In their readings, the Pentecostal community identified God as present and active. Most of their interest in *Isaiah* concerned passages that could resonate with their experience of faith in Christ and pneumatic encounter. The Pentecostal readers identified their experience in the text as they entered the world of the text, emphasizing its immediacy. A corollary of this emphasis is the lack of interest or awareness in the historical context of the passage. The Pentecostal readings as a whole tended to be ahistorical in their approach, with little concern for the social and historical issues from which the text has emerged. This was also highlighted by the negative interest in the original language of the text. The lack of awareness of textual issues perhaps reinforced the ahistorical nature of their readings as each participant tended to identify their particular translation as the "Word of God" rather than an English translation of an ancient text that evolved from a particular historical and social setting. Instead, they read the text for its christological significance and immediate message to their contemporary Christian life.

While some of the readers identified the text as being written for the ancient Israelite community before the coming of Christ, the readers tended to be unsure of the historical location of the text—specifically its significance to the post-exilic community. This meant that a measure of its power as a message of restoration was lost to the Pentecostal readers. While they recognized the themes of compassion, restoration, and forgiveness in the two texts of Isaiah 54 and 61, the detachment of the passage from the historic context of the exilic community meant that the enormity of the judgment and subsequent restoration was absent in their readings. Everything in the text then becomes for the contemporary reader an issue of personal spirituality. Although the experience of oppression and dislocation represented in the text was keenly felt by some of the Pentecostal readers, particularly the men's charismatic group,[25] they each expressed an anticipation of restoration and compassion of God toward which the text points and directs the reader. Yet this approach can be highly problematic as the community can be reading the text in their own image, rather than recognizing the text as representing another cultural world from which they are separated. This literalizing of the text questions the responsible use of scripture by Pentecostal-charismatic readers. While the text can serve semiotically as a symbol for the reader in pointing to principles and truths consistent with the theological worldview of the Pentecostal-charismatic community (as discussed in the previous chapter),[26] the process of literalization of the text identified in these readings may be less innocent. It does not point to principles so much as it imposes contemporary meanings of words or concepts found in the biblical text onto the interpretation.

PROBLEMATIC USE OF LITERALIST READINGS

This literalistic approach evident in the Pentecostal readings is cause for potential disagreement in the triune discussion as the responsibilities of readers is highlighted. The responsibility of readers to value and honor the context of each text is highlighted by scholars of hermeneutics.[27] Yet the readings highlighted above emphasize the purpose of the Pentecostal community in reading biblical texts that potentially conflict with the concerns for responsibility among the wider academy. The Pentecostal readers expect Scripture to speak meaningfully into social settings divergent from those in which it originated.[28] This positively represents the ability of Scripture to transcend historical and social contexts to be relevant to all generations and communities.[29] However, within the

25. See Appendix 1, Ref XA.

26. See Grey, "Burning Tongues."

27. In particular see Thistleton, *New Horizons in Hermeneutics*, 530.

28. Archer, "Early Pentecostal Biblical Interpretation," 39.

29. Ibid.

Pentecostal community it has also allowed a literalistic tendency. This pragmatic approach is noted by Pentecostal scholars as a value of the community inherent in its approach to all Bible reading, not just Old Testament texts. As Wonsuk Ma reflects on Pentecostalism, "The very birth of the movement was connected to a bold literalistic reading of Acts 2. Charles F. Parham, called by some the originator of the Pentecostal 'pragmatic' hermeneutic, argued that the experience of Spirit baptism should be identical with what is found in Acts 2."[30] While this approach of Pentecostal readers positively emphasizes the immediacy of Scripture, it has two major shortcomings of particular concern within the study of hermeneutics. Firstly it does not recognize the hermeneutical distance between the reader and the text, resulting in a confusion of culture. Secondly, and more crucial to the Pentecostal value-system, the literalistic tendency denies the uniqueness and immanence of God's message to the original community.[31] The hermeneutical distance of a reader from the text is the measure of the degree to which historical and cultural differences are recognized. It highlights the cultural and social location of the text as "other" from the situation of the reader. This is an important consideration for Pentecostal readers who have tended to apply the biblical text to their own situation without recognition of these differences. This begins by the Pentecostal reader looking carefully at their own context and the place from which they read.[32] The Pentecostal reader begins with a worldview, values, and interests that reflect their community and influences their reading of the text. They are also part of a wider culture, which (for the Pentecostal community in Australia) is definably secular and postmodern. Their culture and worldview is self-evidently very different to that of the pre-modern, pre-industrialized society of ancient Israel. While the reader cannot but help influence the interpretation through their context and social location (as post-structuralist theories highlight), the imposition of their context onto the text is an injustice to the passage. To not recognize the differences is to misunderstand and potentially misread the text.

There are profound discontinuities between the worldview of ancient Israel and the worldview that informs the Pentecostal community in (post)modern Christian civilization.[33] From an understanding of ancient Israelite culture, the prophet in Isa 54:5 was not referring to God as a husband-mechanic, but rather that God would be all things that a husband, consistent with the culture represented by the text, was.[34] This would

---

30. Ma, "Biblical Studies in the Pentecostal Tradition," 54.

31. According to Ma there are two major effects of a literalistic tendency among Pentecostal-charismatics. He writes, "This literalistic approach had at least two effects in the ensuing Pentecostal-charismatic movement. First, the centrality of Scripture was always stressed. The popular expression of the 'biblical pattern' reflected this focus. Secondly, the gap between clergy and laity was narrowed and prepared a way for the active participation of the lay people in ministry" (Ma, "Biblical Studies in the Pentecostal Tradition," 55).

32. McKinlay, "What do I do with Contexts?" 159.

33. Harrop, *Elijah Speaks Today*, 154.

34. Harrop continues his discussion by noting, "In admitting the profound discontinuity between the 'strange' world of the Bible and the world of modern megalopolis, are we saying that there are no abiding or recurring elements in the human situation and the divine-human encounter? Is there no analogy to be perceived in what happened twenty-eight centuries ago in Jezreel, and what happens in the high-rise offices and dwellings of the Great Society, along its throughways and in its factories, its churches, its hospitals,

include provision and protection, but does not "mean" mechanical assistance directly. The worldview(s) of the biblical writers are so fundamentally different to that of the contemporary Western reader that to simply adopt their worldview or transpose the reader's own location onto the text without recognizing the shifts in culture is to be ignorant of the reader's own identity.[35]

If we do not consider the text on its own terms—culturally and historically—then "a premature fusion of horizons" will occur.[36] This means the reader will have fused their world with the world of the text without respect for the tension between the horizons of the text and the horizon of the reader. The textual horizon will have collapsed into that of the reader's own narrative biography, and is unable to do more than speak back his or her own values and desires.[37] This location of meaning solely on the significance of the text for the individual reader can result in idolatry. We can project our own interests, desire, and selfhood onto that which the biblical text proclaims. In this case, the text no longer acts as an independent authority, nor can it challenge the reader with prophetic integrity but simply mirrors the reader's own assumptions or misassumptions. Thereby we can unsuspectingly re-create the text (and God) in our own image.[38] This approach uses the text to justify our own ideas, concepts and theology. Pentecostal readers can avoid this "affective fallacy" (whereby meaning lies in the affect of the work upon the reader) by reaffirming the historical-cultural distance between their own horizon and the horizon of the text. This recognizes that the meaning the reader brings to the text may not be reminiscent of the cultural and historical assumptions attached to the words or symbols of the text.

The tendency toward literalistic readings by Pentecostal readers also denies the immanence and relevance of God's message to the original community. Ironically, this is an important value to the Pentecostal community: God (it is believed by the community) speaks to believers clearly and comprehensibly. This means that God communicates to the Pentecostal community in a language that is familiar and culturally relevant to them. This highlights the immanence of God. If this value is central to the Pentecostal community, then why should Pentecostal readers deny this experience to previous communities of faith? As Archer notes, to deny this suggests that the Bible had somehow escaped the vicissitudes of historical construction or that the writers of the Bible had not been influenced in any significant way by the setting in which they lived.[39] The fundamental nature of the biblical witness is God speaking to people "where they are at." As we shall see, this is a principle important to the development of a holistic Pentecostal reading

---

schools, and universities? To find the analogy, without ignoring the discontinuities, is the hermeneutical task that must be undertaken by whoever it is that seeks to speak to our time in the name and spirit of the prophets of Israel" (ibid., 156).

35. Ellington, "History, Story, and Testimony," 245.

36. Thistleton, *New Horizons in Hermeneutics*, 530.

37. Ibid.

38. Ibid.

39. Archer, "Early Pentecostal Biblical Interpretation," 36.

model.[40] Yet this recognition of the limited nature of the language of the biblical text to specific communities does not deny its meaningfulness for subsequent communities of faith, such as the Pentecostal-charismatic community.

This tendency to literalize all events, images, and mythic language in the Old Testament observed in these Pentecostal readings, is also reflective of classic Fundamentalism—a community of ideas which early classical Pentecostals shared. As Archer notes, "Like popularistic Fundamentalists and Holiness folk, they [Pentecostals] read the passages in their Bible as sacred Scripture: thus the various biblical genres were absorbed and dissolved into one category—'Holy Scripture.' The Bible was a gold mine. All that was needed to unearth precious gold was the popularistic Bible reading method and sensitivity to the Holy Spirit's present revelatory guidance."[41] For Pentecostal readers, this means that God must not only act exactly like a husband to Gunn in the literalization of biblical imagery, but that the biblical stories had to have actually happened in order to be "true." As Clark notes, the Pentecostal movement stands in the tradition of those groups that maintain the record of Scripture as historically accurate, including the "so-called supernatural stories" such as the Noachian Flood and the ten plagues of Egypt.[42] Literalization occurs as Pentecostal readers impose Modern assumptions of culture and historiography onto ancient texts.[43] However this raises, once again, the relationship between Pentecostal reading practices as demonstrated by the community and the reading approach of Fundamentalism.

DOES A LITERALIST STANCE MAKE PENTECOSTAL READINGS FUNDAMENTALIST?

The label of a "fundamentalist" is a loaded term. As Spittler notes, the term "fundamentalist" is usually a put-down.[44] He writes, "It is applied to those who are seen to be more to the right of the theological spectrum than oneself. Consequently, one person's fundamentalist could be, and certainly has been, another's liberal."[45] Fundamentalism, as defined by Spittler, is "an unbending literalism in biblical interpretation coupled with a theory of inspiration close to dictation."[46] Clark identifies Fundamentalism as a threefold belief in the verbal inspiration of Scripture, a commitment to the literal inerrancy of

---

40. This feature is particularly highlighted by the minimal interest of the Pentecostal-charismatic readers in textual issues, the original Hebrew language or even comparing English translations. They tend to accept whatever English translation they are using (usually NKJV or NIV) as the "Word of God" rather than recognising it as a translation of an ancient text.

41. Archer, "Early Pentecostal Biblical Interpretation," 38.

42. Clark, "An Investigation into the Nature of a Viable Pentecostal Hermeneutic," 55.

43. Archer, "Early Pentecostal Biblical Interpretation," 39.

44. Spittler, "Are Pentecostals and Charismatics Fundamentalists?," 103.

45. Ibid. As Spittler writes, "As stated above, fundamentalism took its name, if indirectly, from the publication of *The Fundamentals*. This series of twelve booklets was distributed with the 'Compliments of Two Christian Laymen,' as the title page relates . . . The exact word fundamentalist, it seems, originated as a descriptor for conservative Christians in the Northern Baptist Convention in 1920" (Spittler, "Are Pentecostals and Charismatics Fundamentalists?" 103).

46. Clark, "An Investigation into the Nature of a Viable Pentecostal Hermeneutic," 111.

the scriptural record, and affirmation of the tenets of the Christian confessions of the immediate post-Reformation era.[47] He writes, "These values are often maintained in a distinctive way, combining a literalistic and uncritical biblicism with an unyielding commitment to the fundamental doctrines."[48]

While there is a resonance between the fundamentalist claims toward scripture and the reading practices of the Pentecostal community, there are key differences in how these two groups arrive at these claims. Fundamentalists arrive at these claims as doctrinal statements whereas the Pentecostal community arrives at these claims through experience.[49] As the Fundamentalist World Conference itself noted in 1928,[50] the notion of the experiential encounter with God, common in the language of the Pentecostal reader, is not consistent with a fundamentalist approach. While, as McKay suggests, no charismatic could prove these fundamentalist claims (like the veracity of the creation narrative in Gen 1) through their prophetic insight, but their experience of the prophetic and pneumatic encounter resonates with the claims. He writes, "Prophetic insight has very little to say about such matters, though it does warm instantly to the emphasis on God's goodness in the creation story or to the message in the book of Jonah about the need for obedience in a prophet."[51] Yet, this does not mean that the Pentecostal community accepts all the claims of Fundamentalism or even that their experience would affirm all their claims. For example, the experience of prophetic proclamation in the Pentecostal community would find it hard to accept the fundamentalist view of literal, mechanical inspiration, as though God had precisely dictated every single word that is spoken.[52]

While the literalist reading of some Old Testament passages by Pentecostal readers does imply a certain amount of sympathy with the concerns of Fundamentalism,[53] however, as discussed in chapter 2, the worldview and emerging theology of the Pentecostal community is not consistent with fundamentalist dispensationalism and its reading purpose. As Spittler asserts, "Pentecostals and Fundamentalists . . . are arch enemies when it comes to such matters as speaking in tongues and the legitimacy of expecting physical

47. Ibid.

48. Ibid., 55. McKay notes, "The fundamentalists maintain a doctrine of literal inspiration of Scripture in all its detail, whether theological, historical or scientific, and so, for example, would argue that the world was created literally in six days, that there actually was a first-created pair named Adam and Eve who originally lived in a garden called Eden which must at one time have been geographically locatable, that people really did begin to speak different languages when a tower project at Babel collapsed, and so forth. To the fundamentalists the laws of Israel were dictated word for word by God to Moses on Mount Sinai, and in a similar fashion the utterances of the prophets are the very speeches of God himself. Thus every word of Scripture is cherished as an infallible word of God to be read, studied, learned and obeyed, but not criticized or questioned" (McKay, "When the Veil is Taken Away," 22).

49. McKay, "When the Veil is Taken Away," 28.

50. Synan, "Fundamentalism," 657.

51. McKay, "When the Veil is Taken Away," 28.

52. Ibid., 29. Though McKay does note that on some rare occasions prophetic inspiration may seem like dictation "but generally the dictum of Paul holds good, that 'the spirits of prophets are subject to the control of prophets' (1 Cor. 14.32)" (ibid., 29).

53. Clark, "An Investigation into the Nature of a Viable Pentecostal Hermeneutic," 108. The enemies of Pentecostal stalwarts have also been the enemies targeted by Fundamentalism.

healing in today's world. But their approaches to the Bible, precritical and uncompli-
cated, are virtually identical. If the word fundamentalism gets defined only by biblical
style, Pentecostals can be labeled fundamentalists without question."[54] The cognitive
approach of Fundamentalism makes the Pentecostal value of charismatic gifting and
pneumatic encounter reducible to propositional truths rather than a dynamic experience of encountering God. Their focus on truth as a set of abstract cognitive absolutes is
alien to the Pentecostal emphasis on experiencing the Spirit.[55] It is the divine experience
and pneumatic encounter of the Pentecostal community that leads them to affirm the
biblical records as true, rather than a strictly intellectual consent. Pentecostalism, unlike
Fundamentalism (and neo-orthodoxy) has distrusted the intellectual enterprise.[56] As
Pentecostal scholar McKay writes, "Charismatics want scholars to begin believing that
what they are analyzing is not just myth, or legend, or the theological ruminations of
pious intellects, if they are liberals, nor simply ancient history or doctrinal presentations,
if they are conservatives, but living Christian experience as it was and as it still should
be."[57] While the pneumatic experience of the Pentecostal community has shifted its focus
towards a more fundamentalist theology concerning the value of the biblical text, it does
not follow that Pentecostal readers readily accept all the historical or theological conclusions of Fundamentalism[58] as the dynamic feature of Pentecostal readings of *Isaiah*
demonstrate.[59]

The key difference is that Pentecostal non-cessationism refuses to operate in the
Modernist paradigm—the location of both Fundamentalism and its archrival Liberalism.
Under the modernist, rationalistic worldview the intervention of God in human history
(including the miraculous reports of the biblical text) must be excluded from any attempt
to establish biblical truth through historical means.[60] In comparison, the Pentecostal
readings we have studied (above) emphasized the ability of God to intervene in human history and to know humanity personally. The Pentecostal community values the
continuation of God's actions in human history and recognizes the involvement of the
spiritual realm in this history. As Archer notes, "Pentecostalism recognizes the interaction between the spiritual realm (whether that is God and good angels or the Devil and
evil angels) and the physical materialistic realm . . . The Pentecostal reading of Scripture
emanated from a popularistic paramodern understanding of Scripture and a paramodern understanding of God and the Devil's participatory interaction and felt influence
upon the created world."[61] Interestingly, many segments of the postmodern community

54. Ibid., 106.

55. Parker, *Led by the Spirit*, 10.

56. Spittler, "Are Pentecostals and Charismatics Fundamentalists?" 108.

57. McKay, "When the Veil is Taken Away," 40.

58. Ibid.

59. In particular, see the Ruthven, *On the Cessation of the Charismata* and Ruthven, "On the Cessation
of the Charismata: The Protestant Polemic of Benjamin B. Warfield," for discussion and polemic against
cessationism.

60. Ellington, "History, Story, and Testimony," 248.

61. Archer, "Early Pentecostal Biblical Interpretation," 38.

express interest in this rejection of Western modern materialism as they recognize the interaction of the spiritual realm in their exploration into New Age spirituality. For the Pentecostal community, this means that they read the biblical text not as a past revelatory document, but as a presently inspired story.[62] In this way, their approach to reading the biblical text diverges significantly from Fundamentalism.

Yet, while the Pentecostal reader approaches the biblical text with a different agenda and concern to Fundamentalism, the assumption of the historical veracity of Scripture is shared by both groups. For the Pentecostal reader, it is a concern that the Bible presents "truth." It is this truth toward which they orient their lives. However for the Pentecostal reader, the truth of scriptural texts is not to be found in their objective historical veracity as determined by contemporary western methods of historiography, but in the truth of their testimony or witness. While it matters to a Pentecostal reader that the blind will see and the deaf will hear according to biblical texts such as Isaiah 61, this proclamation is based on the witness of the covenant community, not on the historical reconstruction of ancient Israelite history. Therefore—in contrast to the modernist paradigm—the text can have meaning separate to the reconstruction of the para-modern author's meaning and the "history" of the text. As Ellington notes, "The problem with locating truth in history in doing biblical hermeneutics is twofold. First, time, distance, and a scarcity of corroborating source materials outside of the Bible have made confirmation and/or reconstruction of the elements of biblical history difficult and, at times, impossible. Second, and more fundamentally, any direct participation by God in the biblical account falls outside of the range of modern historical methodology. God's speaking, acting, and revealing are not so much unscientific as they are ascientific, that is, such events are hardly accessible to examination using conventional historical methods."[63] Pentecostal readers need only look to their own readings and testimonies to see this principle in action. For example, Gunn's testimony of God being a husband cannot be verified by historical reconstruction; the truth of the claim is in her testimony itself.

This raises questions for the Pentecostal community regarding the nature of history and the presentation of "ancient Israel" in Old Testament texts. According to Davies, there is no neutral history since all writing about the past is influenced by the present of the writers. History is as much about the present as it is about the past.[64] Davies writes, "There is no objective history of Israel any more than there is an objective 'ancient Israel.'"[65] Any attempt at recalling the past involves not just description but interpretation and explanation.[66] Old Testament texts are not just interested in history but in community formation. They interpret past events to inform their present community. Therefore their presentation of past events is more than memory but is an impacting, creative act of

---

62. Ibid., 37.

63. Ellington, "History, Story, and Testimony," 250.

64. Davies, "Whose History? Whose Israel? Whose Bible?" 113. As Davies notes, Old Testament "history" is more "historiography" which refers to a narrative which claims to relate the past (ibid., 114).

65. Davies, "Whose History? Whose Israel? Whose Bible?" 111.

66. Whitelam, "Sociology or History," 153.

community identity.[67] And yet, the concept that the biblical witness presents some kind of "truth" is important to the Pentecostal community. According to Croatto, readers need to attach significance to the text, not the author. He writes, "We read a text, not an author. To conceive of biblical inspiration as attaching to the sacred writers is a form of historicism, and this sacred halo leaves the text more unprotected than might be supposed."[68] This means that if the text is inspired, then a re-reading of the Bible can also recover a meaning that is part of the "reservoir of meaning" that was not in the intention of the author.[69]

While Pentecostal readers tend to literalize the text, it is consistent with their concern for the continuing intervention of God in history. The interaction between Pentecostal literalism and Pentecostal dynamism, however, may lead to recognition of this "reservoir of meaning" that does not need to locate truth in the "historical" events but in the testimony of the text. This is also, as Stroup suggests, consistent with the witness of historical narrative of Christianity. Like Old Testament texts, the historical claims of Christianity (of which the Pentecostal community is a part) exist for the purpose of identity formation. Stroup writes,

> Christian narrative is "historical" for two reasons. On the one hand, its claims about reality are based on and appeal to certain event in the communal history of Israel and the personal history of Jesus of Nazareth. But secondly, Christian narrative is not recited in order to amuse or entertain. There is an explicit kerygmatic undertow to Christian narrative. It is told for a reason, to make a point, which of course is that the redemption and salvation of personal and communal histories is to be found in this Christian story. Persons and communities cannot be redeemed without their histories, for their identity is inseparable from them.[70]

The development of a reading model of the Old Testament texts for the Pentecostal community must recognize the kerygmatic nature of biblical texts. For this reason it is important to keep historical distance so the reader can separate "what happens" from the meaning of what happens.[71]

As the proliferation of Pentecostal scholarship indicates, critical reflection does not have to come at the expense of the commitment to the authority of Scripture or loss of the uniqueness of Pentecostal values. This suggests the need to separate the question of inspiration and authority of the Bible from the question of historicity, especially since the Pentecostal reader is not necessarily searching for "scientific" truth as represented by "history." As many postmodern approaches to scripture emphasize, truth is not located exclusively in historical truth,[72] neither is meaning found exclusively in "objective" data. Instead, the interest of the Pentecostal readers of Isaiah 54 in historical matters can be identified as an interest in the testimony of God's actions within the earlier covenant

67. Ellington, "History, Story, and Testimony," 254.

68. Croatto, *Biblical Hermeneutics,* 46.

69. Ibid., 47.

70. Stroup, *The Promise of Narrative Theology,* 94–95.

71. Croatto, *Biblical Hermeneutics,* 6.

72. Ellington, "History, Story, and Testimony," 251.

community. It concerns the interaction of God with people.[73] As Childs concludes, "In short, a theology of the Old Testament is not to be confused with a description of Israel's religion, but is Israel's testimony, a perspective from within the faith(emic)."[74] This involves asking questions about the significance of the text to its original community (as represented in the text) as part of the testimony of God's actions in history and the world. It is this ongoing drama of salvation through God's actions in time and space that the Pentecostal community is a part.

While it can be seen that the Pentecostal reader will express the fundamental truth-claims of the biblical text as a doctrinal position, their reading practice does not reflect a fundamentalist perspective. The dynamic nature of Pentecostal readings demonstrates a tendency to find meaning and value in the biblical text without reference to "what really happened." As Ellington suggests, the truth-claim of the Bible on the Pentecostal reader is unconnected to its historical reference.[75] He writes, "It is my contention that the biblical writers neither understood nor were they interested in writing history in the modern sense of that term. Neither, however, were they simply writing creative stories without any reference to 'real events.' Where, then, is truth to be located in the biblical narrative, and how is it to be accessed and appropriated for Pentecostals?"[76] This suggests the need to separate the question of inspiration and authority of the Bible from the question of historicity, especially since the Pentecostal reader is not necessarily searching for "scientific" truth as represented by "history." As many postmodern approaches to scripture emphasize, truth is not located exclusively in historical truth,[77] nor is meaning found exclusively in "objective" data. Particularly also as previous fundamentalist definitions were made in the fight against historicist liberalism—the current debates are not of the same order. Following the lead of Brueggemann, Ellington proposes a model for Pentecostals that understands the truth-claims of the Bible as testimonies that—while interested in the question of "what really happened"—are more concerned with understanding the interaction of God with people.[78] This suggestion will be explored in the next chapter in the development of a Pentecostal reading model of the Old Testament.

---

73. Ibid., 246.

74. Childs, *Biblical Theology of the Old and New Testaments*, 416. It must be noted, that while Childs differentiates between "emic" (or insider) approaches and "etic" (outsider) approaches to understanding the description of the ancient Israelite faith, he does not reject the valuable input of historical critical reconstruction. He writes, "Historical critical reconstructions can aid the interpreter in understanding Israel's own witness by seeing how its witness to the content of its experience with God over generations led to a reshaping of its faith in a manner often very different from the actual historical development, at times overriding, subordinating or recasting the noetic sequence in the light of a new and more profound ontic interpretation of the ways of God with Israel."

75. Ellington, "History, Story, and Testimony," 246. Instead for postmoderns, truth is located in the functioning of the text rather than in 'historical' truth (ibid., 251).

76. Ibid., 255.

77. Ibid., 251.

78. Ibid., 246.

FROM PRINCIPLE TO PRACTICE

The literalist tendency of the Pentecostal readings studied here is demonstrated in their interpretations of Isaiah 54 and 61. This literalism reads the contemporary understanding of the language and imagery into the interpretation of the biblical text. This process adopted by Pentecostal readers does not recognize the cultural distance between the horizons of the reader and text. Yet, the cultural location and worldview(s) of the biblical writers are fundamentally different from the worldview of the Pentecostal community. This worldview is reflected in the text; each text has its historical and cultural context to which the text is bound. Therefore the recognition of the cultural and historical context of the text is crucial if one is to avoid irresponsible readings. The significance of the text to the original community helps provide boundaries of reasonable interpretation. This involves asking questions about the significance of the text to its original community (as represented in the text). While the Pentecostal readings of Isaiah demonstrated a dynamic quality that resulted in multiple meanings, textual polysemy does not mean simply "what-you-will."[79] The text specifies the limits of its own meaning in order to avoid open-ended subjectivity.[80]

Yet, how does the Pentecostal community achieve this? How does the Pentecostal reader contemporize the Old Testament texts while still respecting the historical-cultural location of the text? Boundaries of reading are provided by recognizing the historical and cultural context and allowing the voice of the text to be heard for its own unique contribution. The text can be contemporized as long as the historical-cultural differences between the text and reader are recognized. Indeed for the text to "live" it is vital that the readings of the Pentecostal community maintain their dynamic quality. However, this must not come at the expense of the horizon of the text. It is crucial that the text is both understood for its significance to the older covenant community but also interpreted and brought into the world of the Pentecostal community who look to the text for guidance.[81] According to Croatto, this is achieved by updating the biblical texts so as to render the biblical kerygma effective for our de facto situations.[82] In this way, the truth of the testimony and the kerygma of the biblical text is relevant to the testimony of the contemporary Pentecostal community. This maintains the value of pneumatic encounter and God's intervention in history in the reading of the biblical text. As Clark asserts, "Most Pentecostals maintain that the movement of God's Spirit in human history, tied as it is to the proclamation and values of Scripture, is not merely another religious phenomenon, but the experiential making-known of the only Way, Truth and Life: Jesus Christ. This means that the search for a pentecostal hermeneutic must take seriously the absolute claims of Scripture and its God: claims which have led its people and their spiritual forebears to sacrifice everything they are and have to live lives of radical discipleship."[83]

79. Croatto, *Biblical Hermeneutics,* 80.

80. Ma, "Biblical Studies in the Pentecostal Tradition," 63.

81. Holmgren, *The Old Testament and the Significance of Jesus,* 29.

82. Croatto, *Biblical Hermeneutics,* 69.

83. Clark, "An Investigation into the Nature of a Viable Pentecostal Hermeneutic," 90–91.

It is crucial for the development of a Pentecostal reading model of the Old Testament that the historical-cultural context of the text be recognized in order to avoid the literalist tendencies identified in their readings. The significance of the text to the original community helps provide boundaries of responsible interpretation. Yet, this recognition should not quench the dynamic nature of their readings as they apply the text through their experience of salvation in Christ and infilling by the Spirit.

From this presentation of the readings of *Isaiah* by the Pentecostal community, the features of their unique reading practices can be articulated. This will not only help the Pentecostal community to understand themselves and their reading practices more critically, but will also assist in the development of a reading model that is representative of the community. However, a model that blindly adopts the culture of its group without reflection and critique is irresponsible. Therefore these readings, voiced from the Pentecostal community, must be categorized and critiqued to not only highlight the dominant features prevalent, but also to evaluate their role in the development of a responsible Pentecostal reading model of the Old Testament.

7

Resolving the Conflict

FOR A READING MODEL to be relevant for a community, it must be consistent with the values and traditions of the movement to which the proposal is being presented and represents. It must also offer a voice of correction (by critical reflection) if it is to develop and enhance the reading experience of a community. It has been the aim of this book to reflect upon the actual reading practices of real Pentecostal communities, using readings of *Isaiah* as a source of data. With these as a foundation, we can present a reading model for the Old Testament that accentuates the strengths and addresses the weaknesses of the community's reading method. In this sense, we move from the questions of "what" and "why" to "how." The conversation between hermeneutics, Pentecostals, and the Old Testament is directed by the pragmatic concern to ensure a responsible reading method. Yet, as we do this, it is important to take into consideration the constructive values of the community, as elucidated from the readings of *Isaiah* and develop them into a reading model that is of critical benefit the Pentecostal reader.

In the study of Pentecostal reading practices, we noted that one of the dominant features of their interpretations of *Isaiah* is their focus on the experience of the individual reader. In this *dynamic* reading, the text serves as a symbol to connect the experience of the Pentecostal reader with their theological understanding of the actions of God in the world. The symbol from the text illuminates the experience of the reader and makes that experience intelligible. The specific historical event or experience in the text thus points to a universal truth or worldview that the Pentecostal reader identifies within their own experience or worldview. This does not provide the Pentecostal reader with "information," so much as an understanding of God and themselves. However (as noted above) by divorcing the text from its historical-cultural moorings, the readings tend towards a literalism that not only imposes contemporary meanings onto the interpretation, but also denies the unique voice of the Old Testament text. Any critical reading model will thus uphold the Pentecostal core values of dynamic reading and christological perspective but also restore a balance by recognizing the intrinsically "different" historical-cultural context represented in the biblical text.

The impetus for reading biblical texts in the Pentecostal community is to obtain transformative encounter with God. However the Pentecostal community does not encounter God in isolation from the acts of God in the past or future, but as part of an ongoing drama in which God interacts with and empowers the church for mission. Land notes this value in the Pentecostal community: "The kingdom of God was at work among God's people, and the evidence was much the same in the twentieth as in the first century."[1] For the Pentecostal community, God has not changed, and therefore the actions, character and intentions of God for humanity are the same today as they were for the biblical communities. Land continues, "Believers today, they reasoned, can, should and must evidence the same longing and power as the first Christians, if they are to be in eschatological continuity with the beginning and end of the church of Pentecost."[2]

This affirms the role of the Pentecostal community as part of the biblical drama and their participation in history as part of God's story.[3] As the story of God unfolds—from creation through Calvary and Pentecost to the present—each person has a part to play. This gives a sense of directedness to individual lives and unites the Pentecostal community in purpose and mission. That the Pentecostal community values the experience of its members (including lay readers) as it focuses on individual encounter[4] is evidenced by the highly individualistic nature of their dynamic readings. Pentecostal readers are not just interested in understanding, but in action and change. Land continues, "Thus the present was to be lived in hope, obedience and holiness. God, who has not changed, will keep the divine promises and give surprises, representations, intimations, glimpses of the future along the way through gifts of the Spirit."[5] The metaphor of participation in God's story is utilized by the Pentecostal community to maintain their core values and can be used to highlight, through this imagery, the necessary corrections to their reading processes.

The participation of the Pentecostal community in the ongoing drama of the salvation of humanity is a key image in this reading proposal. It highlights the involvement and uniqueness of communities of faith in the past, present and future. The question central to this Pentecostal reading model of the Old Testament is: what does the text mean to *me*, to *them* and to *us*? The meaning and significance of the text to the individual reader is highlighted in the dynamic tendencies observed in the Pentecostal readings of

---

1. Land, *Pentecostal Spirituality*, 58.

2. Ibid., 60.

3. Ibid., 70. Land particularly notes the use of biblical metaphors adopted by the Pentecostal community to highlight their participation in the ongoing history of salvation. He writes, "The point was to experience life as part of a biblical drama of participation in God's history. The church was a movement from the outer court to the inner court to the holy of holies; from Egypt through the desert across the Jordan into Canaan; from Jerusalem to Judea, Samaria and the end of the age (and the uttermost parts of the earth); from justification to sanctification to Spirit baptism, and then in justification, sanctification and Spirit baptism into the harvest" (Land, *Pentecostal Spirituality*, 75).

4. Droogers, "The Normalization of Religious Experience," 46.

5. Land, *Pentecostal Spirituality*, 68.

Isaiah. The Pentecostal reading model appreciates the transformative power of the text as the experience of the reader and the text interact, providing meaning and significance to *me* as an individual reader. This is where most of our Pentecostal subjects tended to stop in reading *Isaiah*; they did not read the text beyond its personal significance for themselves, but read the text for a transformative message through their christological glasses, regardless of the historical-cultural context of the older covenant text. This inherent weakness in the Pentecostal reading approach may be addressed in the adoption of this three-tiered model. The model addresses this limitation as the Pentecostal reader does not read in isolation but as part of the wider Pentecostal and Christian community who, in turn, are identified as part of the ongoing people of God. For this reason, it is important to question the significance of the text for *them*—the people of God in previous communities to whom the Old Testament text holds different meaning. More specifically, the significance for "them" refers to the community and culture represented in the text. While the full significance and meaning of the Old Testament text to the previous community may not be known, this question at least respects historical-cultural contextual differences, and differentiates the two horizons of reader and text. Where the significance and meaning of the Old Testament text to the previous community is known, this question allows the unique voice of the previous community of faith (pre-New Testament) to be heard.

This is an approach that does not contradict the legitimacy of the historical and cultural context of the text, but (to use the terminology of Childs) *extends* it.[6] Childs asks, "Specifically in terms of an understanding of God, what features do the two testaments hold in common respecting the mode, intention, and goal of God's self-manifestation? A comparison is being made, but neither witness is absorbed by the other, nor their contexts fused."[7] However, while it is important to appreciate the unique voice of the Old Testament text, the identity of the Pentecostal community is associated with the New Testament people of God. While God is unchanging, the Pentecostal community acknowledges the changed nature of God's covenantal activity as inaugurated by the life and ministry of Jesus Christ. There are both continuities and discontinuities between the older covenant and the newer covenant as embraced by the Christian community. The value of the christological perspective highlighted in Pentecostal reading of *Isaiah* emphasizes the significance of the text to *us*; the Christian community. Although the Pentecostal community provides the "communal consensus" or the boundaries of expectation in reading, this Pentecostal reading model explicitly locates the community in the context of ongoing participation in the story of salvation.

A MODEL FOR READING

The key image adopted in this reading model of the Old Testament is the value that the Pentecostal community place in "being" participants in the ongoing history (God's

---

6. Childs, *Biblical Theology of the Old and New Testaments,* 380.

7. Ibid.

story) of salvation.[8] From this perspective, the Pentecostal community can read the Old Testament as *part of* the people of God. As Childs notes, this designation of the "people of God" (*'am YHWH*) is the most basic Old Testament term to describe God's special relationship to Israel.[9] For Wellhausen, this formulation (of Yahweh as the God of Israel and Israel as the people of God) was the essence of Israel's religion.[10] Childs notes how the New Testament at times continues the conventional terminology of the Old Testament, though he recognizes that "it is not always evident how much weight to attach it."[11] The New Testament church lies in continuity with Israel, not as a historical extension, but through the reality of faith.[12] While there are many claims to continuity with the communities of faith represented in Scripture, the Pentecostal community is one voice that seeks to be identified as being consistent with the New Testament understanding of the "people of God." The validity of their claim is akin to the acceptance of Paul's ministry to the Gentiles by the early church because God had given them the "Holy Spirit just as he did to us" (Acts 15:8). In like manner, the Pentecostal community appeals to the creative role of the Spirit in bringing forth new forms of the church as the "people of God"[13] through the Lukan narrative. This reading of the narrative does not replace the Jewish people, but rather "Israel is now divided into repentant and unrepentant Jews, and the church consists of both those believing Jews and Gentiles who together form the one true Israel."[14]

The corporate identity of the Pentecostal community is thus in positive continuity with Israel and the New Testament worshippers. Participation as the "people of God" is

---

8. This perspective of Scripture being the ongoing story of God's purposes and plans for redemption is highlighted by Bird ("Paul Ricoeur's Hermeneutical Theory and Pentecostal Proclamation," 39) as a feature of the early church and pre-critical era.

9. Childs, *Biblical Theology of the Old and New Testaments,* 421.

10. Ibid.

11. Ibid., 428. Childs notes the importance when relating the New Testament to the Old Testament to account for the influence of Hellenistic Judaism preceding and contemporaneous with the New Testament. However, he also recognizes that "the implication cannot be drawn that the only proper, scientific method of relating the testaments now lies in tracing a historical trajectory which spans Old Testament, Hellenistic Judaism, and the New Testament. Rather, the reflective, critical task of biblical theology remains as to how to relate the two canonical testaments theologically which is not the same as merely sketching a historical development. In sum, the issue continues of relating the Old Testament's own witness to that of the New, whose voice bears the unmistakable accents of first-century Judaism, especially in the manner in which the Old Testament was heard and transmitted' (ibid., 429).

12. Ibid., 435.

13. Ibid., 448.

14. Ibid., 436. The writings of Paul in the New Testament present the church as the eschatological Israel, "whose entire existence is characterized by life in the Spirit" (ibid., 435). This does not mean that God has rejected Israel. For Paul, as Childs continues, "From his encounter with the exalted Lord he confesses the creation of a totally new and eschatological people of God, brought forth by the power of Christ's Spirit. It is not fully clear how Paul understands the relation of this new people with the Jews, 'his kinsmen by race' (Rom 9:3). He confesses it to be a mystery how 'all Israel will be saved,' which is grounded in the inscrutable will of God, and he is content to allow God full freedom as he concludes his chapter with a doxology (11.33ff.)" (ibid., 448). For discussion of the theme of the "people of God" in the synoptic and fourth Gospels, see ibid., 428–34.

a present reality for the Pentecostal community. Pentecostals value "the notion that the history of God with his people, as narrated in Scripture, still continues now, in the same manner and accompanied by similar phenomena."[15] As Clark notes, the Pentecostal movement has a strong sense of continuity with God's action in history.[16] He writes, "In solidarity with their antecedents, Pentecostals stress their *continuity* with the personal dynamic action of the saving God through the intervention of his Spirit in human history, and that through a called and empowered priesthood of individual believers."[17] If the Pentecostal community is to participate in this ongoing history of God, they need to live in obedience and engagement with God and Scripture. Indeed the Pentecostal community identifies itself as an active rather than passive participant, which partners with God to transform both contemporary society and thus the future with the gospel. The Bible is not merely a textbook of human history, but the testimony of God's relationship with humanity; a history that continues in the present community of faithful believers. As Johns notes, "Historically, Pentecostals have subscribed to a dispensationalism that emphasizes a progressive unfolding of revelation and the interrelation of the ages. All events, past, present, and future are related to a single master plan of God that will be consummated at the second coming of Christ."[18] The aim of the Pentecostal community is not to compile dogma and confessions but to *live* and *act*.[19] For Clark, this includes making visible the powerful presence of God through the operation of the charismata.[20]

The concept of *participation* in this ongoing drama of history is crucial to the Pentecostal identity. The Pentecostal reader discovers their role in the activity of God as they take on the mantle of mission and evangelism from the New Testament writers and the Christian church throughout history. McKay writes of "a discovery that one has stepped out of the audience into the play where one shares in so many, if not ultimately all, of the experiences of the actors, particularly of the charismatics/Pentecostals of the last act in the New Testament church."[21] This is reflected in the eschatological urgency of the Pentecostal community for evangelism and mission. The general pattern of the re-

15. Clark, "An Investigation into the Nature of a Viable Pentecostal Hermeneutic," 24.

16. Ibid., 37.

17. Ibid., 39.

18. Johns, "Yielding to the Spirit," 52.

19. Clark, "An Investigation into the Nature of a Viable Pentecostal Hermeneutic," 40. Clark notes this same interest in the contemporary community as participants in the ongoing history of God with earlier Christian communities, such as Anabaptist, Wesleyan groups, and nineteenth-century Holiness movements. These groups are identified by Clark as antecedents of Pentecostalism (ibid., 40).

20. Ibid. The Pentecostal community is not only in continuity with the New Testament church, but that the latter provides the model for Christian living. As Roelofs notes, "The charismatic model of thought is furthermore inspired and reinforced by 'a surrender to . . . the First Century Christian Schema.' This schema is said to be found in the texts of the New Testament, starting with the description of Pentecost in the Acts of the Apostles. Here, charismatics find the 'authentic model' of a Christian community after the resurrection of the Messiah. It offers them a blueprint for strong experiences of God. Many of them testify that they recognize themselves in these texts. For these people, what happened among the first Christians does not belong to a different and past culture. It is 'everyday reality.'" (Roelofs, "Charismatic Christian Thought," 226).

21. McKay, "When the Veil is Taken Away," 39.

ception of the Spirit by the early church was identified from the Lukan narrative as normative and to be replicated in the life of each individual believer.[22] Dayton also notes this appropriation of the experiences of the Old Testament "people of God" by the nineteenth century antecedents to Pentecostalism. In this sense, each encounter with God presented in the Old Testament provides a pattern or testimony for the Pentecostal community to participate in or learn by.[23] For example, the exodus from Egypt, the wilderness wanderings, and crossing the Jordan River into the Promised Land all became stages in the normative pattern of the spiritual pilgrimage from conversion into the "second blessing" of "Beulah Land."[24] In this way, every pattern and act of participation as the people of God in the continuation of history points to the director and activator of those events: God.

The hermeneutical key for the "people of God" motif is the unchangeableness of God. This makes normative God's interaction with the communities of faith in both testaments to be normative. McLean notes, "The Pentecostal will insist on the continuity of the mode of God's presence in and among the faithful from creation down to this very day."[25] From this premise, God is as much an active, causative agent in the contemporary church as God is in the biblical writings.[26] This conviction of the unchangeableness of God is important in Pentecostal readings as the dynamic feature of their reading practice demonstrates: the text points to a greater reality of God's actions in the world. The Pentecostal reader assumes this continuity of the character of God as they apply principles from the text to their contemporary situation. As participants in salvation history, the Pentecostal community expects to follow in the footsteps of Jesus, empowered by the Spirit to teach, preach, and heal as commanded.[27] The question remains as to how, and how much, the Pentecostal community should follow in the footsteps of the community of faith of the *older* covenant.

This concept of the continuity of the "people of God" is a unifying factor between the older and newer testaments for the Pentecostal community.[28] However, while there

---

22. Dayton, *Theological Roots of Pentecostalism,* 23.

23. As Wonsuk Ma notes, "The Bible was read as a record of God's interaction with, and revelation to, his people. Pentecostals readily accepted not only the validity of the supernatural events described in the Bible but also God's ability to do similar miracles in their midst" (Ma, "Biblical Studies in the Pentecostal Tradition," 55).

24. Dayton, *Theological Roots of Pentecostalism,* 23–24.

25. McLean, "Toward a Pentecostal Hermeneutic," 38.

26. Ibid.

27. Roelofs, "Charismatic Christian Thought," 229.

28. Croatto acknowledges that "To continue to speak of an 'Old' and a 'New' Testament has its practical utility for distinguishing textual blocks, traditions, and eras, but it undermines the hermeneutic effort of the primitive church to constitute a *single* text. Thus it is the better to employ such terms as 'Bible' and 'Scriptures' . . . If the Bible, then, is a *single* text, it is not the cumulative sum of a plurality of literary units. It is the unification of a linguistically coded central kerygma. Henceforth it is possible to recognize, in this one, extended account, the 'semantic axes' orientating the production of meaning that is our reading of the Bible" (Croatto, *Biblical Hermeneutics,* 57). For Croatto, one of the "axes of meaning" in the Bible as a totality would be the kerygma of the liberation of the oppressed (ibid., 58). These "axes" structure the Bible as a single, lengthy account. For Pentecostal readers concepts of continuity as the people of God and testimony to this activity function as Croatto's semantic axes. In the quest for "semantic axes," the Bible produces a

are certain continuities evident in this designation as the "people of God" (such as worship and election)[29] there are also discontinuities. Childs notes:

> there is a dialectical pattern which is reflected in both testaments. Within the Old Testament Israel is portrayed as a concrete, historical nation, as well as a trans-historical, even ideal reality. It has both a political past and an eschatological future. The "people of God" comprises "all Israel," but at times this is only a faithful remnant. The nation chosen by God can be described according to a quality of response as a holy and obedient people. It is a social entity and an invisible fellowship. It can describe its identity over against the Gentiles, but then again to define its mission as a "light to the nations." Likewise the New Testament can speak of an old and new Israel, a people of the flesh and of the spirit. The church both defines itself in complete solidarity as well as in radical discontinuity with the ancient people of God.[30]

The importance of the discontinuities is highlighted by the significance of the Old Testament text to both "them" and "us." While the significance of an Old Testament text may be meaningful to the "people of God" represented in the text in their establishment and maintenance as a socio-political entity, this significance is clearly not continued in the New Testament. The New Testament teaches a newer covenant in which the people of God do no obtain membership in the kingdom of God as a socio-political unit, but in a kingdom of God which is in the hearts of the believer. For the Pentecostal community, God does not work through a chosen nation, but a chosen people comprised from the nations of the world. The significance of the text to "us" will therefore reflect this new covenant understanding, in the coming of the Pentecostal community as the "people of God."

This adoption of the "people of God" as the framework for a Pentecostal reading model of the Old Testament establishes the biblical text as a meta-narrative, in which the Pentecostal reader can locate themselves. As Goldingay writes, "In general, the biblical story is designed to enable us to discover who we are. We do that by telling our own story, but by telling it in the context of the Bible story. We find ourselves by setting ourselves in that other story."[31] The narratives of the Pentecostal reader ("me") are told in the context of the meta-narrative of the Bible ("them" and "us"). Counter to the postmodern trajectory, the Pentecostal community recognizes the meta-narrative in the history of which they are a part. Indeed, it points out the irony of this rejection of meta-narrative by postmodernism in that postmodernity is itself located in a meta-narrative. The term "postmodern," after all, presupposes a meta-narrative that includes pre-Modernism and Modernism. The ludic nature of this self-critical movement is that its last laugh is at itself.

---

new meaning effect (ibid., 58). For the Pentecostal community, that meaning is found in their experience as the people of God.

29. Noting from the "Introduction" the Armenian flavor of Pentecostal theology that tends to define their understanding of "election" as being chosen for the purpose of calling others into the kingdom of God. This is in contrast to other theological reflections of "election" including Calvinism.

30. Childs, *Biblical Theology of the Old and New Testaments,* 442.

31. Quoted in Ellington, "History, Story, and Testimony," 258–59.

While it cannot share postmodern irony, Pentecostal reading models share a historical concern with the dominance of scientism, and so are not just concerned with scientific method but with total human experience. The Pentecostal community is not concerned with amassing knowledge for knowledge's sake but from the desire to "know" God. As Pentecostal readers approach the Old Testament text with the desire to hear God speak to them they do in a vibrant relationship of forming and informing meaning through the interaction of the significance of the text to these three entities: "me," "them," and "us." Each entity (of "me," "them," and "us") is important and cannot be ignored or isolated. As Poythress writes, "God meets us and speaks to us in power as we read the Bible. God's power and presence must be taken into account from the beginning, just as we take into account all that characterizes a human author of any human text. We cannot, with perfect precision, analytically isolate God's propositional content from his personal communion. To attempt to perform grammatical-historical exegesis by such an isolating procedure is impious."[32] The significance of each entity is crucial in the search for a balanced voice and balanced reading for the Pentecostal community. To hear only "me," "them," and "us" in isolation is to miss part of the conversation. The tendency of many of the Pentecostal readings of *Isaiah* noted above (chapter 3) was to disregard or be ignorant of the voices of "them," and "us," hearing only the voice of "me." All the voices should be heard in a Pentecostal reading of Old Testament texts to provide boundaries of responsible reading. The interaction of these voices provides controls against the loud domination of a single voice and offers "check points" against each other.

By appreciating all three voices, this reading model also recognizes that God speaks to people where they are at. Just as God spoke to the community of "ancient Israel" in their own language, setting, culture, and context with a message relevant to their situation, so God also speaks to a "located" Pentecostal community. This emphasizes the immanence of God. It reminds the Pentecostal reader that Scripture did not "fall from heaven" but was the product of the historical and cultural context of the community that received it.[33] In this sense, the Bible is not trans-historical or trans-cultural[34] but the meaningful message from God to a community located in a specific historical and cultural setting. It is the same way, in essence, that the Pentecostal community understands God to speak to them in their language, cultural and time.

"Me"

The meaningfulness and message of the biblical text to the individual reader is a core value of the Pentecostal community and needs to be incorporated into any reading model of the Old Testament. The description of the Pentecostal reading approaches of *Isaiah*, discussed in the previous chapters, demonstrated this foundational premise of the Pentecostal community: that God speaks to them through Scripture. The illumination of the biblical text by the Spirit is anticipated. By reading with an open heart and mind, the

---

32. Poythress, "Divine Meaning of Scripture," 112.

33. This highlights the irony that the Pentecostal reader does not read the text in its historical context.

34. Archer, "Early Pentecostal Biblical Interpretation," 39.

Pentecostal reader trusts the Holy Spirit to speak directly from the text of Scripture into their own lives.[35] Therefore the significance of the biblical text to the individual reader ("me") is a crucial element of this reading model. As the Pentecostal reader approaches the biblical text with the goal of hearing from God, they read the text seeking the significance of the words for "me." While the potentiality for literalism and fundamentalism in this approach has been discussed, this tendency can be addressed through the dialogue (reading in conversation with "us" and "them") that this model proposes, so controlling the potential for rampant subjectivism.

As discussed previously, within this dynamic reading approach, the Pentecostal reader identifies themselves and their experience in a particular biblical text. From this association or resonance, they identify a particular universal truth or experience to which the text points; the text acts as a sign that points to God's interaction with—and laws governing—the world. In this sense, there is a referential function of the text that points to a larger pattern of meaning that exists in the worldview of the Pentecostal reader(s). This is the meaning of the text to the Pentecostal reader; to "me." The text highlights an important truth in God's interactions in the world (including their context and situation). The biblical text highlights a spiritual principle that resonates with the experience of the Pentecostal reader in Christian living. The text provides the symbol by which the reader can understand or view their world. It opens a new way of living and invites the reader to participate in this world to which the text points. It suggests a new way of living, thinking, being and acting[36] through its directive. This was portrayed in Diagram 2 as a dynamic interaction of personal experience, Pentecostal value system (or worldview of the Pentecostal community in which the reader is placed) and the text. The symbol (text), experience of the reader and the Pentecostal value-system interact to produce the meaning and significance for the individual reader (me). Reading is not a passive process or simply an issue for the mind. This diagram highlights the role of the reader as they contribute to the meaning of the text. The reader associates, remembers, imagines, expects, and concludes.[37] It represents a wholeness of meaning for the Pentecostal reader that incorporates all three elements of the reading experience. The aim of this process is to extract from the text the meaning for the individual reader, not just explain its content.[38] This allows for exciting possibilities in the reading of biblical texts.

While the dynamic personal reading for "me" is affirmed by this Pentecostal reading model it is important to recognize that the principles the text points to must have connection, or be analogous, to the meaning of the text for "them" and "us." Pentecostal reading is a process of both "self-realization" and "other-realization-in-self." The determination of analogy is decided by the reading community, which must be accountable to the wider ecumenical dialogue. The reading of the text by *me* must be part of the bigger story; the story of God's interaction with the people of faith and present interaction within the community of Pentecostal readers. As Johns notes, "To encounter God is to know oneself

35. Fee, "History as Context for Interpretation," 11.

36. Smit, "Biblical Hermeneutics," 301.

37. Ibid., 308.

38. Ibid., 299.

as a subject and object in history."[39] Yet, even though the personal significance of the text must be located in the general narrative of salvation history, the significance of the text to "me" is also a private question. The significance of the text to "me" is determined according to the identity and context of "me;" it will be different for each reader. Although each "me" is located in a community of readers, making the outcome and application of their reading a public issue as they live and act in a wider community, this aspect of the reading model addresses them as unique individuals. While capacity of all people for self-deception generates a role for the community in providing accountability,[40] the significance of the text to "me" limits meaning of the text from being universally applicable to all other believers, even while the reader shares with others their experience of reading Scripture.[41] This approach requires personal engagement with the text and involves an active response in the application of the text to the unique location of the reader. As Johns notes, "if a person knew God, he or she was encountered by One who lived in the midst of history and who initiated covenant relationship which called for a response of the total person. Knowledge of God, therefore, was not measured by the information one possessed, but by how one was living in response to God."[42] The unique situation and context of the reader is addressed through the voice of the Spirit, who speaks to the reader through the text and applies it to their Christian living.

This role of the Holy Spirit is crucial as the Pentecostal reader seeks to hear the Spirit's voice speaking to them through the pages of Scripture. Scripture is sterile unless it discloses true knowledge of the self to the individual reader and to their community. As Clark writes, "The Holy Spirit is regarded as far more than the source of light shed on the text: He is expected to offer personal and corporate guidance, to grant discernment between true and false, to empower Christian witness based upon the message of the text, and to demonstrate the ongoing involvement of the God of the Bible with needy humanity."[43] The text speaks to the Pentecostal reader with insight into the reader's own context and situation. This model proposes that the Pentecostal reader asks: what does the text mean to *me*? Through this process, the text can speak to the Pentecostal reader. This aspect of the model highlights the reading experience of the Pentecostal community as an opportunity to encounter God in the text event as individual readers who corporately form a reading community. This emphasizes the continuing activity of the divine speaker and the necessity of an encounter with that speaker in the heart of the believer.[44] The Pentecostal reader anticipates transformation and renewal from the

39. Johns, "Yielding to the Spirit," 76.

40. Stroup, *The Promise of Narrative Theology*, 129. Stroup continues his discussion by noting that while entire communities can suffer self-deception. When this happens, he suggests, the only hope for the community is in the prophet to highlight and point the community to the truth (ibid., 130). However it would be hoped that the involvement of the community in the ecumenical dialogue would also be a voice of balance.

41. Fee, "History as Context for Interpretation," 11–12.

42. Johns, "Yielding to the Spirit," 78.

43. Clark, "An Investigation into the Nature of a Viable Pentecostal Hermeneutic," 206.

44. Bird, *The Bible as the Church's Book,* 47. As Bird notes, this shifts the authority so that it is not exclusively located in either the words themselves or in the historical authors, but in the divine author (ibid., 47).

encounter. The significance of the text for "me" is identified for the purpose of shaping Christian identity and behavior ("us") and participation as the ongoing "people of God." While the Pentecostal reader ("me") encounters God in the text, the challenge for the Pentecostal community is to broaden their expectation that the spirit may also speak through the reflection of the significance of the text for "them" and for "us."

"Them"

The observation of Pentecostal reading practices from *Isaiah* highlights the need for the community to appreciate the cultural-historical context of Old Testament texts. The task of interpretation requires the Pentecostal community to overcome the historical weakness in their reading practices and to bridge the historical and cultural gap between "them" and "me," without merely absorbing the culture of the older text into the culture of the reader. As our subject pool of Pentecostal readings of *Isaiah* tended to disregard or be ignorant of this step, it is a crucial corrective. By doing this, the reader can hear and understand how God spoke to "them" through the testimony of the older covenant text. Rather than subsume the culture and historical situation of the text into the situation of the reader (literalism) the context of the text and its meaning for "them" must be voiced. Fee notes "Because its human authors spoke their own language, out of their own culture and in their own history, we must go back to them and listen to what they meant in their own historical contexts if we are going to hear the word of the living God—both to them and us. Precisely because God spoke his eternal word to them within their own particular history, we can take great confidence that he will speak again out of that context into lives all over the globe."[45] The unique voice of the Old Testament text must be heard by the contemporary Pentecostal community. Yet, while the cultural-historical context of "them" is recognized as important for the Pentecostal reading model, the question must be raised: who is "them"? As Davies asks concerning the designation of "ancient Israel" as a historical term, "what sort of identity, if any, was implied by the self-designation 'Israelite' in ancient times? Where and when does 'Israelite culture' begin and end, and how does one characterize and identify it? This last question is surely the fundamental question for a modern historian of ancient Israel: what exactly do we now mean by 'Israel'?"[46] As Conrad suggests, "Texts from the past are not reflections of history; they are artifacts of its construction."[47] Who, then, is this construction of "them"? In the same way, what does the term "them" refer to in this Pentecostal reading model of the Old Testament?

While the term "them" generally refers to the community addressed by the author, it is clear within the realm of biblical studies that the identification of the recipients of biblical texts is typically *unclear*. Is it the community addressed by the (possibly) oral tradition, or by the author(s) or by the redactor(s) of the Old Testament text? For example, is

45. Fee, "History as Context for Interpretation," 13. Fee continues his discussion by noting that "because God's eternal word was given in human words in history, those words were themselves conditioned by the culture, background and speech patterns of the author. God's eternal word was spoken in historically particular moments" (ibid., 13).

46. Davies, "Whose History? Whose Israel? Whose Bible?" 112.

47. Conrad, "Prophet, Redactor and Audience," 314.

the "them" of the Pentateuch referring to the community of the oral tradition(s), the community of the author(s) or the community of the redactor(s)? Depending on how "them" is designated, the community addressed by the Pentateuch could be located anywhere in the pre-monarchic, or exilic, or even post-exilic context. The identification of "them" will differ according to the critical skills, knowledge and resources of the Pentecostal reader. For a lay reader with little knowledge of the scholarly debates regarding authorship and redaction, the meaning for "them" may refer to the "old testament times" generally (i.e., the ancient society before the coming of Christ).[48] In comparison, for a reader exposed to more scholarly issues, the "them" of a text may be more specific. Yet as Conrad notes, the historical-critical reading of Old Testament texts is often inaccessible to the lay reader due to the adoption of reading strategies that require highly technical skills.[49] Despite this variance of knowledge, the purpose of appreciating the meaning of the text for "them" is the attempt to understand the text from the general historico-cultural location and worldview of the older covenant text.[50] The Pentecostal reader enters the world of the older covenant testimony. This process highlights the differences between the world of the Pentecostal reader and the world of the Old Testament text. In this way, the reading for "them" is not a domestication of the world of the Old Testament making it simply a mirror reflection of contemporary culture and its values and worldview.[51] The meaning of the Old Testament text to "them" is the significance of the text to the older covenant people of God. This appreciates the uniqueness of the testimony of ancient Israel in the Old Testament, as distinct from a New Testament or Christian reading.

The significance of the text to "them" recognizes the voice of an ancient community. For example, the testimony of *Isaiah* may be the voice of the community in the context of pre- and post-exile. The testimony of Isaiah 61 presents itself as an utterance to the post-exilic community. While this general context may be inadequate for academic study of the text, it sufficiently separates it as other than the horizon of the general Pentecostal reading community. The recognition of such differences, and active pursuit of an understanding of the context of "them" (the older covenant community), creates a faithful yet critical edge to the reading practices of the Pentecostal community. A more simple reflection on the context of Old Testament Scripture should not obstruct academics, and more detailed "scientific" study of context should not intimidate lay readers. Neither should

---

48. Dyck writes concerning the reading of Genesis: "The book of Genesis refers to the patriarchs. Whatever position one may take regarding the historicity of these accounts, one must admit that the text shows not a trace of interest in the context of the narrator of the accounts. Yet, our exegetical task, as normally defined, tells us to be primarily interested in the narrator's context, the very context with respect to which the text is mute" (Dyck, "Canon as Context for Interpretation," 43).

49. Conrad, *Reading Isaiah*, 25.

50. This understanding of the "historical context," as represented by Conrad, includes dialogue with archaeology and social historians. He writes, "Reading prophetic books in their historical context necessitates dialogue with archaeological studies, which in turn are encountering archaeological remains of the past as texts requiring interpretation. It means dialogue with historians of ancient Palestine, many of whom are stressing the need to understand the social dimension of history rather than focus strictly on religious or theological matters" (Conrad, "Prophet, Redactor and Audience," 317).

51. Stroup, *The Promise of Narrative Theology*, 27.

the simple reflection encouraged by this proposal be equated with simplistic theories of historical development.[52] After all, the Pentecostal community needs to recognize the evolution of the final testimony of Israel in the constant re-working of their "testimony." It also recognizes that it is not the prerogative of all Pentecostal readings, such as devotional readings, to engage in technical issues. While there may be a contrast between these level of enquiry from an academic and lay level, all levels of reading need to value each other and take seriously the important insights each study provides.[53] The symbolic world of Old Testament texts is available for all readers and faith communities to construct; the raw material through which they can hear themselves addressed by God.[54] However, encouragement for the Pentecostal community to engage in the comparison of responsible English translations of the Old Testament and awareness of the Hebrew text may also assist in the recognition of the unique voice of the ancient community.

The significance of the text to "them"—the older covenant people of God—does not uniquely preference the veracity of the historical account (as discussed previously) but rather hears the voice of their "testimony." The message of "them" is a past testimony and an authoritative (canonical) testimony of God's actions. As Ricoeur notes, any testimony is interpretation.[55] The testimony of "them" is the selective remembering and beliefs of the witnesses incorporated into references to events that are believed to be true.[56] According to Brueggemann, the central truth-claims of Israel in the Old Testament are not about historical truth, but the truth offered by the testimony of witnesses. Therefore, the truth of the older covenant is not in the historical events that may or may not lie behind the offered testimony, but is in the testimony itself. Brueggemann writes, "What happened, so our 'verdict' is, is what these witnesses said happened. In complementary fashion, this means that theological interpretation does not go behind this witness with questions of ontology, wondering what is 'real.' What is real, so our 'verdict' is, is what these witnesses say is real. Nothing more historical or ontological is available."[57] While the proper setting of testimony may be a court of law in which various witnesses are called to give their version of the events that have transpired, Brueggemann notes that the use of testimony in any trial situation is a mixed meeting of memory, reconstruction,

---

52. Childs, *Biblical Theology of the Old and New Testaments*, 352. Childs notes that while the Old Testament texts, particularly narratives, cannot be easily dated, this is not license to adopt simplistic theories of the historicity or historical development of the texts. He writes, "In spite of the usefulness of a historical reconstruction in some contexts, it gives a very false impression of Israel's faith if such a development is construed as a unilinear trajectory within a historical continuum" (ibid., 352).

53. Brueggemann in particular notes the need for interaction between academic and ecclesial circles. See Brueggemann, *Theology of the Old Testament*, 774.

54. Melugin, "Figurative Speech and the reading of Isaiah 1 as Scripture," 295. In his study of the figurative language of Isa 1, Melugin notes, "I am convinced that communities of faith must participate imaginatively in the Isaianic symbolic world in order to be transformed profoundly by that prophetic book" (ibid., 305).

55. Ricoeur, "The Hermeneutics of Testimony," 123.

56. Ellington, "History, Story, and Testimony," 262.

57. Brueggemann, *Theology of the Old Testament*, 68.

imagination, and wish.[58] It is then the purpose of the court to determine, with no other data except testimony, which version of the testimonies witness to reality. Brueggemann writes, "It is on the basis of *testimony* that the court reaches what is *real.*"[59] Like in a court of law, there is no access to the "actual event" besides the testimony.[60] In the same way, the Pentecostal community listens to the testimony of "them" to discover the truth of God's past actions and character. This highlights the dual nature of testimony; there is the one who testifies and the one who hears the testimony.[61] The Pentecostal community hears the report for "them."

The development of the concept of "testimony" in the work of Brueggemann and other scholars is part of the trajectory of postmodernity and literary criticism in biblical studies called narrative criticism[62] (or narrative theology). This approach treats the biblical text as a story; the text invites readers into its story-world and makes claims upon the reader's perception of reality.[63] While some narrative theologians, such as Stroup highlight the foundation of the historical events on which the narratives of the Christian Scripture and tradition are told,[64] other narrative critics such as Gunn consider this historical underpinning as unnecessary for the task of narrative criticism since the foundation for meaning is created by the world of the narrative.[65] While the use of narrative criticism in biblical studies ranges widely from the observation of the mechanics or artistry of authors[66] to the study of plot functions by structuralists[67] to the exposure of agendas in more deconstructive approaches,[68] they all locate the meaning of the text in its final form. In extreme examples, narrative criticism completely disconnects the meaning of the text from questions of history so that, for example, the character and actions of God is simply a literary device of the biblical writers.[69] Yet this approach also allows for the simplistic acceptance of the claims of the story as real, so resonating with the Pentecostal tendency towards literalism. Pentecostal readers must be aware that the adoption of "tes-

58. Ibid., 120.

59. Ibid.

60. Ibid., 121.

61. Ricoeur, "The Hermeneutics of Testimony," 123.

62. As Gunn notes, the term "narrative criticism" in biblical studies is loose term used since the 1970s to differentiate approaches based on the literary nature of the text rather than the historical nature of the text (Gunn, "Narrative Criticism," 210). It sees the meaning of the text to be located in its final form, rather than in the understanding of its development.

63. Ellington, "History, Story, and Testimony," 253.

64. Stroup, *The Promise of Narrative Theology*, 17. Stroup writes "Narrative theology is not simply a matter of storytelling. Narrative theology does recognize, however, that Christian faith is rooted in particular historical events which are recounted in the narratives of Christian Scripture and tradition, that these historical narratives are the basis for Christian affirmations about the nature of God and the reality of grace, and that these historical narratives and the faith they spawn are redemptive when they are appropriated at the level of personal identity and existence' (ibid., 17).

65. Gunn, "Narrative Criticism."

66. See Alter, *The Art of Biblical Narrative*; Sternberg, *The Poetics of Biblical Narrative*.

67. See Patte, "Structural Criticism," 183–200; Bal, *Death & Dissymmetry*.

68. See Fewell, "Reading the Bible Ideologically: Feminist Criticism," 268–82.

69. Ellington, "History, Story, and Testimony," 253.

timony" is not an excuse for literalism under the guise of postmodern methodology. While Pentecostal readers also focus on the final form of the text, it is important for them to recognize the text as the result of historical and cultural development.[70] While focusing on the speech of Israel tends to bracket out questions of historicity, it does not deny that the experience of Israel was deeply rooted in the socio-economic-political realities; that which comprises history.[71]

The model of testimony, according to Brueggemann, asks not "What happened?" but "What is said?"[72] As Childs writes, "it is incumbent on the interpreter, especially of the Old Testament, not to confuse the biblical witness with the reality itself. In order to hear the voice of each biblical witness in its own right, it is absolutely necessary to interpret each passage within its historical, literary, and canonical context . . . There is no legitimate way of removing the Old Testament's witness from its historical confrontation with the people of Israel."[73] While the Old Testament text is presented as a unified voice that witnesses to the actions and character of God, the often contradictory and perplexing voices of individual witnesses found in its pages (especially to the contemporary reader) must not be silenced. This also helps to recognize that the testimony of the Old Testament is located in a specific cultural-historical period with a worldview peculiar to that time. This highlights the "other"-ness of the "them."[74] Conrad suggests readers engage biblical texts as "alien" or "unfamiliar" rather than domesticating them.[75] He writes, "Often biblical scholarship has obliterated the 'other' voices of biblical texts by making them speak a familiar language, reducing a dialogue with past texts to a monologue about them."[76] For example, the worldview of the contemporary Pentecostal community is not equivalent to an ancient Israelite cosmology in which the world is viewed as a flat disc with water above and below.[77] This simply reflects a cultural-historical location among biblical writers which contemporary readers cannot imitate or expect to be congruent with. However, the testimony of "them" points to principles of God's character and relationship with the world. As reflected in Pentecostal values, the testimony of ancient Israel highlights Yahweh as an active agent who is the subject of an active verb. They witness to the God of Israel acting in decisive and transformative ways.[78] Speaking of God as the subject helps the Pentecostal reader to recognize that ancient Israel's testimony of God is

---

70. According to Ellington (ibid., 262), the adoption of narrative theology for the Pentecostal community is only helpful to the extent that it is grounded in the concern for 'what happened' and not isolate the text completely from any historical context.

71. Brueggemann, *Theology of the Old Testament*, 118.

72. Ibid.

73. Childs, *Biblical Theology of the Old and New Testaments*, 379.

74. Conrad, "Prophet, Redactor and Audience," 315.

75. Ibid.

76. Ibid.

77. Clark, "An Investigation into the Nature of a Viable Pentecostal Hermeneutic," 87–88.

78. Brueggemann, *Theology of the Old Testament*, 123.

not a description of God *per se*, but of God engaged transformatively with and on behalf of the object, ancient Israel.[79]

Brueggemann notes the basis of the older covenant's speech as a testimony to their encounter with God. Their testimony has become text, now studied by subsequent communities.[80] This concept of testimony resonates with the reading practices of the Pentecostal community. Due to the oral nature of their community and emphasis on the "experience" of the Spirit, the Pentecostal reader tends to offer a "testimony" of experience rather than reasoned answers to theological inquiry.[81] The Pentecostal community accepts the testimony of the biblical text, because it is the witness of the covenant "people of God" with whom they identify. The testimony of the Old Testament text creates a picture of the nature and actions of God as they witness to the intervention of God in the realm and experience of the covenant people. This testimony, then, becomes the reality for the Pentecostal community. As a testimony points to the characteristic actions of another (or an other, namely God) in the Old Testament, and functions on the assumption of the consistency of person and character, it may be assumed that for the Pentecostal community the actions of God in their present context will be consistent with those which are the object of the biblical witness. This approach promotes God as an active agent in both the biblical story and the Pentecostal community.[82] The recognition of God as an active agent, for the Pentecostal community, includes the miraculous intervention of God operating outside a rationalist worldview. And yet, this active agency of God is relevant to and operates within the particular historical-cultural context of the people of God, whether that is an ancient Israelite or a contemporary Pentecostal reader. While there are distinctions between the testimonies of the two covenants, it does not negate the meaningful voice that the witness of the older covenant provides.

It is this concept of Yahweh as the object and purpose of the testimony of ancient Israel that resonates with the key Pentecostal reading purpose of the desire to know God. The witness to the reality of God is central to the Old Testament's understanding.[83] However, this is not a private knowledge. The Pentecostal community identifies with the evangelistic mandate given to the ancient Israelite community to proclaim God's character and salvation for the "other." For the Pentecostal community, the mandate of "them" continues through "us" and "me" to reach the "other." In this way, each voice and testimony in the Pentecostal reading model must be heard for its unique contribution and function as balancing factors in the reading process. The Pentecostal reader is not an isolated reader, but part of the Pentecostal and Christian community. The New

---

79. Ibid., 125. This is also highlighted by Childs who writes, "The biblical language of depicting God in human form is not an unfortunate accommodation to human limitation, but a truthful reflection of the free decision of God to identify with his creation in human form and yet to remain God" (Childs, *Biblical Theology of the Old and New Testaments*, 358). Even the examples of such subjectification of God (such as Isa 6:1: "I saw the Lord") where the "I" conditions "saw" intend objectification.

80. Brueggemann, *Theology of the Old Testament*, 118.

81. Parker, *Led by the Spirit*, 9.

82. Ellington, "History, Story, and Testimony," 262.

83. Childs, *Biblical Theology of the Old and New Testaments*, 358.

Testament provides the interpretive lens through which they also read the older covenant text. Therefore this voice must also be heard in the dialogue of reading. The voice of "us" promotes a concern for the "other" as the mission and vision of the church is articulated through readings of Old Testament texts.

"Us"

While the Pentecostal reading model recognizes the importance of the unique voice of "them" in reading Old Testament texts, the identification and location of the Pentecostal community as the post-Pentecost "people of God" distinguishes them from the older covenant "people of God." The Pentecostal community is not only interested in what the text meant to "them" and "me," but also in the christological implications of the older testament—what the text means to "us" as a Christian community. As Dyck writes, "the Christian interpreter is not interested only in what words meant to another audience but in what they continue to mean to the believing community, today's believers included."[84] The Christian community is the continuation of God's story expressed through the newer covenant inaugurated by the life and ministry of Jesus Christ. The Christ-event presented in the New Testament is an unfinished event as the Pentecostal community takes on the mission of the New Testament community in expanding the kingdom of God. This mandate can also be seen as a continuation of the older covenant testimony of the Abrahamic covenant: that through the seed of Abraham (Jesus Christ) all the nations of the earth will be blessed. However, this new covenant inaugurated by Christ as described in the New Testament text is not identical with the covenant represented in the Old Testament text, but also has discontinuities. This Pentecostal reading proposal highlights, through the significance of the text to "us" (the Christian community), both the continuity and discontinuity of the Pentecostal community with the community of faith represented in the older covenant text. This requires a clear concept of the canon as a whole.[85] For the Pentecostal reader, this has traditionally been the Protestant canon.

The new covenant identity of the Pentecostal (and Christian) community is not based on their socio-political status as a chosen nation, but by their identity as a chosen people with the kingdom of God in their hearts—a people not constituting a nation but comprised from the nations of the world. This discontinuity with the older covenant must also inform the Pentecostal reading model of Old Testament texts, as well as its continuity. The Old Testament presents a physical kingdom; a physical, geographical location that was fought for and defended against flesh and blood enemies (as in the ethically-challenging testimony of *Joshua*). The Old Testament ends with the expectation of a Messiah who will come and save them from their enemies and establish a kingdom of peace centered in the Temple in Jerusalem—God's dwelling place. However, this expectation was transformed by the life and ministry of Jesus Christ who inaugurated a new kingdom; not a political or geographic kingdom but a spiritual kingdom established through the defeat of the spiritual powers at work in the world. Through the exorcism of

84. Dyck, "Canon as Context for Interpretation," 37.
85. Bird, *The Bible as the Church's Book*, 42.

evil spirits, healings and acts of public righteousness, the testimony of the New Testament "people of God" presents Jesus as fighting spiritual enemies to establish this new kingdom.[86] Worship is no longer a physical act, but "in Spirit and in truth." God's presence no longer just dwells in the Temple (the geographical location of Jerusalem) but in the heart of every believer. The climax of the new kingdom comes at the cross and resurrection when Jesus triumphs over the enemy, becoming the first-fruits of a new community.

The Pentecostal community identifies themselves with this new community and with the continuing work in the expansion of the kingdom of God through evangelism and spiritual warfare—not fighting against flesh and blood but against the spiritual enemies of God. By allowing the unique voice of "them" to be heard, the Pentecostal community can hear the testimony of the community of faith represented in the older testament with whose story they participate. Yet, the christological standpoint from which the Pentecostal community reads, throws into relief the discontinuities with this earlier community. This conditions the testimony of the older covenant in its application to the life of the Pentecostal reader—the testimony of "them" must be voiced in dialogue with "us" to determine the direct relevancy and application of the text. For example, while the voice of the testimony of the conquest texts in Joshua can be appreciated (within its ancient Near Eastern context) for their significance to "them," its significance in dialogue with "us" requires acknowledgement that the Pentecostal community is no longer fighting for a physical territory but is engaged in a spiritual battle. Therefore the principles that the unique voice of "them" highlights from their testimony may be applied to this new context, such as holiness, but a direct application of "holy war" is discontinuous with the newer covenant as represented in the New Testament text. Dyck notes that, "Continuity and discontinuity are therefore affirmed, both in the New Testament itself and in the titles by which the two are recognized."[87] However, this requires knowledge of the wider framework of salvation history by the Pentecostal reader, to recognize the continuities and discontinuities and so avoid the potential pitfalls of a simplistic spiritualizing of the earlier testimony or the literal application of the older covenant text to the newer covenant context.

This reading model requires the Pentecostal community to place their reading within the wider framework of the redemptive-historical perspective of the two testaments. As discussed previously, the redemptive-historical framework provides the wider context for reading Old Testament (and New Testament) texts. The testimony of the older covenant text can be voiced by the Pentecostal community as an epic story. The testimony begins at Creation, with the celebration of humanity as the special act of God's deliberate work. Their story then centers on one family, led by Abraham, and his descendants. According to the testimony of the biblical texts, they become slaves in Egypt but are miraculously liberated so they can worship God. Once liberated from Egypt they enter into a covenant relationship with God which recognizes their identity as a unique nation: as noted above, they are "God's people." This community records that they settled

---

86. Longman, *Making Sense of the Old Testament*, 83–86.

87. Dyck, "Canon as Context for Interpretation," 35.

in the Fertile Crescent and eventually (under their first stable king, David) established a united monarchy. This kingdom however was soon divided, followed by a cycle of apostasy, decline, and renewal amidst which the voice of prophets (such as Isaiah) was heard. Being small fish in the big pond of the world of ancient Near Eastern politics, the two kingdoms were continually caught up in the web of political intrigue.

Their testimony records that eventually, due to the violation of their covenant stipulations, the two kingdoms fell. First the Northern kingdom was taken by Assyria then the southern kingdom was captured by Babylon and taken into exile. While the southern kingdom, Judah, was in captivity, the Babylonians were overthrown by the Persians. After a period of time, the Persians allowed the Judeans to return to their homeland to rebuild the city and Temple. They introduced many religious and social reforms but always struggled in their worship and political independence. Throughout these events, as described in the biblical text, the community of faith continued to voice their prayers of complaint and praise to their God and source of all wisdom in the various psalms and wisdom literature.[88] This epic testimony of the older covenant "people of God" is not simple, but important for the Pentecostal community to grasp in order to understand their identity as participants in this drama, and to locate the context of the unique witness of individual Old Testament texts in this meta-narrative. However, according to the New Testament, in the fullness of time, God sent his son to save Israel and the nations from the cycle of sin. Christ, called Immanuel, is the ultimate evidence of "God with us" and God for us. This highlights the necessity of reading the biblical text in the light of the fuller knowledge of God's reality gained from the entirety of Scripture.[89] This approach does not rival the historical study of the biblical text and significance of the text for "'them,'" but complements or extends it.[90]

This reading model proposes that the Pentecostal community question the meaningfulness of the Old Testament text for not only "me" and for "them," but also for "us." What is the significance of the older covenant text for the Christian community? How does it bear on an understanding the life and ministry of Christ, and on the continued mandate of extending this kingdom? As the Pentecostal community continues the ministry of Christ, they also read the Old Testament text as ongoing participants in this meta-narrative. The earlier confessions of the Pentecostal movement highlight their particular christological emphasis and role in the continuation of the mission of Christ. The earlier Pentecostals identified Jesus Christ as Savior, Healer, Baptizer in the Holy Spirit, and Coming King—the so-called "four-square" formula.[91] As Clark notes, this

---

88. It is acknowledged that while this testimony of the Old Testament texts concentrates on the presentation of a meta-narrative, this model generally fails to incorporate adequately other elements of the Old Testament testimony such as wisdom literature and some poetic literature such as the Psalms. However, this contribution of this framework of meta-narrative to the Pentecostal community is enormous in establishing the context of individual texts in a basic (though limited) framework.

89. Childs, *Biblical Theology of the Old and New Testaments*, 381.

90. Ibid.

91. Clark, "An Investigation into the Nature of a Viable Pentecostal Hermeneutic," 23. This is generally considered the defining action of the Spirit—in both constituting the Pentecostal community and "continuing the ministry of Jesus."

Christology "implies a dynamic Christ, who is currently and consistently saving, healing, and baptizing in the Holy Spirit, and whose imminent return supplies urgency to pentecostal preaching and missions."[92] In this continued vocation of Christ, the Pentecostal community participates as they also preach salvation in Christ, pray for healing in the name of Jesus Christ, baptize believers in the Holy Spirit, and anticipate the Parousia. Therefore the Pentecostal community reads the Old Testament text for the understanding and articulation of their experience as the "people of God" and identity in the ongoing drama of history. At the core of the Pentecostal experience is an eschatological urgency and passion for evangelism. Through the testimony of the community of faith in the older covenant, the Pentecostal community articulates their Christian life and pneumatic experience through the symbols, events, and figures of its pages. This kind of analogous reasoning is not limited to identifying Jesus Christ in the Old Testament but in some cases, the Pentecostal community also sees themselves or their situation addressed in ancient Scripture.

CONCLUSION AND FIELD TEST OF THE MODEL

To extend the metaphor of dialogue in this book, the Pentecostal reading model proposed by this study is a harmonious song between the voices of "me," "them," and "us." Each voice comes as a participant in the ongoing drama of history and as a witness to the actions of God. The reading of the Old Testament by the Pentecostal community should be an ongoing and melodious interaction between these three elements, each one informing the other. Each voice provides the boundaries of reading. The model allows a reading to correct itself from its own internal dialogue as the voices engage. Within this model none of the voices can be heard on their own but require listening and interaction. The testimony of "them" and "us" provides the boundary by which the meaning of the text to the reader (me) can be evaluated. The voice of "them" alone is stagnant without the dynamism and immediacy of its significance to the individual (me) and Pentecostal community (us). The voice of "us" requires the foundation and unique voice of "them" to be heard and personal application to the life of the believer (me). A responsible and balanced reading requires participation in the formation of a harmony that respectively includes the reality of the Pentecostal situation, the newer covenant experience, and the text.

Yet while the three voices of "me," "them," and "us" engage in harmonization, what if the music turns sour? What if the vibrant song is disharmonious and flat? What if cooperation fails? Should there be a soloist or dominant "voice" if this situation arises? Clark suggests that where there is conflict and discrepancy, the priority should be given to the "literal" meaning of the text in to avoid the worst excesses of subjectivity.[93] That is, the voice of "them" provides the secure underpinning for a responsible reading. However the domination of the literal meaning of the text can lead to irresponsible outcomes if the literal meaning reinforces prejudices or actions which are ethically dubious to one of the

92. Ibid., 23.
93. Ibid., 206.

dialogue partners. As Conrad writes, "When reading past texts as 'other,' however, neither the texts nor the reader should be given an omnipotent status in the dialogue. The voices of the past, as in any good dialogue, need to be questioned."[94] This questioning each of the voices in the harmony highlights the priority of listening to the voice of "us" that reinterprets the testimony of "them" in the light of the newer covenant. In contrast to Clark's suggestion, the actual reading practices of the Pentecostal community observed in the readings of *Isaiah* suggest that the dominant voice (and sometimes *only* voice) in their approach is the voice of "me." In the situation of the decline of harmony in a Pentecostal reading practice, it is the community and their ethical values that provide the boundaries rather than the domination of one voice. The community of Pentecostal readers, and its participation in the wider Christian dialogue, provides the requisite safeguards. This is not to suggest that the song must reach a unified conclusion in which the three voices are fused, but that each voice is respected and understood for their unique contribution to maintain a deliberate unity. The intention of this reading model is not the fusing of the three voices, but for each distinct voice to be heard in harmony of song, that each voice resonates with the tone and pitch of each other. In this way, the voices of the Pentecostal reading model can also respect the voice of the "other" in the wider dialogue with the ecumenical community and with scholarly discipline.

The unity of the voices of "me," "them," and "us" in reading Old Testament texts should also lead to a concern for the "other." The purpose of the "people of God" continually affirmed in the meta-narrative of the biblical text involves a concern for the "other" who is invited to join the community of faith.[95] The challenge for the Pentecostal community is to engage, and yet still remain distinct from, the "other"—those outside its community.[96] While at times the differentiation of ancient Israel from others led to exclusion, separation and violence in their testimony, such as their anti-Canaanite polemic during the conquest,[97] the boundary markers between "them" (ancient Israelites) and "others" (non-Israelites) was not always clear.[98] As the testimony of "us" in Acts 15 highlights, texts such as Amos 9 are understood by the Christian community as a mandate to embrace the Gentile, the "other." The voices of "us" (the Christian community represented in the New Testament text), "them" (the testimony of the Old Testament text), and "me" (the experience of conversion of Gentiles) resonates in a harmonious interplay that leads to a concern for the "other."

The challenge for the Pentecostal community will be to hear the voice of the "other" and have concern for their welfare without the pre-requiring the "other" to

---

94. Conrad, "Prophet, Redactor, and Audience," 316.

95. While the concern for the "other" is expressed in numerous Old Testament texts, there is also a recognition in recent studies of the deliberate exclusion of others as a legacy of monotheism. For an engaging discussion on this issue, see Schwartz, *The Curse of Cain*.

96. Johns, "Yielding to the Spirit," 81.

97. McKinlay, "What do I do with Contexts?" 164.

98. As McKinlay suggests, the employment of a hermeneutic of suspicion, for example, can question the power structures of these exclusivist witnesses (ibid., 165).

joining or convert to "us" (the Christian community).[99] This is a major challenge to the Pentecostal community in the adoption of this model. One of the ironies for a Pentecostal reading of the Old Testament is the potential for dismissal of Jewish readings; the insider of Old Testament readings has become the outsider in Christian and Pentecostal readings.[100] It is crucial for Pentecostal readings to respect the voices of other traditions and be willing to harmonize with those outside its immediate community. Even though the values of mission and evangelism are recognized in the Pentecostal community, the voice of the Pentecostal reading model must not be used to silence the "other," but allow an engagement in song that can be mutually informing. In this way there can be a correlation between confession and conduct[101] as the Pentecostal reader embraces the voice of the "other."

The voice of the Pentecostal reading community is a reminder to the wider ecumenical dialogue of the claims that God still speaks to and through human beings.[102] Their value is reflected in this Pentecostal reading model, which affirms the priority of pneumatic encounter while addressing the inherent weaknesses of the reading practices of the community. While this Pentecostal reading model of the Old Testament has been developed from the foundation of the values and practices of actual readers, it is important to test the model with a similar process. Therefore, the Pentecostal reading model developed in this study will be applied below by members of the Pentecostal reading community to test its effectiveness for actual readers. The application of this model to three Old Testament texts will be explored through an informed discussion group. This group of three young Pentecostal women, have been acquainted with this reading model through discussion and reading. While two of the lay readers have limited theological training all three are young professionals. The group was asked to apply the model to a diverse group of texts: Isa 6:1–8, Gen 22:1–19 and Deut 28:1–6. Each text represents a different genre of prophetic narrative, "historical" narrative and didactic orientation. They were selected for their literary diversity but basic familiarity to the Pentecostal readers. The following applications are a summary of their use of the model and the testing of the model by and for actual readers (including the writer) within the Pentecostal community. While it is acknowledged that the Pentecostal reader will generally begin with the significance of the text to *me* as an individual reader—and often stop there—it is not the only beginning point for the Pentecostal reading model. If the reading partners ("me," "them," or "us") are truly in harmony, it should be possible for the model to begin at any point of the significance of the text—to '("me," "them," or "us"). At whatever point it begins, the other elements must be engaged to provide balance and control in the reading. The application of the model to these Old Testament texts will thus deliberately

---

99. McKinlay adopts the images of Jezebel and Rahab as representatives of a foreigner or "other" who, for one woman, remains outside the boundary of community (Jezebel) and another who through assimilation is embraced by the community (Rahab) (ibid., 166–67).

100. Brueggemann, *Theology of the Old Testament*, 745.

101. Mudge, "Gathering around the Center," 395.

102. Clark, "An Investigation into the Nature of a Viable Pentecostal Hermeneutic," 209.

begin with a different starting point for each text.[103] The Isaiah passage will begin with the significance of the text for "me," the Genesis passage will begin with the significance for "them" and the Deuteronomy passage will begin with the significance for "us." The following discussion presents a reading by lay members of the Pentecostal community applying the Pentecostal reading model suggested by this thesis.

APPLICATION OF MODEL TO AN ISAIAH TEXT: ISAIAH 6:1–8

The three questions from the Pentecostal reading model were asked of the discussion group:

- What does the text mean to *me*?
- What does the text mean to *them*?
- What does the text mean to *us*?

The following response is an attempt to reflect the discussion and voice of the Pentecostal readers (the individual voices of the three participants of the group discussion represented by P1, P2, and P3) to appreciate the significance of the text of Isa 6:1–8 for these readers.

What Does the Text Mean to Me?

The question of the significance and meaning of the text to *me* as an individual reader resulted in a varied response from the group. For P1, the immediate significance of the text was in the calling of the prophet. From this, the text spoke to her own sense of calling: "I am called—there is a calling. I am set apart for a specific purpose. And God can deal with the sin in my life to fulfill that call." The personal revelation of God's majesty reflected in the text reinforced the purpose of that calling for P1; that she is to proclaim the glory of God. As P1 continued to reflect on the text, she recalled a previous "revelation" that Isaiah's vision came in the year that King Uzziah died. She reflected: "Uzziah was a good king, and revered by the people. That sometimes moving on into the prophetic destiny of a person or group is the letting go of the previous move or previous season that may have been very good and very beneficial, but God is taking him on from that. It's about moving on with God rather than being stuck in the familiar." This principle identified in the text informed and was informed by P1's experience of Christian living.

There was also an identification of the inter-relation between earthly happenings or historical events and the spiritual realm in the personal reading by P1. As the text witnesses to an earthly event of the death of Uzziah, it then immediately follows that the prophet has a vision of the heavenly, eternal king. From her reflection, P1 identifies that "The spiritual realm is the determining factor of what goes on in the world. It means that my response to the spiritual realm can have a direct impact on earthly events. The way I abdicate responsibility spiritually—such as not responding to the call of God—can

---

103. Each text was read using the NIV translation in the discussion group, a common translation utilized in the Pentecostal community.

actually have an effect on earthly happenings." For P2, the personal significance of the text was in the revelation of the grace of God. The text "spoke" to her that: "None of us is unclean enough that God would never use us." She continued, "It comes down to a choice—God said: 'whom will I send?' we have a choice to respond to God. Will we respond to God?" The passage leads P2 to respond positively and be a messenger for God in ways which resonate with the prophet's description. The Spirit spoke to her through the text asking: will you go for me? "Its personal." The significance of the text to P3 was also similar to this reading by P2. The lips that once were unclean are now used to proclaim the message of God. For P3, "Those same lips that may have been used for selfish gain and self-promotion are now used for God. I can't read the Bible and say I meet God's standards of holiness. We're all sinners, but God doesn't leave us there—he provides for us. God provides for me." As God met Isaiah in his context so God also meets us in our context; revealing our heart condition and transforming us. God takes that same life, now transformed, and uses it as an instrument to proclaim God's glory and God's word to the people where they are at. The text resonates with their experience of grace and Christian living, pointing to the principles of calling and prophetic vocation.

What Does the Text Mean to Them?

The significance and meaning of the text to *them* (the people of God represented by the text), was particularly focused on the role of Isaiah as a prophet speaking on behalf of God. As P2 highlights, in the Old Covenant, God spoke through spokespersons. To "them" he was a man God had chosen, a prophet, to tell them what was coming if they didn't repent. This was also emphasized by P1, "For Isaiah, in responding to the call, it meant being marginalized in his society. He had a revelation of the greatness of God but he was also accepting a lifestyle of rejection because he is the prophet of God speaking of the sin of the people who did not want to hear that message." As the prophetic word was only given to a specific few individuals in the older testament, rather than to the whole community, it means that Isaiah had a unique role. For someone to be "called" to be a prophet in ancient Israel implies that others are *not* called. In other words, it was a special role that only a select few or "special" people could fill. The revelation of God to the prophet was considered pertinent to his calling. As P2 noted, "Isaiah's getting a massive revelation of the holiness and majesty of God. He's completely overcome because he's so aware of his sinfulness. Entering the presence of God with sin would result in death. But God sends an angel to show his grace—in a moment he goes from being woeful and devastated to understanding God's grace over his life. With the revelation of God's grace, he's able to respond to God. He is able to rise up and go to tell this people of God."

The location of this testimony of Isaiah at the death of King Uzziah was considered important to the readers for understanding the significance of the text to "them." For P1, the death of the king represented a period of transition and uncertainty. She noted, "A great king had died, a king of Judah, so the people are feeling it. It's a period of change and possible uncertainty. Because when there's a change of leadership there is a period of uncertainty." The significance of this context is also noted by P3: "Isaiah is mourning the loss of a good king when God comes to him and reveals himself as THE king—seated on a throne, wearing kingly garments. God revealed himself in a way that Isaiah could understand: not as a prime minister in his office, or a president in the White House, or a CEO in a suit—God revealed himself in a way that was familiar to the prophet." The discussion group also noted the significance of the symbolism in the prophetic narrative that would have been pertinent to "them." Images such as the "throne" and "robe" have limited meaning to us, but for "them" it would have had an embedded meaning that we don't have direct access to. For example, P1 noted that the seraph would have been reminiscent of the Ark of the Covenant—all pointing to covenant relationship. She noted, "Because these symbols aren't in our culture we miss a lot of it." This highlights the importance of covenant in the significance of the text for "them." As Isaiah at the time of his call encountered the holy God in the sanctuary, this encounter determined his whole preaching and the way he understood God. For P3, this also determined what the appropriate response of the people toward God and others should be. If Isaiah understood God as "holy, holy, holy," then God's followers should reflect this holiness in their social, political, and economic lives. She commented, "Isaiah places before the people the standard of divine holiness—reflected in the covenant writings. It is the standard by which the people should be living their lives; in conformity with the holy character of God." Therefore the prophetic vocation of Isaiah was to call the people to this moral standard and pronounce judgment on the inability of Judah to truly reflect the holiness of God. The testimony of the people of Judah in the biblical text witnesses to their continued inability to reform that led to the ultimate curse of the covenant: exile.

What Does the Text Mean to Us?

The significance and meaning of the text to *us* as Christian readers was perceived through the life and ministry of Jesus Christ, and the continuation of that mission embraced by the Pentecostal community, including the women of this group. While it speaks so much of the majesty and power of God that he would draw close to humanity, for "us" this relationship is achieved by the atoning work of Christ on Calvary. As P2 noted, "We can go into the throne room of God and enter his throne of grace freely because of the new covenant." This was reinforced by the contribution of P3 that "God wants us to be restored and transformed. For us, it comes through the cleansing work of Christ on the cross." For the Pentecostal readers, Jesus is the burning coal of the Isaiah passage: his blood cleanses us. Under the new covenant Jesus gives the believer access to what Isaiah had access to: the presence of the living God. For P1, this grace that is so freely available through the death and resurrection of Jesus Christ is not an excuse for unholy living. Instead, "Even though we are in a covenant of grace, God is still the 'holy, holy, holy' Lord."

While the atoning work of Jesus Christ was recognized as providing access to the presence of God, the group also noted the response of believers to this grace as exemplified by the volunteerism of Isaiah. For P1, the Christian community reads the "send me" section of the Isaiah text as part of the Great Commission in Matt 28. She noted, "it's the idea of the 'sent ones'—being a disciple—we are sent ones." The sense of calling of the

Old Testament prophet was also drawn upon by P2 as significant to the Christian reader: "It's a call to the people of God—we are chosen." However, rather than the task of the prophet being a unique role, the prophetic vocation for the newer covenant community is now understood as the vocation of the entire post-Pentecost Christian community as the spirit empowers all believers for the task of witnessing.

The interaction of the three voices of "me," "them," and "us" in the application of this Pentecostal reading model highlights the different meanings of the text to the different communities of faith. Yet in the midst of the distinctions, there was also a resonance in the constancy of the holiness of God, the provision of God expressed in the various means of atonement throughout the history of God's people, and a sense of the "calling" of God to a specific task, albeit democratized in the contemporary Christian community. The sense of the "special" nature of the call is retained by the expansion of the "all" from ancient Israel to the global society, rendering Pentecostals an equivalent "few." The reflection of "them" emphasizes the differences of the prophetic vocation and calling for the Old Testament prophet and the Pentecostal reader, highlighting the deliberate voice of "us" rather than the simplistic appropriation of the older covenant calling. While Pentecostal readings of the Old Testament have tended to focus on the significance of the text to the individual reader ("me"), this model forces the reader to consider the additional meanings of the text for "them" and "us" as a guide in their personal reading. This reading differs from those described in chapter 3 as the personal immediacy and application of the passage is not removed from the historical context ("them") and the redemptive history represented by the text. Instead the significance of the text to "me" and "us," is heightened by acknowledgment of the themes and issues of the text for "them."

APPLICATION OF MODEL TO ANOTHER OLD TESTAMENT TEXT: GENESIS 22:1–19

The three questions of the Pentecostal reading model were asked of the discussion group:

- What does the text mean to *them*?

- What does the text mean to *us*?

- What does the text mean to *me*?

Although "them" is not necessarily the natural beginning point for many Pentecostal readers, this use demonstrates the flexibility of the model. By beginning with the significance of the text to the ancient community, the consideration of this question first may be a good starting point for a Pentecostal reader aiming to intentionally engage more directly with historical-critical concerns.[104]

---

104. My thanks to Dr John Squires for this observation.

What Does the Text Mean to Them?

The significance and meaning of the text to the people of God represented by the "histori-cal" narrative ("them") was identified by the discussion group as an example of obedience and faith. The narrative highlighted the unfailing obedience of Abraham in the story, which was a model of faith for the ancient community. For P2, God was seen as testing the faith of Abraham to see if he would believe in God's ability to provide. P2 suggested that, "In the context of 'them' it is for Abraham being tested in his obedience to God." She continued, "It's like God has given him a promise already about his descendants but then God is saying what if I say take your son (v. 2) and sacrifice him? Yet God had given him the son as the fulfillment of this promise but was now being asked to sacrifice him. Yet Abraham followed through and trusted God completely. He was very attentive to God's voice." While Abraham did not have to actually complete the sacrifice of his son through the interception of the angel of the Lord (v. 11), it was a testing of his obedience and loyalty. Once Abraham's faith was confirmed, God provided for their worship and sacrifice with the discovery of the ram. The testimony of obedience and trust was to be an example for the ancient community.

Yet the significance of the text for "them" was also highlighted by the dense refer-ence to ancient practices of worship and ceremonial sacrifice that are not practiced by contemporary Christian communities of faith. As P1 noted, "It relies on an understand-ing of offerings and ceremonial sacrifice and the function and purpose of a sacrifice in worship. It relies on an inherent cultural understanding of offerings—a concept in all the Middle Eastern religions of that time and the significance of blood offerings." The offering required of Abraham was identified as a personal challenge. It was a test of trust that God would provide an offering. God worked through the culture of "them"; the institutions of sacrifice and worship, and family orientation. As P1 described, "to take your son and be willing to offer it to God is a powerful concept." This involved Abraham giving back to God the promised child received after the long period of waiting. Through trust in God, there could be no obstacle to the fulfillment of covenant that couldn't be overcome. As P3 noted, this was part of the bigger promise that through Abraham all the nations of the world would be blessed. Isaac was the first fruit of that, yet even this promise was not fulfilled through the works of Abraham but the ability of God. In the lineage of Abraham and Isaac, the nation of Israel identified its roots. The testimony of "them" highlights that the older covenant was fulfilled through obedience. For Abraham, it was a test of his loyalty; did he fear God more than the pagan gods of other people? His example was for the benefit of the older covenant community in teaching obedience and the provision of God.

What Does the Text Mean to Us?

The significance of the text to *us* as Christian readers resonated with the meaning of the text for "them": obedience and faith. However, the object of that faith and obedience is focused on the person of Jesus Christ. As P2 reflected, "The first thing I noticed for 'us' is that it's a foreshadowing of the new covenant." Abraham is asked to sacrifice his *only* son, who he loves (conveniently no mention of Ishmael is made in this reference), just as God sacrificed his only begotten son, Jesus Christ. The messianic resonances in the text was also highlighted by P1 who noted, "it starts with the mention of the response to a call from God in verse 2, to take your only son (with the emphasis on the only son) that will later have resonance in the New Testament. Abraham is called to sacrifice him on a mountain, being reminiscent of Calvary." The narrative was replete with symbols recognized by the Christian readers. For P3, it was the particular image of Isaac carrying the wood with which he would be potentially sacrificed that was highlighted as analogous to Jesus carrying the cross to Calvary on which he would be sacrificed. Similarly the relationship between Abraham and Isaac was considered representative of the relationship between Jesus and the "heavenly father"; the trust exhibited in both sons in submitting to their father's will. Abraham reaching out and slaying his son has resonance with God the father being willing to slay his own son for the good of the covenant—the new covenant. For the Christian reader, Jesus is the ultimate sacrifice; he was obedient unto death. Just as Isaac was symbolically resurrected, so Jesus was also literally raised to fulfill the new covenant.

The narrative also establishes for the Christian reader paradigms of giving what is precious and the first-fruits of a promise. While the promise to Abraham was of literal descendants and a physical homeland, this same promise is spiritualized by the New Testament community. As P1 highlighted, "Corporately, we come under the blessing of the Abrahamic covenant. In being grafted into the Jewish lineage, these promises are pertinent to us as well. That we will be a blessing to the nations and other people groups through our obedience. We will bless them, bringing the blessing of Jesus Christ, and a blessed life—family relations, children, material wealth—all the blessings that Abraham had."

What Does the Text Mean to Me?

The significance of the text to *me* as individual readers continued to resonate with the meaning of the text for "them" and "us." As P2 expressed, "It speaks to me about the same things: faith and obedience. Having such a relationship with God that I would trust him that deeply to go and do something that is illogical in my own human mind. It speaks to me about God providing, just as the mountain is called. We can trust God to provide—his plans are perfect, so I can trust his plans. It's when you don't understand God's ways, which are higher than our ways, that the challenge comes to trust him and have faith until he shows you the next step." For P1, the significance of the text was also in the personal challenge of obedience. However, it was obedience of a high level. As she commented, "The more that God wants to give you then higher the cost can be. It wasn't just a corporate cost, but a deep personal cost to Abraham. So what God wants to do sometime comes at a deep personal cost."

The call to follow Christ was identified by the readers as having deep personal costs which involved laying down their own dreams and desires in obedience. This may also mean the laying down of divinely inspired dreams, such as what Isaac represented to

Abraham. For P1, "even things God has promised and then delivered need to be given back to God in an act of obedience if he requires them—like a husband, ministry or a child. Nothing should be held too tightly—everything must be surrendered to God, even the things that are closest to us." This personal significance was also reflected in the contribution of P3. For her, it was the deliberate action of Abraham and willingness to sacrifice his own greatly loved son that particularly spoke to her. She noted: "In the same way, for us as contemporary readers, we must be willing to lay down the things dearest to us for the glory of God." She recalled specific events in her life in which she had felt compelled to "lay down" dreams and hopes for her life. In particular, the hope for a romantic relationship was laid down in the expectation that if God was the author of this promise, he would raise it again, just as Abraham experienced. The event of it not being "raised up" was an indication of that relationship not being the will or plan of God for her life. As P3 highlighted, "This forces us to rely on God." While the cost of personal obedience to the readers was recognized as high, the gains of this sacrifice were similarly identified as enormous. For P1, the benefits had generational implications. She noted that her decision will affect future generations, "Abraham's faith is imitated by Isaac in that he trusts his father for a sacrifice to be provided. He accepts the word of his father and in his father's faith. We are the spiritual covering for our children. Because of Abraham's obedience then future generations will be blessed, so my obedience will have implications for my children and the generations after me." The benefits of sacrificial obedience were also identified in the provision of God. By being obedient, the lack or need which this emphasized was perceived by the readers as an opportunity for God to provide. For P1, "In whatever area the need is, God can provide for it out of his resource, but he requires our obedience and trust in that."

This conversation of Pentecostal readers highlighted the significance of the text in promoting exclusive loyalty and obedience to God. Although this is expressed in different ways in the two covenants, the principle of trust is emphasized.

APPLICATION OF MODEL TO ANOTHER OLD TESTAMENT TEXT: DEUTERONOMY 28:1–6

The three questions of the Pentecostal reading model were asked of the discussion group:

1. What does the text mean to *us*?

2. What does the text mean to *them*?

3. What does the text mean to *me*?

What Does the Text Mean to Us?

The significance and meaning of this Old Testament text to *us* as new covenant readers is the spiritual blessing that results from active obedience to God. As P1 noted, "God is putting forward a proposal to us to come under his blessing. But he allows us, or requires us to choose and enact our own obedience and diligence to follow his commands. He initiates the proposal, he allows that space to choose and then he actually outlines the blessing that we will receive under his covenant." For P1, the embracing of God's covenant by the Christian believer involves a process of consecration. It is this consecration that distinguishes the Christian believer. She notes, "He sets us apart as there is a distinction between those who have chosen God and those who haven't that is demonstrated by the blessing and prosperity of God. There is a holistic prosperity that's indicated in this passage for people who are living under God's covenant. The details of that blessing are not bound geographically because it's not a physical kingdom, it's not cultural." The new covenant believer receives the blessings of God, outworked in all areas of their lives as represented in the holistic blessing of the Deuteronomy text. This highlights the holistic nature of God's blessings that are not limited to the spiritual or physical realm, but encompasses the whole person. However, as P3 noted, the nature of the two covenants is different and therefore the blessings will be different. And yet, the whole person is called to obey God and therefore the call and blessings will overflow to the whole person.

The blessing of God is holistic; there is no compartmentalization of sacred and secular, but every part of the Christian life can overflow with divine meaning and contact. The provision and blessing incorporates all genders, ages and occupations; whether it is in the city or country, doing what may be women's work (bread-making) or men's work, they will be blessed. It is a reversal of the curse upon humanity represented in Genesis 3. For P1 this means that, "God wants to and seeks to bless every area of our lives—whether that's our leisure, family, relaxation or work—everything comes under the covenant. You are a carrier of the covenant—it's upon your life and not the geographic location—being the temple of the Holy Spirit, so we are mobile blessing carriers." For P2, this represented a challenge to the Christian church to live a lifestyle of obedience and blessing. She described it as a "call to rise up for us—to rise up and dare to really obey God. It's a challenge to carefully follow his commands: does the church see this? It's our place to live in this blessing."

What Does the Text Mean to Them?

The meaning of the text to *them* (the people of God represented by the text) was identified as the preparation for entry into the Promised Land. The passage presents itself as the speech of Moses to the people of Israel on the plains of Moab prior to their entrance to the Promised Land. As P3 noted, it is portrayed as a covenant renewal in which the blessings for covenant loyalty and curses for disobedience are established. According to the testimony of the Deuteronomy passage, the blessing of food and provision is promised the people upon entrance to the Promised Land. Moses emphasizes the faithfulness required of the people. That obedience is necessary for the fulfillment of the divine promises. It follows that the provision of manna in the wilderness would cease once the people entered a place in which they could produce their own "manna." God would bless their hands and ability to produce food and provide raw materials—it would be like the same direct supernatural provision as before, but provision in the ability to produce the food rather the food itself. The same God who provided them with manna, quail and water from the rock, now provides them with houses, vineyards and crops and cisterns already built—the instruments of production and the ability to feed themselves (highlighted by the fact that as soon as they entered the Promised Land the manna stopped). However, as the Christian reading emphasized, the blessing required obedience. This obedience is to the conditions implied by the older covenant. As P2 highlighted, "This is before they go into the land, so God is preparing them for living in the land. The principles set out for them to live in the land is to love and obey God first and then the result is that the land will be blessed, and they will be blessed because the land produces good harvest, produce and multiplication." The requirement of this covenant people, as emphasized by P1, was their separation and consecration as a distinct people group. The evidence of their consecration to God was these blessings. This separation of the ancient community from the other nations was perceived by the discussion group not to be a negative separation or ostracism, but an elevation through the blessings and prosperity promised. However this prosperity required the full obedience to the older covenant.

The significance the imagery to "them" was noted by the readers for its agrarian nature. As P1 noted, "we treat it as metaphoric, but for them it was literal. The blessing of the fruit of their womb would have been highly salient as fertility was seen in all ancient cultures as important." The literal blessing for "them" established a generational community blessing, not just an individual blessing. The literal blessing for "them" was also located in the specific geographical realm for the establishment of the physical kingdom of ancient Israel.

What Does the Text Mean to Me?

The meaning of the Deuteronomy text to the individual readers ("me") also resonated with the significance of the text for "them" and "us." The readers highlighted the principles of obedience observed in the text. For P2, this principle was personalized: if she will put God first in her life, then she will be blessed by God. However, the challenge of this principle is in obedient living. She noted, "Carefully following his commands is a challenge. How much do you respect all the words God has said and how willing are you to follow all of them? I think it comes down to a choice." For P3, this text emphasized the fruitfulness of obedience. Although it may not be seen in success as judged by the world, it is the blessing that comes from relationship and acceptance from God.

In contrast, the personal significance of the text for P1 was in the revelation of the holistic nature of God. She emphasized that "in God's blessing under his covenant, he blesses every part of life, there is no sacred or secular. There are physical ramifications of the spiritual blessing." While the blessings of God for the Pentecostal reader are identified as spiritual in nature, these spiritual blessings have implications in the physical and material realm. Just as the Christian is called to live an obedient life in the physical realm (which includes morality and character integrity) so also the blessings overflow into the physical realm. For example, the physical and material impact of a spiritual choice of being in covenant with God will be a blessed life, including a healthy marriage and family that are prospering materially, relationally, psychologically. Again, this blessing requires obedience consecration. For P1, this means that, "I should be distinct and set apart from those not living under covenant. That doesn't mean that I don't associate with them or that they're not in my friendship circle, but there should be something tangibly different about me. Not weird or in a loopy way, but like in Psalm 45 the covenant person is obviously different."

The text of Deuteronomy is meaningful to the Pentecostal readers in emphasizing the blessing of God that follows obedient believers. While the blessings may be different according to each covenant, the women highlighted the holistic nature of God's blessing. Every part of the Christian life can overflow with divine meaning as believers demonstrate exclusive loyalty to God. Yet the voice of other traditions may challenge this meaning to the Pentecostal reader. The voice of the "other," such as a third-world reading may question the inherent materialism of reading by Western Christians and challenge the responsibility of the community to an ethical reading in which the resources of the "kingdom" are distributed equitably and justly. The voice of the third world reminds the Pentecostal community in Australia not to hoard the bread from the wider community. This is true not only for the Pentecostal community in Australia which is part of a global movement, but for the role of the Pentecostal community in ecumenical dialogue. This reminds the Pentecostal reader of the importance of reading the biblical text with "others." [105] As Smit writes, "As people who read these documents from our own social locations, from the places we are, we cannot ignore our own experiences and questions and the experiences and questions of the people around us with regard to these documents."[106] The voice of "others" must be engaged, and the responsibility to actively pursue righteousness and justice by the Pentecostal community. In this sense, it causes the Pentecostal reading to focus on the purpose of the blessing (to glorify God), rather than the object of blessing (prosperity). This correction of the reading is not to contradict it,[107] but to further foster meaning that is more true to the gospel.

From the above discussion of the three biblical texts, certain similarities and dissimilarities between "me," "them" and "us" emerge. The dynamic engagement of the text for "me" highlights the personal relevancy of Scripture for the contemporary Christian life. It embraces the playfulness and openness of texts[108] and challenges the limits of historical-critical readings. It seeks to understand what the text has to say to the individual reader. Yet, this application is dissimilar to the voice of "them" that requires a separation of horizons and covenant values to appreciate the voice of the ancient faith community. In this way, the Pentecostal reader exhibits respect for the "other"-ness of the ancient literary texts. These texts speak to the contemporary reader over centuries of and from cultural worlds far different to their own.[109] Together, the voices of "them," "us," and "me" resonate in a harmonious interplay of meaningful engagement. From this

---

105. Smit, " Biblical Hermeneutics," 314.

106. Ibid.

107. Mudge, "Gathering around the Center," 393.

108. Havea, "[Y]our Book, [Y]our Reading: Writing Täsilisili Readings," 186.

109. Smit, " Biblical Hermeneutics," 314.

vibrant song, the Pentecostal reader engages holistically with the biblical text resulting in understanding and transformation.

While the "voice" of the Pentecostal community can be sharpened and transformed through the dialogue process, their unique approach can also offer an important contribution. As Pentecostal scholar Robert Baker asserts "Clearly the Scriptures are special texts, having been inspired by the Holy Spirit. Truly to *understand* the message of biblical texts, one must submit to the Spirit who breathed the Scriptures and indwells the reading process. A reading strategy that coheres with and is informed by Pentecostal spirituality is a treasure that Pentecostal scholars can offer the church and its scribes."[110] Pentecostals need to make their own voice heard in the conversation by bringing their Pentecostal emphases as reflected in their reading approaches. By articulating the unique emphasis on the dynamic of the Holy Spirit in the reading process that points to the broader worldview of this christological Pentecostal community, they can offer a freshness of approach to the wider interpretive community. This approach of seeking to understand the text for its significance to the individual reader, rather than just content, is necessary for the development of a Pentecostal reading model of the Old Testament.[111] But what would such a model look like? Now that the actual reading practices of the Pentecostal community have been described, this study is in a position to *prescribe* a reading model that is informed by both the values of the Pentecostal community and the ethical responsibility of the wider ecumenical reading community.

---

110. Baker, "Pentecostal Bible Reading," 47.

111. Smit, "Biblical Hermeneutics," 299.

8

Friends for Life

THE NUMERICAL GROWTH OF the Pentecostal movement as a significant segment of Christianity in Australia means that their "voice" can no longer be ignored in the ecumenical dialogue. Having developed from a sect-like movement among the margins of society, the Pentecostal community has grown to become a global movement. However this growth and "blessing" of the Pentecostal and charismatic movements is not necessarily a corollary of good hermeneutics. While the Pentecostal community has grown, the need for critical self-reflection on their own unique "voice" has likewise grown as a reflection of their growing academic responsibility. This is should (but has not necessarily) involved engaging with the actual Pentecostal community to elucidate their practices and values in this process of articulation, rather than imposing ideal versions and academic musing separate to the workings of the grass-roots reader. On the other hand, a Pentecostal construction of responsible critique is necessary in order to allow defensible public engagement. This book has sought to take this challenge seriously. It has proposed a reading model of the Old Testament that begins with the actual reading practices of the Pentecostal community in order to allow the "voice" of the community to be heard.

The "voice" of the Pentecostal community is heard within the matrix of a predominantly oral culture in the context of worship, liturgy, and small group Bible discussion. The importance of Scripture in the corporate worship of the church is highlighted by Bird[1] as the primary way in which the Bible is transmitted to its community of readers. The use of Scripture in private devotions is an extension of this primary usage.[2] By the examination of selected reading practices of the Pentecostal community in its liturgy, small group discussion and (limited) published studies, the "voice" and values of the group have emerged. From this description, the reading practices of the community have

1. Bird, *The Bible as the Church's Book,* 19.
2. Ibid.

been critically examined for their strengths and weaknesses. The dominant features of Pentecostal readings have been evaluated and corrected as they are incorporated into an effective reading model of the Old Testament. This book has not assumed that the voice of the community is either correct or responsible, but that its principles and practices are an important foundation from which to build a model that reflects, in a responsible method, the values of the community. From this reflection, the book has proposed a reading approach to the Old Testament that incorporates the values of the community. Describing, evaluating and prescribing a Pentecostal hermeneutic will also assist those outside the community to understand their "voice" in the wider ecumenical dialogue.

The study of the interpretations of actual readers highlights the false perception that Pentecostal reading of biblical texts is simple and its message obvious. The role of the interpreter is crucial to the elucidation of meaning in the text. The Bible is not a self-interpreting book,[3] but is read through the values, culture, and presuppositions of the Pentecostal community. These presuppositions influence the interpretation as they create expectations of reading. The expectation of the Pentecostal reader as evidenced through their readings of *Isaiah* has been that they will encounter the living God as reflected in their own pneumatic experience. The Pentecostal reader expects to see Christ and his mission echoed through the pages of the Old Testament and to live that text in their contemporary setting. As the Pentecostal readers studied here brought this presupposition of charismatic experience to their reading of biblical texts, their readings of *Isaiah* demonstrated an expectation that the Spirit would be encountered in the reading process. As the prophet Isaiah encountered God in his vision of the eternal king in Isa 6, so also the Pentecostal reader anticipates encountering God in their reading of Scripture. Just as the prophet's lips were touched by the burning coal and his lips seared and life transformed, so also the Pentecostal reader anticipates transformation in their reading of Scripture. This is an inherent value for Pentecostal readers—the transformational encounter of God, identified here in the readings of *Isaiah* by an actual Pentecostal community.

However, while Isaiah was chosen as a spokesperson for his community in the unique role of the prophet, a further value identified by the Pentecostal community is the universality of the prophetic calling and role. For the Pentecostal community, all believers can encounter God and have a prophetic message from God burning on their lips. This means that God speaks to and through all members of the Pentecostal community, rather than just the professional clergy. One does not have to become a student to be a reader,[4] nor a professional minister to have a voice in the community.[5] The democratization of the Spirit installed at Pentecost (Acts 2), highlights the active role of lay membership in prophetic utterance as symbolized by the outpouring of the *charismata*, especially the gift of tongues. This empowering is for the purpose of building the kingdom of God. The Spirit empowers the Pentecost community to be witnesses of the

---

3. Ibid., 81.

4. Havea, "[Y]our Book, [Y]our Reading: Writing Täsilisili Readings," 182.

5. However, it is noted that the learned reader does have a responsibility of guidance to the readers who are not students.

gospel of Jesus Christ and to fulfill the christological mission. The Pentecost community identify themselves as participants—as the "people of God"—in the ongoing drama of salvation outworked in human history. Their lips burn with the message and good news of the gospel of Jesus Christ. The empowered speech and impetus for mission is what results from this pneumatic encounter. The Pentecostal values of prophetic transformation can be articulated in this reading model of the Old Testament: what does the text mean for "me," "them," and "us"?

The significance of the Old Testament text for "me" emphasizes the values of dynamic encounter and personal application. The reader, as Bird has elsewhere noted, seeks "God's purpose and plan for their lives in the prescriptions, admonitions, and examples of Scripture."[6] The Pentecostal reader identifies with the figures and events in the Bible and sees their experience analogously reflected in the biblical text. The biblical text provides guidance for Christian living and spiritual formation. The Pentecostal reader approaches the text to encounter God, highlighting the Pentecostal value of transformational encounter of God in their personal reading. The significance of the text to "me" varies according to the situation and context of the individual reader: the context of "me." This produces multiple interpretations according to the experience and situation of each individual reader. In comparison, the significance of the text for "them" emphasizes the cultural and historical location of the older covenant text. This "voice" attempts to address the tendencies toward literalism inherent in the Pentecostal reading practices that emphasize personal appropriation of the biblical text. Instead, the cultural-historical location of the Old Testament is emphasized to highlight the "other"-ness of the text. Although the identification of "them" will differ according to the research skill and resources of the Pentecostal reader, it emphasizes the cultural worldview of the ancient society represented by the text, before the coming of Christ. This process highlights the difference between the world of the Pentecostal reader and the world of the Old Testament text and allows the unique testimony of the older covenant text to be voiced. The uniqueness of this voice must be separate from a New Testament or Christian witness to the Old Testament text: the voice of "us."

The christological value of the Pentecostal reading community is an important recognition of the life-engaging transformation of the Christian gospel experienced by the Pentecostal community. The identification of the Pentecostal community as the post-Pentecost "people of God" distinguishes them from the older covenant "people of God." This Pentecostal reading proposal highlights through the significance of the text to "us" (the Christian community) both the continuity and discontinuity of the Pentecostal community with the community of faith represented in the older covenant text. This reading model requires that the Pentecostal community place their reading within the wider framework of the redemptive-historical perspective of the two testaments. Through the testimony of the community of faith in the older covenant, the Pentecostal community articulates their Christian life and pneumatic experience through the symbols, events, and figures of its pages. As Bird writes, "To be a Christian is to belong to

---

6. Bird, *The Bible as the Church's Book*, 27.

a community whose identity and vocation have been deeply and decisively shaped by the Bible and whose present self-understanding and life before God and in the world continue to bear the stamp of its witness. That communal reality affects each of us individually as Christians."[7] Therefore, this reading model of the Old Testament operates as the Pentecostal reader asks: what does the text mean to "me"? What does the text mean to "them"? And, what does the text mean to "us"? Together, the voices of "them," "us," and "me" resonate in a harmonious interplay of vibrant song. The model can begin with any "voice." The reading can start with the significance of the text to either "me," "them," or "us," however, the unity of these voices in reading Old Testament texts should also lead to a concern for the "other."

While this reading model proposes to liberate the "voice" of the Pentecostal community and allow them to participate in the dialogue of the wider reading community, the responsibility and legitimacy of this reading approach must be questioned. Biblical interpretation influences lives; it is a social activity and therefore requires responsible methods for the community of readers it addresses. Obviously different people will read, interpret and apply the same texts in different ways.[8] Therefore, it must be asked: where are the boundaries of a legitimate reading? Who determines the definition of a "responsible" interpretation? Is one reading more legitimate than another? Is the Pentecostal community a valid or invalid reading community? And, more importantly, who decides?

From the broader dialogue of hermeneutics, it can be observed that the decision as to a "correct" reading does not come from a study of the text, but comes from an extra-textual authority.[9] The basis for the legitimacy of a Pentecostal reading can come from one of two sources. Either it comes from the postmodern concern for the marginalized voice, or their concern to contribute to the ecumenical dialogue (either directly or filtered through institutional formation). Although these options are not contradictory, the basis for legitimacy ultimately comes from either inside or outside the dialogue of biblical interpretation. For some postmodern approaches, such as ideological criticism[10] and the "hermeneutics of suspicion," their legitimacy is based on their location of powerlessness; their location outside the margins of dialogue. Within this framework, the only legitimate readers are the powerless, representing the "epistemological privilege of the poor."[11] In other words, it is the poor, the marginalized and suffering people of the world who are the valid readers of biblical texts as their context provides the only legitimate context.[12] This approach questions whose interests are being served by a reading[13] and

---

7. Ibid., 22–23.

8. Smit, "Biblical Hermeneutics," 302.

9. Croatto, *Biblical Hermeneutics*, 21.

10. Readers such as feminist and liberationist that have questioned the power structures of readings must also be included in this matrix.

11. Smit, "Biblical Hermeneutics," 306.

12. Ibid. This is particularly highlighted in the approaches of Black Theology, Liberation Theology, Feminist Theology, Womanist Theology, African Theology, and others. One is also reminded of the contribution of people such as Martin Buber, whose studies of the Hasidic communities of Eastern Europe have likewise challenged over-nationalist approaches to theology.

13. Exum, "Feminist Criticism," 67.

attempts to critique the power structures at play. As Gutiérrez writes, "To support the social revolution means to abolish the present status quo and to attempt to replace it with a qualitatively different one; it means to build a just society based on new relationships of production; it means to attempt to put an end to the domination of some countries by others, of some social classes by others, of some persons by others."[14] The liberation of the "voice" of the marginalized is to end the domination of other voices or dialogue. Therefore in this matrix, a legitimate reading is one that undermines or exposes the structures that serve the powerful.

These approaches rely on an unchosen social status applied to the reader in community, such as being female or indigenous. While the Pentecostal community may fit this category of marginalization due to their status as part of the disenfranchised of society, the difference for the Australian Pentecostal community is that their status is often a choice. Rejection of the world and a marginalized social status go hand in hand with the embracing of God's activity in the Pentecostal community. As they reject the world and embrace God, their social status and respectability declines.[15] Therefore the validation of a Pentecostal reading approach is not based on the powerlessness of their social position but based on the quest of Pentecostal readers to "know" God. Their social marginalization is considered a choice. This does not mean that the Pentecostal community should not heed the voice of postmodern approaches. As noted previously in the "conversation" with hermeneutics (chapter 6), the ability for self-delusion is always possible. As Stroup asserts, "The question that endures and which must be answered by every Christian individual and community is the degree to which its self-understanding has been shaped by its knowledge of the God who is Creator and Redeemer and the degree to which it uses 'God' only as religious dress for its own moral, political, and cultural values."[16] Instead the voice of ideological criticism and postmodern methods must still be heard by the community as a critique of their approach in the dialogue of biblical interpretation rather than as a *justification* for the legitimacy of their "voice." Therefore the validity of the voice of the Pentecostal community must come from another source. The basis for validity in the engagement with ecumenical dialogue is the contribution of each dialogue partner. The Pentecostal community is a valid reading community as they emerge from the margins and participate in the wider dialogue of readers of biblical texts. Engagement with the wider dialogue highlights the social implications of readings and requires responsibility for the reading outcomes of the Pentecostal community. Pentecostalism has much to offer the conversation with the wider ecumenical dialogue, including the dialogue with Hermeneutics and the Old Testament.

Bird offers three principles as guidelines for the determination of a responsible reading that are helpful for the Pentecostal reader in the adoption of this reading model that is accountable to the wider reading community. She firstly highlights the principle of Bible reading, study, and understanding as a life-long process. Bird writes, "Bible study

14. Gutiérrez, *A Theology of Liberation*, 31.

15. Poloma particularly highlights this aspect of the Pentecostal community in her sociological study of the Assemblies of God in North America.

16. Stroup, *The Promise of Narrative Theology*, 20.

is more a process of hearing and responding than the acquisition of a body of facts and propositions, a conversation rather than a collection of right answers."[17] This process, or conversation, is a life-long journey over terrain that can be difficult or uneasy, but which builds the strength, confidence, and ability of the traveler.[18] This is crucial for the Pentecostal reader as their continued experience and encounter of God impacts their worldview which also informs their Bible reading. Likewise, their Bible reading impacts their experience which informs their worldview. Within this mutually informing dynamic the recognition of theological formation as a life-long process is crucial. A Pentecostal reading of the Old Testament should not be allowed to become static or "arrive," but be worthy of its description: dynamic. This also requires humility on behalf of the Pentecostal reader to recognize the partiality (in the sense of both limitation and preference) of their readings. And in this journey, the travelling is made lighter by the conversation of travelling partners.[19]

Secondly, Bird suggests that Bible study should always be undertaken in the context of community: the community to which the reader is a member as well as the wider reading community.[20] This means that the voice of the Pentecostal reading is accountable to the partners of the ecumenical dialogue. Without conversation with the ecumenical church, the Pentecostal reading model cannot claim to represent the Christian church; it cannot validly speak for "us." As Bird notes, "if it is Christ that we have met and the Christian Bible that has been the agent of transformation, then we will be led into the community whose book this is to continue our journey of understanding in company with that community, that people."[21] The ecumenical dialogue to which the Pentecostal community voices its reading must allow for the freedom and uniqueness of interpretation while still seeking the contribution of each voice.[22] In an ecumenical dialogue, all readings are potentially valid and represent the potential for mutual enrichment. However, as reading has a social effect, readings of the biblical text need to be responsible. In this way, the interpretive community (of which the Pentecostal community is a part) has a responsibility to be socially and ethically accountable to their dialogue partners and wider society. As Thistleton notes of biblical interpretation, the same can be said of interpretive communities: "the biblical texts themselves function with greatest integrity and coherence with their directedness when they function (where appropriate) as illocutionary acts of address, promise, commission, decree, praise, celebration, pardon, liberation, and authorization."[23] An interpretation can be legitimate, though not exclusive or exhaustive of the meaning, but must be socially responsible to promote the freedom, transformation and grace reflective of the gospel of Jesus Christ, which it pertains to

---

17. Bird, *The Bible as the Church's Book*, 83.

18. Ibid.

19. Ibid.

20. Ibid.

21. Ibid., 85.

22. Ibid., 84.

23. Thistleton, *New Horizons in Hermeneutics*, 615.

represent. It must also allow Pentecostal readers to continue to be who they are, and admit that they were partially created by ecumenical rejection.

The purpose of a Pentecostal reading is for the transformation of the reader and community. Their reading should result in the transformation and lifestyle that reflects the values of the Pentecostal community and character appropriate of disciples of Jesus Christ.[24] By engaging in this process and dialogue of critique—correcting and informing—the Pentecostal community can be enriched and transformed. While no approach to Scripture has an absolute guarantee against misuse,[25] the ecumenical community can mutually inform the reading communities through dialogue. A fully critical theological hermeneutic will demand that the Pentecostal community engage with the wider dialogue of biblical interpretation to listen to the voices of others in the delineation of their own voice and unique perspective; and in this way expand their theological reflection. Reading is a community activity with a corporate responsibility; it has important social consequences.[26] The social consequences of a Pentecostal reading need to be evaluated and their reading outcomes judged by the norms of faith, hope, and love[27] represented by the Christian gospel.[28]

Bird suggests the third guideline for the determination of a responsible reading as the principle of compatibility of experiential knowledge.[29] This means that the understanding obtained in Bible study should be compatible with the community's knowledge and experience of God obtained through other sources, including church tradition. The truth a reader identifies in a text must be tested against the traditions of the church, experience, and reason but not forced to conform to these sources completely,[30] thus providing a check to the voice of "us." As Bird writes "the Bible must also be allowed its own voice, to awaken senses deadened by the familiar, to press the church to reassess inherited views."[31] This guideline highlights the ability of biblical readings to challenge the routinization and domestication of interpretation, even susceptible to the "dynamic" approach of Pentecostal readings. This allows for a holistic reading of the biblical text and inquiry of interpretation as it affirms the integration of human reason, experience, imagination, affections, tradition, and pneumatic encounter. Bird concludes, "The demand for understanding does not do away with the realm of the incomprehensible or inexpressible, with the reality of mystery and limits. But it does mean that the effort to understand is dissolved by encounter with the mystery of God, nor opposed to it.

24. Smit, "Biblical Hermeneutics," 305.

25. Holmgren, *The Old Testament and the Significance of Jesus*, 36.

26. Smit, "Biblical Hermeneutics," 311.

27. Bird, *The Bible as the Church's Book*, 42.

28. Bird ascribes this rule of reading to Augustine, in which these norms of faith, hope and love guided the reader. However she also notes that this required a clear concept of the canon as a whole, knowledge of the original languages and the ability to distinguish between the literal and derived sense (Bird, *The Bible as the Church's Book*, 42).

29. Bird, *The Bible as the Church's Book*, 85.

30. Ibid.

31. Ibid.

Silence may alternate with speech and inform speech, but the speech must make sense."[32] Although silence may be uncomfortable to the oral community of Pentecostal readers it affirms the fundamental mystery of pneumatic encounter and ineffable experience of the divine. To this dialogue of speech and silence, the Pentecostal community also energetically contributes their voice; speech inherently loaded with the values and culture of their community that they contribute to this wider community of readers.

The Pentecostal reading model of the Old Testament, which is partially constitutive for the Pentecostal community, offers a diversity of contribution to the dialogue partners with which it engages as a "prophetic" voice informing and informed by these co-readers. The community brings their voice to the various dialogue partners who read the text: the church, academy, and society.[33] Yet, what does the Pentecostal reading model offer these three groups? While this reading model will not be appropriate for all communities of readers[34] (it is not for instance, a universal model for all readers of the Old Testament)—it can challenge the three-fold areas of *church*, *academy*, and *society* with a legitimate and constructive voice. These different worlds can learn from each other and benefit from the articulation of a Pentecostal reading model of the Old Testament. Just as the mouth of the prophet Isaiah was touched by the burning coal from the altar of God, so also burning lips of the Pentecostal community are raging with the life of pneumatic experience to share with the wider reading community.

For the reading community of the wider *society*, the Pentecostal reading model of the Old Testament can offer an articulation and experience of the living God. Just as Isaiah encountered the divine presence and was transformed by the vision of the holy God, so also the Pentecostal community can share their encounter with the living and holy God as they voice their readings of the Old Testament. This contributes to the wider society the value and authority of the testimony of Scripture. The biblical text is not just a religious document or a cultural classic[35] but presents an opportunity to encounter the living God. The significance of the Pentecostal community for contemporary hermeneutics and the wider reading community is the claim that God still speaks to and through human beings.[36] Yet, the voice of the wider community also informs the Pentecostal reading model as the voices of "others" are engaged. They hold the Pentecostal community accountable to the pursuit of holiness, righteousness, and justice that reflects this transformational encounter with the living God. Even though the voice of the Pentecostal community resonates with the impetus for mission and evangelism, the voice of the Pentecostal reading model must not be used to silence the "other," but to allow an engagement in dialogue that is mutually informing.

This transformational encounter with God, represented in the Pentecostal reading model of the Old Testament is trans-rational. It represents devotion to God and the testimony of Scripture. This contributes to the *academic* community the voice of the subjec-

32. Bird, *The Bible as the Church's Book*, 85.

33. Smit, "Biblical Hermeneutics," 304.

34. Havea, "[Y]our Book, [Y]our Reading: Writing Tāsilisili Readings," 191.

35. Smit, "Biblical Hermeneutics," 313.

36. Clark, "An Investigation into the Nature of a Viable Pentecostal Hermeneutic," 209.

tive encounter and pneumatic experience. While there are various voices in the academy that emphasize the subjective nature of interpretations and bring readings from various perspectives such as feminist, Womanist, and third world, the Pentecostal reading offers the experience of pneumatic encounter. The affective reading also highlights that the biblical text is not just an ancient literary collection,[37] but a testimony of God's participation in the history of humanity. The reading of biblical texts is not just a scientific, objective quest, but a subjective enterprise that involves heart and mind. Yet, this reading model also does not deny the benefits of critical reflection. In this way, the worlds of scholarly reflection and the Pentecostal community can be mutually beneficial. The lay readers adopting this model can benefit from the critical reflection it represents, and scholars can benefit from listening to the approach and values of the Pentecostal community.

For the wider *church*, the voice of the Pentecostal community confronts the ecumenical dialogue with the experience of the charismata. Their voice reminds the dialogue partners of the democratization of the spirit that has resulted in a prophetic community, not just a prophetic professional clergy. This model requires that the Pentecostal community take care to preserve their historic self-understanding as a prophetic movement— the humble who speak with and for God.[38] The Pentecostal reading model highlights the role of the Christian community as a prophetic voice in and to their generation. As the Pentecostal community reads the Old Testament seeking the significance of the text for "me," "them," and "us" they uphold their values of pneumatic encounter and continue the testimony of the people of God established by the older covenant community, transformed by the inaugurate kingdom of Jesus Christ, and renewed by the Spirit in the post-Pentecost church. As Pentecostalism engages with the dialogue partners of the Old Testament and Hermeneutics, a future ongoing friendship is made possible. The engagement of these three dialogue partners suggests that three is not a crowd, but a company for the sharing of ideas, mutual encouragement, and transformational reading.

---

37. Smit, "Biblical Hermeneutics," 313.

38. Johns, "Pentecostalism and the Postmodern Worldview," 71.

Appendix

Table of Sample Groups

AS NOTED IN CHAPTER 1, the aim of this study is to critically examine the differing factors and concerns that contribute to the "voice" of a Pentecostal hermeneutic and, from this reflection, to propose a responsible reading approach to the Old Testament that reflects the values of the community.[1] This includes the reading approaches of both clergy and lay readers, to determine principles or symbols used in their hermeneutic, and to provide a vehicle for the "voice" of the Pentecostal community to emerge. To do so, it employs both a meta-critical study of the hermeneutical approaches observed in the history of Pentecostal publications and an ethnomethodological approach that seeks to highlight the attitudes of sample groups as representative of the community. The "voices" of the Pentecostal community utilized in this study are tabled below with cross-referencing in order to assist in tying the methodology of this study with its tabulated analysis.

The publications represented below are from populist publications within the Pentecostal community, primarily the *Australian Evangel*, the official publication of the Assemblies of God in Australia. This study also recognizes the importance of the liturgy with the Pentecostal community in informing the reading processes of its members, and therefore includes a study of collected sermons. These sermons were collected by invitation. There were approximately 1,400 ordained ministers (pastors) of the Pentecostal churches of various Pentecostal denominations (predominantly AG) contacted by the researcher through a written letter which requested them to forward copies of sermons and songs presented in their churches relating to *Isaiah*. Although many responses acknowledged the importance of the study, most declined involvement due to lack of dedication in their messages to any particular text of *Isaiah* or lack of availability of recorded/written material. Of the fifteen responses, nine were considered to significantly engage with a section of *Isaiah*.

---

1. Geertz, *The Interpretation of Cultures*, 95.

APPENDIX

Through an accepted ethnomethodogical approach, the researcher aimed to highlight the attitudes of sample groups as representative of the community.[2] Through the use of guided group discussion from populations chosen because of this "statistical normativity," the reading and reasoning processes in interpreting the text of *Isaiah* were derived. Since a "community" shares certain principles of interpretation which reflect its values, viewing both Pentecostal traditional and present interpretations through the prism of *Isaiah* helps highlight the values consistent within the development of the movement and potentially throw light on this development for future analysis and was given adequate oral instruction as to the purpose of the research. The participants were recruited as members of bible study groups from existing Pentecostal churches. Each member of the group consented to participate. The guided group discussion took place in the context of existing church bible study groups on the "home ground" of the group with the normal leadership and membership there to enable the research to be conducted within the context of its normal rituals of bible study or cell group meetings. The study was approved by the Charles Sturt University's Ethics in Human Research Committee.

Reference	Resource	Context	Reference	Description
Isaiah (general)				
A	J. S. Eastman	Article	"Bible University," *Australian Evangel* 30.3 (Oct 1973).	Male pastor/clergy
B	Aeron Morgan	Article	"A Clarion call to the Church," *Australian Evangel* 48.9 (Oct 1991), 5–7.	Male pastor/clergy
C	Author unknown	Poem	"The Books of the Bible," *Australian Evangel* 29.20 (1972), 9.	unknown
D	Eustace Illman	Poem	"The Prophet Isaiah," *Australian Evangel* 37.11 (1980), 2.	Female
E	Ken Legg	Teaching	2003	Male pastor/clergy
Isaiah 6				
F	Donald Gee	Article	*Australian Evangel and Glad Tidings Messenger*, http://evangel.webjournals.org.	Male pastor/clergy
G	Ron Hoffman	Article	"The Next Step," *Australian Evangel* 42.8 (1985), 14–15.	Male pastor/clergy

2. Mackay, Hugh, *Reinventing Australia: The Mind and Mood of Australia in the 90s* (Pymble: Angus & Robertson, 1993).

Reference	Resource	Context	Reference	Description
H1	Charismatic Ladies Group	Group discussion— meeting 1	2003	Charismatic bible study group of predominantly older ladies (primarily over 55) in a semi-rural area. Included 6 participants in the group.
I	Youth Cell	Group discussion	2004	A youth cell meeting of a Pentecostal Cell Church. The group contained primarily high school students of mixed gender. Included 8 participants in the group.
J	Henry Seeley & Nathan Rowe	Song	"Lift Up Your Eyes" © Planet Shakers Ministries International, 2002.	Male youth leaders
K	Rod Allen	Sermon	2004	Male pastor/clergy
L	Chris Falson (1993)	Song	"I See the Lord" © Seam of Gold, 1993.	Male pastor/clergy
M	Sam Evans and Henry Seeley	Song	"Send Me" © Planet Shakers Ministries International, 2001.	Female and male youth leaders
Isaiah 9				
N	L. A. Wiggins	Article	"His Government," *Australian Evangel* 22.12 (Dec 1965), 6–7.	Female writer
O	Gerald Stewart	Article	"His Name Shall Be Called—'Wonderful,'" *Australian Evangel* 27.11 (Dec 1970), 20–21.	Male pastor/clergy
P	W. G. Hathaway	Article	"The Prince of Peace," *Australian Evangel* 27.11 (Dec 1970), 22–23.	Male pastor/clergy
Q	Jenny Complin	Article	"The Feast of Lights," *Australian Evangel* (Dec 1993), 5–6.	Female pastor/clergy
R	John F. Harvey	Article	"World Government and World Events," *Australian Evangel and Glad Tidings Messenger* (March 1944), 16–17.	Male pastor/clergy

APPENDIX

Reference	Resource	Context	Reference	Description
S	Pentecostal cell church meeting	Group discussion	2004	Pentecostal "cell church" cell meeting, comprised of mainly professional and working-class laypeople aged from 25–35. Included 6 participants in the group.
T	Francis M. Burg	Poem	*Australian Evangel* 33 (Feb 1976), 1.	Female poet
U	Raymond Badham	Song	"Emmanuel" © Hillsong Publishing, 2000.	Male pastor/clergy
Isaiah 25				
V	John Ollis	Article	"The Sovereign God," *Australian Evangel*, Sept 1992, p31.	Male pastor/clergy
W	Jim Williams	Article	"An Open Heaven," *Australian Evangel* 42 (Jan 1985), 3–5.	Male pastor/clergy
X	Ashleigh McKenzie	Article	"The Development of Christ-Like Character," *Australian Evangel* 38.8 (August 1981) 12–13.	Male pastor/clergy
Y	David Mead	Sermon	Chester Hill, NSW, 2002.	Male student
Z	Girls Youth Group Bible Study	Group discussion	2004.	Pentecostal Youth group bible study in Western Sydney. Included 5 participants in the group.
Isaiah 40				
AA	A. T. Davidson	Article	"If I Were to Begin Again!," *Australian Evangel* 37.7 (July 1980), 3–8.	Male pastor/clergy
BA	P. B. Duncan	Article	"Our Pentecostal Destiny," 29.2 (1972), 6.	Male pastor/clergy
CA	Andrew Mina	Sermon	Auburn, NSW. 2003.	Male student
DA	Michael C. Smith	Article	"Soar Like an Eagle," *Australian Evangel* 45.7 (July 1988) 15–17.	Male pastor/clergy
EA	Harold Bartholomew	Editorial	*Australian Evangel* 42.3 (March 1985), 2.	Male pastor/clergy

Reference	Resource	Context	Reference	Description
FA	Ps Fred Evans	Article	"Waiting Upon the Lord—Part One," *Australian Evangel* 42.5 (May 1985), 5–6.	Male pastor/clergy
GA	Ps Fred Evans	Article	"Waiting Upon the Lord—Final Part," *Australian Evangel* 42.6 (June 1985), 19–20.	Male pastor/clergy
Z	Girls Youth Group Bible Study	Group discussion	2004	Pentecostal female Youth group bible study in Western Sydney. Included 5 participants in the group.
Isaiah 53				
HA	Moshe Elijah	Article	"Jesus—the Jewish Messiah of Israel," *Australian Evangel* (April 1993), 30–31.	Male Evangelist
IA	William Booth-Clibborn	sermon	"A Joyful Jesus" (1931) http://evangel.webjournals.org.	Male pastor/ Evangelist
JA	David Cartledge	Teaching on Healing	Chester Hill, NSW, 2003.	Male pastor/clergy
KA	Harold Harvey	Sermon: "The Unfair exchange"	AOG, WA, 2003.	Male pastor/clergy
LA	Chris Mulhearn	Sermon	New Hope Church, QLD, January 2003.	Male pastor/clergy
MA	Andrew Evans	Article	*Australian Evangel* (Feb 1992), 50.	Male pastor/clergy
NA	Harriet Bainbridge	Article	*Australian Evangel* (1935) http://evangel.webjournals.org.	
OA	Hoover	Article	*Australian Evangel* (1930) http://evangel.webjournals.org.	
PA	Alex Grancha	Personal correspondence	Bankstown, NSW. 2003.	Male pastor/clergy
QA	Thomas Attebery	Article	*Australian Evangel* (1930) http://evangel.webjournals.org.	
RA	Dave Logan	Personal correspondence	2003	Male pastor/clergy

APPENDIX

Reference	Resource	Context	Reference	Description
H1	Charismatic Ladies Group	Group discussion—meeting 1	2003	Charismatic bible study group of predominantly older ladies (primarily over 55) in a semi-rural area. Included 6 participants in the group.
I	Youth Cell	Group discussion	2004	A youth cell meeting of a Pentecostal Cell Church. The group contained primarily high school students of mixed gender. Included 8 participants in the group.
S	Pentecostal cell church meeting	Group discussion	2004	Pentecostal "cell church" cell meeting, comprised of mainly professional and working-class laypeople aged from 25–35. Included 6 participants in the group.
Isaiah 54				
SA	Ps Harold Harvey	Sermon	Koongamia, WA. 2003.	Male pastor/clergy
H2	Charismatic Ladies Group	Group discussion—meeting 2	2003	Charismatic bible study group of predominantly older ladies (primarily over 55) in a semi-rural area. Included 6 participants in the group.

Reference	Resource	Context	Reference	Description
TA	Pentecostal Women's Group	Group discussion	2004	Pentecostal (G-12 model church) women's cell-type meeting. The Group comprised of both new Christians and non-Christian women of working-class and middle-class backgrounds. A mix of married and single women, the average age being approximately 28 years. Included 4 participants in the group.
UA	Ishbel Gunn	article	"God Takes Special Care of Widows," *Australian Evangel* 41.2 (1984), 7.	Female writer
VA	Professional Women's Cell	Group discussion	2004	A cell group of young, single, professional women from a Pentecostal church in middle-class Sydney, the average age being 25 years. Included 5 participants in the group.
Isaiah 61				
WA	Editor	Enquiry Column	*Good News* (1924), 19.	unknown
H2	Charismatic Ladies Group	Group discussion—meeting 2	2003	Charismatic bible study group of pre-dominantly older ladies (primarily over 55) in a semi-rural area. Included 6 participants in the group.

APPENDIX

Reference	Resource	Context	Reference	Description
VA	Professional Women's Cell	Group discussion	2004	A cell group of young, single, professional women from a Pentecostal church in middle-class Sydney, the average age being 25 years. Included 5 participants in the group.
XA	Charismatic Men's bible study	Group discussion	2004	Charismatic bible study group of predominantly older men (primarily over 55) from a migrant background (mainly Indian and Malaysian) in urban Sydney. Included 4 participants in the group.
PC Reading Model				
YA	Discussion Group	Group Discussion	2004	A discussion group of single, 30-something professional women in middle-class Sydney. Included 3 participants in the group.

Bibliography

Achtemeier, Elizabeth. *The Community and Message of Isaiah 56–66: A Theological Commentary*. Minneapolis: Augsburg, 1982.

Ackerman, Susan. "Isaiah." In *The Women's Bible Commentary*, edited by Carol A. Newsom and Sharon H. Ringe, 169–77. London: SPCK, 1992.

Aichele, George. *Sign, Text, Scripture: Semiotics and the Bible*. Interventions 1. Sheffield: Sheffield Academic, 1997.

Albrecht, Daniel E. *Rites in the Spirit: A Ritual Approach to Pentecostal / Charismatic Spirituality*. Journal of Pentecostal Theology Supplement Series 17. Sheffield: Sheffield Academic, 1999.

Anderson, Allan H. "Introduction: World Pentecostalism at a Crossroads." In *Pentecostals after a Century: Global Perspectives on a Movement in Transition*, edited by Allan H. Anderson and Walter J. Hollenweger, 19–32. Sheffield: Sheffield Academic, 1999.

———. "Dangerous Memories for South African Pentecostals." In *Pentecostals after a Century: Global Perspectives on a Movement in Transition*, edited by Allan H. Anderson and Walter J. Hollenweger, 89–107. Journal of Pentecostal Theology Supplement Series 15. Sheffield: Sheffield Academic, 1999.

———. "Global Pentecostalism in the New Millennium." In *Pentecostals after a Century: Global Perspectives on a Movement in Transition*, edited by Allan H. Anderson and Walter J. Hollenweger, 209–23. Journal of Pentecostal Theology Supplement Series 15. Sheffield: Sheffield Academic, 1999.

Archer, Kenneth J. "Early Pentecostal Biblical Interpretation." *Journal of Pentecostal Theology* 18 (2001) 32–70.

———. *A Pentecostal Hermeneutic for the Twenty-First Century: Spirit, Scripture and Community*. Journal of Pentecostal Theology Supplement Series 28. London: T. & T. Clark, 2004.

Arrington, French L. "Hermeneutics, Historical Perspectives on Pentecostal and Charismatic." In *Dictionary of Pentecostal and Charismatic Movements*, edited by Stanley M. Burgess et al., 376–89. Grand Rapids, Zondervan, 1988.

———. "The Use of the Bible by Pentecostals." *Pneuma* 16:1 (Spring 1994) 101–7.

Autry, Arden C. "Dimensions of Hermeneutics in Pentecostal Focus." *Journal of Pentecostal Theology* 3 (1993) 29–50.

Avis, Paul D. L. *God and the Creative Imagination: Metaphor, Symbol and Myth in Religion and Theology*. London: Routledge, 1999.

Baker, Robert O. "Pentecostal Bible Reading: Toward a Model of Reading for the Formation of Christian Affections." *Journal of Pentecostal Theology* 7 (1995) 34–48.

Beale, G. K. "Did Jesus and His Followers Preach the Right Doctrine from the Wrong Texts?" In *The Right Doctrine from the Wrong Texts? Essays on the Use of the Old Testament in the New*, edited by G. K. Beale, 387–404. Grand Rapids: Baker, 1994.

Bergunder, Michael. "Constructing Indian Pentecostalism: On Issues of Methodology and Representation." In *Asian and Pentecostal: The Charismatic Face of Christianity in Asia*, edited by A. Anderson and Edmond Tang, 177–214. Regnum Studies in Mission. Asian Journal of Pentecostal Studies Series 3. Oxford: Regnum, 2005.

Bird, Phyllis A. *The Bible as the Church's Book*. Library of Living Faith 5. Philadelphia: Westminster, 1982.

Briggs, Richard S. *Words in Action: Speech Act Theory and Biblical Interpretation*. Edinburgh: T. & T. Clark, 2001.

Brueggemann, Walter. *Theology of the Old Testament: Testimony, Dispute, Advocacy*. Minneapolis: Fortress, 1997.

Bibliography

———. *Isaiah. Vol. 1, Isaiah 1–39.* Westminster Bible Companions. Louisville: Westminster John Knox, 1998.

———. *Isaiah. Vol. 2, Isaiah 40–66.* Westminster Bible Companions. Louisville: Westminster John Knox Press, 1998.

Byrd, Joseph. "Paul Ricoeur's Hermeneutical Theory and Pentecostal Proclamation." *Pneuma* 15:2 (Fall 1993) 203–14.

Cargal, Timothy B. "Beyond the Fundamentalist-Modernist Controversy: Pentecostals and Hermeneutics in a Postmodern Age." *Pneuma* 15.2 (Fall 1993) 163–87.

Cartledge, Mark J. "Charismatic Prophecy: A Definition and Description." *Journal of Pentecostal Theology* 5 (1994) 79–120.

———. "Empirical Theology: Towards an Evangelical-Charismatic Hermeneutic." *Journal of Pentecostal Theology* 9 (1996) 115–26.

———. *Practical Theology: Charismatic and Empirical Perspectives.* Studies in Pentecostal and Charismatic Issues. Carlisle: Paternoster, 2003.

Cerillo, Augustus. "The Beginnings of American Pentecostalism: A Historiographical Overview." In *Pentecostal Currents on American Protestantism*, edited by Edith L. Blumhofer et al., 229–60. Urbana: University of Illinois Press, 1999.

Chan, Simon. *Pentecostal Theology and the Christian Spiritual Tradition.* Journal of Pentecostal Theology Supplement Series 21. Sheffield: Sheffield Academic, 2000.

Chant, Barry. "The Spirit of Pentecost: Origins and Development of the Pentecostal Movement in Australia, 1870–1939." PhD diss., Macquarie University, 1999.

Childs, Brevard S. *Biblical Theology of the Old and New Testaments: Theological Reflections on the Christian Bible.* London: SCM, 1992.

———. *Isaiah.* Old Testament Library. Louisville: Westminster John Knox, 2001.

Clark, Matthew S. "An Investigation into the Nature of a Viable Pentecostal Hermeneutic." DTh diss., University of Pretoria, 1997.

Cleary, E. L. "Latin American Pentecostalism." In *The Globalisation of Pentecostalism: A Religion Made to Travel*, edited by Murray W. Dempster et al., 131–50. Carlisle, UK: Regnum, 1999.

Clements, Ronald E. "Isaiah 53 and the Restoration of Israel." In *Jesus and the Suffering Servant: Isaiah 53 and Christian Origins*, edited by William H. Bellinger et al., 39–54. Harrisburg, PA: Trinity, 1998.

Clifton, Shane. "Pentecostal Theological Method: A Colourful and Creative Approach." BTh (honours) diss., Sydney College of Divinity, 2001.

Conrad, Edgar W. *Reading Isaiah.* 1991. Reprinted, Eugene, OR: Wipf & Stock, 2002.

———. "Prophet, Redactor and Audience: Reforming the Notion of Isaiah's Formation." In *New Visions of Isaiah*, edited by Roy F. Melugin and Marvin A. Sweeney, 306–26. Journal for the Study of the Old Testament Supplement Series 214, Sheffield: Sheffield Academic, 1996.

Coulter, Dale M. "What Meaneth This? Pentecostals and Theological Enquiry." *Journal of Pentecostal Theology* 10 (2001) 38–64.

Cox, Harvey. *Fire from Heaven: The Rise of Pentecostal Spirituality and the Reshaping of Religion in the Twenty-First Century.* Reading, MA: Addison-Wesley, 1995.

———. "Pentecostalism and Global Market Culture: A Response to Issues Facing Pentecostalism in a Postmodern World." In *The Globalization of Pentecostalism: A Religion Made to Travel*, edited by Murray W. Dempster et al., 386–96. Carlisle, UK: Regnum, 1999.

Croatto, J. Severino. *Biblical Hermeneutics: Toward a Theory of Reading as the Production of Meaning.* Translated by Robert R. Barr. Maryknoll, NY: Orbis, 1995.

Davies, Andrew. *Double Standards in Isaiah: Re-evaluating Prophetic Ethics and Divine Justice.* Biblical Interpretation Series 46. Leiden: Brill, 2000.

Davies, Philip R. *In Search of "Ancient Israel."* Journal for the Study of the Old Testament Supplement Series 148. Sheffield: JOST, 1992.

———. "Whose History? Whose Israel? Whose Bible? Biblical Histories, Ancient and Modern." In *Can a "History of Israel" Be Written?*, edited by Lester L. Grabbe, 104–22. Journal for the Study of the Old Testament Supplement Series 245. Sheffield: Sheffield Academic, 1997.

Dayton, Donald W. *Theological Roots of Pentecostalism.* Studies in Evangelicalism 5. Metuchen, NJ: Scarecrow, 1987.

Del Colle, Ralph. "Postmodernism and the Pentecostal-Charismatic Experience." *Journal of Pentecostal Theology* 17 (2000) 97–116.

Dempster, Murray W. "Paradigm Shifts and Hermeneutics: Confronting Issues Old and New." *Pneuma* 15.2 (Fall 1993) 129–35.

Dempster, Murray W. et al., editors. *The Globalization of Pentecostalism: A Religion Made to Travel.* Carlisle, UK: Regnum, 1999.

Droogers, André. "The Normalization of Religious Experience: Healing, Prophecy, Dreams, and Visions." In *Charismatic Christianity as a Global Culture*, edited by Karla O. Poewe, 33–49. Columbia: University of South Carolina Press, 1994.

Dyck, Elmer. "Canon as Context for Interpretation." In *The Act of Bible Reading*, edited by Elmer Dyck, 33–64. Downers Grove, IL: InterVarsity, 1996.

Ellington, Scott A. "Pentecostalism and the Authority of Scripture." *Journal of Pentecostal Theology* 9 (1996) 16–38.

———. "History, Story, and Testimony: Locating Truth in a Pentecostal Hermeneutic." *Pneuma* 23:2 (2001) 245–64.

Ervin, Howard M. "Hermeneutics: A Pentecostal Option." *Pneuma* 3:1 (Fall 1981) 11–25.

Evans, Craig A. *To See and Not Perceive: Isaiah 6.9–10 in Early Jewish and Christian Interpretation.* Journal for the Study of the Old Testament Supplement Series 64. Sheffield: Sheffield Academic, 1989.

Exum, Cheryl. "Feminist Criticism: Whose Interests Are Being Served?" In *Judges and Method: New Approaches in Biblical Studies*, edited by Gail A. Yee, 65–90. Minneapolis: Fortress, 1995.

Fee, Gordon D. "Hermeneutics and Historical Precedent—A Major Problem in Pentecostal Hermeneutics." In *Perspectives on the New Pentecostalism*, edited by Russell P. Spittler, 118–32. Grand Rapids: Baker, 1976.

———. "History as Context for Interpretation." In *The Act of Bible Reading*, edited by Elmer Dyck, 10–32. Downers Grove, IL: InterVarsity 1996.

Fee, Gordon, and Douglas Stuart. *How to Read the Bible for All Its Worth.* Grand Rapids: Zondervan, 1982.

Fishbane, Michael A. *The Garments of the Torah: Essays in Biblical Hermeneutics.* Indiana Studies in Biblical Literature. Bloomington: Indiana University Press, 1989.

Fogarty, Stephen. "Toward a Pentecostal Hermeneutic." *PCBC Journal* 5:2 (2001). Online: http://webjournals .alphacrucis.edu.au/journals/PCBC/vol5-no2/toward-a-pentecostal-hermeneutic/.

Freston, Paul. *Evangelicals and Politics in Asia, Africa and Latin America.* Cambridge: Cambridge University Press, 2001.

Gadamer, Hans-Georg. *Truth and Method.* Translated by Garrett Barden and John Cummings. New York: Crossroad, 1975.

Geertz, Clifford. *The Interpretation of Cultures: Selected Essays.* New York: Basic, 1973.

Goldingay, John. *Isaiah.* New International Biblical Commentary Old Testament Series 13. Peabody, MA: Hendrickson, 2001.

Graham, Stephen R. "'Thus Saith the Lord': Biblical Hermeneutics in the Early Pentecostal Movement." *Ex Auditu* 12 (1996) 121–35.

Grey, Jacqueline. "Torn Stockings and Enculturation: Women Pastors in the Australian Assemblies of God." *Australasian Pentecostal Studies* 5/6 (2001). Online: http://aps.webjournals.org/articles/4/1/2002/2969 .htm/.

Gunn, David M. "Narrative Criticism." In *To Each Its Own Meaning: An Introduction to Biblical Criticisms and Their Application*, edited by Steven L. McKenzie and Stephen R. Haynes, 201–29. Revised and expanded. Louisville: Westminster John Knox, 1999.

Gunn, David M., and Dana Nolan Fewell. *Narrative in the Hebrew Bible.* Oxford Bible Series. Oxford: Oxford University Press, 1993.

Gutiérrez, Gustavo. *A Theology of Liberation.* Rev. ed. Translated by Sister Caridad Inda and John Eagleton. Maryknoll, NY: Orbis, 1988.

Hagner, Donald A. "When the Time Had Fully Come." In *A Guide to Biblical Prophecy*, edited by Carl Edwin Armerding and W. Ward Gasque, 89–100. Peabody, MA: Hendrickson, 1989.

Hanson, Paul D. "The World of the Servant of the Lord in Isaiah 40–55." In *Jesus and the Suffering Servant: Isaiah 53 and Christian Origins*, edited by William H, Bellinger et al., 9–22. Harrisburg, PA: Trinity, 1998.

Bibliography

Harrington, Hannah K., and Rebecca Patten. "Pentecostal Hermeneutics and Postmodern Literary Theory." *Pneuma* 14.1 (1994) 109–14.

Harrop, G. Gerald. *Elijah Speaks Today: The Long Road into Naboth's Vineyard.* Nashville: Abingdon, 1975.

Havea, Jione. "[Y]our Book, [Y]our Reading: Writing Täsilisili Readings." In *Methodist and Radical: Rejuvenating a Tradition,* edited by Joerg Rieger and John Vincent, 181–91. Nashville: Kingswood, 2003.

Hays, Richard B. *Echoes of Scripture in the Letters of Paul.* New Haven: Yale University Press, 1989.

Hey, Sam. "Contemporary Developments in Pentecostal Hermeneutics." *PCBC Journal* 5 (2001). Online: http://webjournals.alphacrucis.edu.au/journals/PCBC/vol5-no2/contemporary-developments-in-pentecostal-hermeneut/.

Hirsch, E. D. *Validity in Interpretation.* New Haven, CT: Yale University Press, 1967.

Hollenweger, Walter J. "The Critical Tradition of Pentecostalism." *Journal of Pentecostal Theology* 1 (1992) 7–17.

———. "The Pentecostal Elites and the Pentecostal Poor." In *Charismatic Christianity as a Global Culture* edited by Karla O. Poewe, 200–214. Columbia: University of South Carolina Press, 1994.

———. "The Black Roots of Pentecostalism." In *Pentecostals after a Century: Global Perspectives on a Movement in Transition,* edited by Allan H. Anderson and Walter J. Hollenweger, 33–44. Journal of Pentecostal Theology Supplement Series 15. Sheffield: Sheffield Academic, 1999.

———. "Crucial Issues for Pentecostals." In *Pentecostals after a Century: Global Perspectives on a Movement in Transition* edited by Allan H. Anderson and Walter J. Hollenweger l, 176–96. Journal of Pentecostal Theology Supplement Series 15. Sheffield: Sheffield Academic, 1999.

Holmgren, Fredrick C. *The Old Testament and the Significance of Jesus: Embracing Change—Maintaining Christian Identity.* Grand Rapids: Eerdmans, 1999.

Hwa, Yung. "Pentecostalism and the Asian Church." In *Asian and Pentecostal: The Charismatic Face of Christianity in Asia,* edited by Allan Anderson and Edmond Tang, 37–58. Regnum Studies in Mission. Asian Journal of Pentecostal Studies Series 3. Oxford: Regnum, 2005.

Israel, Richard D., et al. "Pentecostals and Hermeneutics: Texts, Rituals and Community." *Pneuma* 15.2 (1993) 137–61.

Johns, Jackie D. "Pentecostalism and the Postmodern Worldview." *Journal of Pentecostal Theology* 7 (1995) 73–96.

———. "Yielding to the Spirit: The Dynamics of a Pentecostal Model of Praxis." In *The Globalization of Pentecostalism: A Religion Made to Travel,* edited by Murray W. Dempster et al., 70–84. Carlisle, UK: Paternoster, 1999.

Johns, Cheryl Bridges, and Jackie D. Johns. "Yielding to the Spirit: A Pentecostal Approach to Group Bible Study." *Journal of Pentecostal Theology* 1 (1992) 109–34.

Johns, Cheryl Bridges. *Pentecostal Formation: A Pedagogy among the Oppressed.* Journal of Pentecostal Theology Supplement Series 2. Sheffield: Sheffield Academic, 1993.

———. "A Pentecostal Perspective." In *Pentecostal Movements as an Ecumenical Challenge,* edited by Jürgen Moltmann and Karl-Josef Kuschel, 45–51. London: SPCK, 1996.

Johnston, Robert K. "Pentecostalism and Theological Hermeneutics: Evangelical Options." *Pneuma* 6 (1984) 51–66.

Kärkkäinen, Veli-Matti. "Pentecostal Hermeneutics in the Making: On the Way from Fundamentalism to Postmodernism." *Journal of the European Pentecostal Theological Association* 18 (1998) 76–115.

Kelley, Page H. "'Doing It God's Way': Introduction to Isaiah 50–55." *Review and Expositor* 88 (1991) 167–76.

Klaus, Byron D. "Pentecostalism as a Global Culture: An Introductory Overview." In *The Globalization of Pentecostalism: A Religion Made to Travel* edited by Murray W. Dempster et al., 127–30. Carlisle, UK: Paternoster, 1999.

Klein, William W. et al. *Introduction to Biblical Interpretation.* Dallas: Word, 1993.

Knowles, Brett. "'From the Ends of the Earth We Hear Songs': Music as an Indicator of New Zealand Pentecostal Spirituality and Theology." *Australasian Pentecostal Studies* 5/6 (2002) 3–16.

Kristeva, Julia. *The Kristeva Reader.* New York: Columbia University Press, 1986.

LaCugna, Catherine Mowry. *God for Us: The Trinity and Christian Life.* San Francisco: HarperSanFrancisco, 1991.

Lakoff, George, and Mark Johnson. *Metaphors We Live By.* Chicago: University of Chicago Press, 1980.

Lancaster, Sarah Heaner. *Women and the Authority of Scripture: A Narrative Approach.* Harrisburg, PA: Trinity, 2002.

Land, Steven J. *Pentecostal Spirituality: A Passion for the Kingdom.* Journal of Pentecostal Theology Supplement 1. Sheffield: Sheffield Academic, 1993

LaPoorta, Japie. "Unity or Division: A Case Study of the Apostolic Faith Mission of South Africa." In *The Globalization of Pentecostalism: A Religion Made to Travel,* edited by M. W. Dempster, B. D. Klaus, and D. Petersen, 151–69. Carlisle, UK: Paternoster, 1999.

Lee, Hong Jung. "*Minjung* and Pentecostal Movements in Korea." In *Pentecostals after a Century: Global Perspectives on a Movement in Transition,* edited by Allan H. Anderson and Walter J. Hollenweger, 138–60. Journal of Pentecostal Theology Supplement Series 15. Sheffield: Sheffield Academic, 1999.

Li, Yue Hong. "The Decline of Confucianism and the Proclamation of the Gospel in China." In *Pentecostalism in Context: Essays in Honor of William W. Menzies,* edited by Wonsuk Ma and Robert P Menzies, 238–64. Journal of Pentecostal Theology Supplement Series 11. Sheffield: Sheffield Academic, 1997.

Lindars, Barnabas "The Place of the Old Testament in the Formation of New Testament Theology." In *The Right Doctrine from the Wrong Texts? Essays on the Use of the Old Testament in the New,* edited by G. K. Beale, 137–45. Grand Rapids: Baker, 1994.

Loades, Ann. "Feminist Hermeneutics." In *The Cambridge Companion to Biblical Hermeneutics,* edited by John Barton, 81–94. Cambridge Companions to Religion. Cambridge: Cambridge University Press, 1998.

Longenecker, Richard N. "'Who Is the Prophet Talking About?' Some Reflections on the New Testament's Use of the Old." In *The Right Doctrine from the Wrong Texts? Essays on the Use of the Old Testament in the New,* edited by G. K. Beale, 375–86. Grand Rapids: Baker, 1994.

———. *Biblical Exegesis in the Apostolic Period.* 2nd ed. Grand Rapids: Eerdmans, 1999.

Longman, Tremper III. *Making Sense of the Old Testament: Three Crucial Questions.* Grand Rapids: Baker, 1998.

Ma, Julie. "Pentecostal Challenges in East and South-East Asia." In *The Globalization of Pentecostalism: A Religion Made to Travel,* edited by M. Dempster, B. Klaus, and D. Petersen, D, 183–202. Oxford: Regnum, 1999.

Ma, Wonsuk. *Until the Spirit Comes: The Spirit of God in the Book of Isaiah.* Journal for the Study of the Old Testament Supplement Series 271. Sheffield: Sheffield Academic, 1999.

———. "Biblical Studies in the Pentecostal Tradition: Yesterday, Today, and Tomorrow." In *The Globalization of Pentecostalism: A Religion Made to Travel,* edited by Murray W. Dempster et al., 52–69. Carlisle, UK: Paternoster, 1999.

———. "Asian (Classical) Pentecostal Theology in Context." In *Asian and Pentecostal: The Charismatic Face of Christianity in Asia,* edited by Allan Anderson and E. Tang, 59–92. Regnum Studies in Mission. Asian Journal of Pentecostal Studies Series 3, Oxford: Regnum, 2005.

Macchia, Frank. "Groans Too Deep for Words: Towards a Theology of Tongues as Initial Evidence." *Asian Journal of Pentecostal Studies* 1 (1998) 149–73.

———. "The Struggle for Global Witness: Shifting Paradigms in Pentecostal Theology." In *The Globalization of Pentecostalism: A Religion Made to Travel,* edited by Murray W. Dempster et al., 8–29. Carlisle UK: Paternoster, 1999.

Mackay, Hugh. *Reinventing Australia: The Mind and Mood of Australia in the 90s.* Pymble: Angus & Robertson, 1993.

Martin, David. "Evangelical and Charismatic Christianity in Latin America." In *Charismatic Christianity as a Global Culture,* edited by Karla O. Poewe, 73–86. Columbia: University of South Carolina Press, 1994.

———. *Pentecostalism: The World Their Parish.* Religion and Modernity. Oxford: Blackwell, 2002.

Massey, Richard D. "The Word of God: 'Thus Saith the Lord.'" In *Pentecostal Perspectives* edited by Keith Warrington, 64–79. Carlisle, UK: Paternoster, 1998.

McKay, John. "When the Veil Is Taken Away: The Impact of Prophetic Experience on Biblical Interpretation." *Journal of Pentecostal Theology* 5 (1994) 17–40.

McKinlay, Judith E. "What Do I Do with Contexts? A Brief Reflection on Reading Biblical Texts with Israel and Aotearoa New Zealand in Mind." *Pacifica* 14 (June 2001) 159–71.

Bibliography

McKnight, Edgar V. "Reader-Response Criticism." In *To Each Its Own Meaning*, edited by Stephen R. Haynes and Steven L. McKenzie, 230–54. Louisville: Westminster John Knox, 1999.

McLean, Mark D. "Toward a Pentecostal Hermeneutic." *Pneuma* 6.2 (Fall 1984) 35–56.

McQueen, Larry R. *Joel and the Spirit: The Cry of a Prophetic Hermeneutic.* Journal of Pentecostal Theology Supplement Series 8. Sheffield: Sheffield Academic, 1995.

Melugin, Roy F. "Introduction." In *New Visions of Isaiah* edited by Roy F. Melugin and Marvin A. Sweeney, 13–29. Journal for the Study of the Old Testament Supplement Series 214. Sheffield: Sheffield Academic, 1996.

———. "Figurative Speech and the Reading of Isaiah 1 as Scripture." In *New Visions of Isaiah* edited by Roy F. Melugin and Marvin A. Sweeney, 282–305. Journal for the Study of the Old Testament Supplement Series 214. Sheffield: Sheffield Academic, 1996.

———. "On Reading Isaiah 53 as Christian Scripture." In *Jesus and the Suffering Servant: Isaiah 53 and Christian Origins*, edited by William H. Bellinger, Jr., and William R. Farmer, 88–103. Harrisburg, PA: Trinity, 1998.

———. "Texts to Transform Life: Reading Isaiah as Christians." *Word & World* 19 (1999) 109–16.

Menzies, Robert P. *The Development of Early Christian Pneumatology: With Special Reference to Luke-Acts.* Journal for the Study of the New Testament Supplement Series 54. Sheffield: JSOT Press, 1991.

———. "Jumping Off the Postmodern Bandwagon." *Pneuma* 16.1 (Spring 1994) 115–20.

Moltmann, Jürgen "A Pentecostal Theology of Life." *Journal of Pentecostal Theology* 9 (1996) 3–15.

———. *The Trinity and the Kingdom: The Doctrine of God.* Translated by Margaret Kohl. London: SCM, 1981.

Moore, Rick D. "Deuteronomy and the Fire of God." *Journal of Pentecostal Theology* 7 (1995) 11–33.

Motyer, J. Alec. *The Prophecy of Isaiah: An Introduction & Commentary.* Downers Grove, IL: InterVarsity, 1993.

Mudge, Lewis S. "Gathering around the Center: A Reply to Thomas Oden." *Christian Century*, April 12, 1995, 392–96.

Oswalt, John N. *Isaiah.* NIV Application Commentary. Grand Rapids: Zondervan, 2003.

Owens, Robert. "The Azusa Street Revival: The Pentecostal Movement Begins in America." In *The Century of the Holy Spirit: 100 Years of Pentecostal and Charismatic Renewal, 1901–2001*, edited by Vinson Synan, 39–68. Nashville: Nelson, 2001.

Nicole, Roger. "The New Testament Use of the Old Testament." In *The Right Doctrine from the Wrong Texts? Essays on the Use of the Old Testament in the New*, edited by G. K. Beale, 13–28. Grand Rapids: Baker, 1994.

Paul, Ian. "Metaphor and Exegesis." In *After Pentecost: Language and Biblical Interpretation*, edited by Craig Bartholomew et al., 387–402. Scripture and Hermeneutics Series 2. Grand Rapids: Zondervan, 2001.

Parker, David. "Studies in Pentecostal Bible Reading." Unpublished notes, 2004.

Parker, Stephen E. *Led by the Spirit: Toward a Practical Theology of Pentecostal Discernment and Decision Making.* Journal of Pentecostal Theology Supplement Series 7. Sheffield: Sheffield Academic, 1996.

Peterson, David. *Christ and His People in the Book of Isaiah.* Leicester, UK: InterVarsity, 2003.

Pinnock, Clark H. "The Work of the Holy Spirit in Hermeneutics." *Journal of Pentecostal Theology* 2 (1993) 3–23.

Plüss, Jean-Daniel. "Globalization of Pentecostalism or Globalization of Individualism? A European Perspective." In *The Globalization of Pentecostalism: A Religion Made to Travel*, edited by Murray W. Dempster et al., 170–82. Carlisle, UK: Regnum, 1999.

Poloma, Margaret M. *The Assemblies of God at the Crossroads: Charisma and Institutional Dilemmas.* Knoxville: University of Tennessee Press, 1989.

Powery, Emerson B. "The Spirit, the Scripture(s), and the Gospel of Mark: Pneumatology and Hermeneutics in Narrative Perspective." *Journal of Pentecostal Theology* 11 (2003) 184–98.

Poythress, Vern Sheridan. "Divine Meaning of Scripture." In *The Right Doctrine from the Wrong Texts? Essays on the Use of the Old Testament in the New*, edited by G. K. Beale, 82–113. Grand Rapids: Baker, 1994.

Ricoeur, Paul. *Essays on Biblical Interpretations.* London: SPCK, 1981.

Roelofs, Gerard. "Charismatic Christian Thought: Experience, Metonymy, and Routinization." In *Charismatic Christianity as a Global Culture*, edited by Karla O. Poewe, 217–33. Columbia: University of South Carolina Press, 1994.

Sepúlveda, Juan. "Indigenous Pentecostalism and the Chilean Experience." In *Pentecostals after a Century: Global Perspectives on a Movement in Transition*, edited by Allan H. Anderson and Walter J. Hollenweger, 111–34. Journal of Pentecostal Theology Supplement Series 15. Sheffield: Sheffield Academic, 1999.

Schwartz, Regina. *The Curse of Cain: The Violent Legacy of Monotheism*. Chicago: University of Chicago Press, 1997.

Seitz, Christopher R. *Isaiah 1–39*. Interpretation. Louisville: John Knox, 1993.

Sheppard, Gerald T. "Pentecostals and the Hermeneutics of Dispensationalism: The Anatomy of an Uneasy Relationship." *Pneuma* 6.1 (1984) 5–33.

———. "Biblical Interpretation after Gadamer." *Pneuma* 16.1 (1994) 121–41.

———. "Pentecostals, Globalization, and Postmodern Hermeneutics: Implications for the Politics of Scriptural Interpretation." In *The Globalisation of Pentecostalism: A Religion Made to Travel*, edited by Murray W. Dempster et al., 289–312. Carlisle, UK: Regnum, 1999.

Smit, Dirkie J. "Biblical Hermeneutics: the 20th Century." In *Initiation into Theology: The Rich Variety of Theology and Hermeneutics*, edited by Simon Maimela and A. König, 337–47. Pretoria, South Africa: Van Schaik, 1998.

Snodgrass, Klyne. "The Use of the Old Testament in the New." In *The Right Doctrine from the Wrong Texts? Essays on the Use of the Old Testament in the New*, edited by G. K. Beale, 29–51. Grand Rapids: Baker, 1994.

Spittler, Russell. "Scripture and the Theological Enterprise: View from a Big Canoe." In *The Use of the Bible in Theology: Evangelical Options*, edited by Robert K. Johnston, 56–77. Atlanta: John Knox, 1985.

———. "Are Pentecostals and Charismatics Fundamentalists? A Review of American Uses of These Categories." In *Charismatic Christianity as a Global Culture*, edited by Karla O. Poewe, 103–16. Columbia: University of South Carolina Press, 1994.

Stiver, Dan R. *The Philosophy of Religious Language: Sign, Symbol, and Story*. Oxford: Blackwell, 1996.

Stroup, George W. *The Promise of Narrative Theology: Recovering the Gospel in the Church*. Atlanta: John Knox, 1981.

Synan, Vinson. "The Pentecostal Century: An Overview." In *The Century of the Holy Spirit: 100 Years of Pentecostal and Charismatic Renewal, 1901–2001*, edited by Vinson Synan, 1–14. Nashville: Nelson, 2001.

———. "Fundamentalism." In *The New International Dictionary of Pentecostal Charismatic Movements*, edited by Stanley Burgess, 655–58. Grand Rapids: Zondervan, 2002.

Tanner, Kathryn. "The Bible as a Popular Text." *Modern Theology* 14 (1998) 279–98.

Tarr, Del. "Transcendence, Immanence and the Emerging Pentecostal Academy." In *Pentecostalism in Context: Essays in Honour of William W. Menzies*, edited by Wonsuk Ma and Robert P. Menzies, 195–222. Journal of Pentecostal Theology Supplement Series 11. Sheffield: Sheffield Academic, 1997.

Thiselton, Anthony. *New Horizons in Hermeneutics*. Grand Rapids: Zondervan, 1992.

———. *Interpreting God and the Postmodern Self: On Meaning, Manipulation, and Promise*. Grand Rapids: Eerdmans, 1995.

Thomas, John C. "Women, Pentecostals and the Bible: An Experiment in Pentecostal Hermeneutics." *Journal of Pentecostal Theology* 5 (1994) 41–56.

Thompson, Alden L. *Who's Afraid of the Old Testament God?* Exeter, UK: Paternoster, 1988.

Watts, John D. W. *Isaiah 1–33*. Word Bible Commentary 24. Waco, TX: Word, 1985.

———. *Isaiah 34–66*. Word Bible Commentary 25. Waco, TX: Word, 1987.

———. *Isaiah*. Word Biblical Themes. Waco, TX: Word, 1989.

Webb, Barry. *The Message of Isaiah*. The Bible Speaks Today. Leicester, UK: Inter-Varsity, 1996.

White, Hayden V. *The Content of the Form: Narrative Discourse and Historical Representation*. Baltimore: Johns Hopkins University Press, 1987

Whitelam, Keith W. "Sociology or History: Towards a (Human) History of Ancient Palestine." In *Words Remembered, Texts Renewed: Essays in Honour of John F. A. Sawyer*, edited by Jon Davies et al., 149–66. Journal for the Study of the Old Testament Supplement Series 195. Sheffield: Sheffield Academic, 1995.

Yong, Amos. *Discerning the Spirit(s): A Pentecostal-Charismatic Contribution to Christian Theology of Religions*. Journal of Pentecostal Theology Supplement Series 20. Sheffield: Sheffield Academic, 2000.

Zimmerli, Walther. "Promise and Fulfillment." In *Essays on Old Testament Interpretation*, edited by Claus Westermann, 89–122. London: SCM, 1963.